Implementing an ISO 9001:2000-Based Quality Management System

Including Safety and Environmental Considerations

Raymond J. Murphy

ABS Consulting

Government Institutes
Rockville, MD

ABS Consulting

Government Institutes
4 Research Place, Rockville, Maryland 20850, USA
Phone: (301) 921-2300
Fax: (301) 921-0373
Email: giinfo@govinst.com
Internet: http://www.govinst.com

ISBN: 0-86587-827-7

This book is dedicated to my wife,
Mary Noah Murphy,
for her loving support and the blessing
she has been and continues to be in my life.

Summary of Contents

Contents

List of Figures

Preface

Have you been searching around for an easy way to gain a better understanding of Management Systems and Processes? Have you or your staff attended numerous courses on ISO 9000 (the model adopted by over 400,000 businesses worldwide) and read books and publications that partially cover some of the subject? Are you frustrated with trying to find what you need to know in order to implement such a system into your organization in a simple and cost effective manner?

It seems that most ISO 9001:2000 training courses or seminars imply that you will walk away with the ability to implement a Quality Management System which will meet ISO 9001:2000 requirements, yet the courses leave you disappointed and in need. I have found that you don't need to invest a large amount of time, you don't need to spend a fortune to design, plan, and implement good management systems and processes, and you don't have to pay to upgrade systems that are currently in place within your organization. What you do need is a very clear commitment from your organization and an equally clear understanding of how to achieve the continual improvement of your current management systems and processes.

If you are searching for a comprehensive, step-by-step management system and process implementation guidance that will not leave you disappointed, then this book is exactly what you need. If you are seeking an understanding of quality, environmental, and safety management systems, then this book is what you need.

This book contains a wealth of information coupled with "how-to" details for every aspect of quality management systems, including the integration of safety and environmental considerations and requirements.

This book is:

- A Reference
- A Guide
- A Training Manual
- A Success Story
- A Model

About the Author

Raymond J. Murphy is the Senior Vice President of the Management Systems Division of ABS Consulting, headquartered in Houston, Texas. Previously, he was the Director of Quality for the American Bureau of Shipping.

He is a seasoned continual improvement process leader and practitioner. He has more than 30 years of hands-on experience in planning and implementing management systems and process improvements in challenging environments. His experience includes orchestrating/sustaining process improvement through the involvement of people; strategic planning; and managing all phases of operations, including Engineering, Research and Development, Manufacturing, Quality Assurance, Project Management, Material Control, Engineering Support, Document Control, and Technical Publications. He directed the establishment of a Total Quality Improvement Process in several international organizations and has served as an engineer, manager, senior executive, and consultant.

Mr. Murphy is a skilled facilitator and communicator with the ability to identify and resolve complex problems using a wide range of tools and techniques. He is known for his reputation as a process improvement pioneer and leader who works effectively with all levels of people and "walks the talk." Mr. Murphy has taught the subject of Continual Improvement in over 60 classroom sessions involving over 800 people.

Mr. Murphy served as a Malcolm Baldrige National Quality Award Examiner for four years and has received the Instrument Society of America's Excellence in Documentation Award. He is the author of two books on implementing ISO 9000 quality management standards. He resides in Spring, Texas with his wife.

Introduction

The format and content of this book are very straightforward, containing no superfluous information. The format was chosen to allow each chapter and each subject within the book to be self-contained. It is a walk through a management system implementation process, based on the ISO 9001:2000 International Standard, and follows the flow diagrams displayed in Figures I-1 through I-4 of this Introduction.

The Quality Management System as contained in this book was implemented in the American Bureau of Shipping (ABS) during a 15-month period, thanks to the commitment of the ABS Chairman and CEO, Frank J. Iarossi, and his entire staff. The ABS Quality Management System implementation story is told as an application example of the Implementation Method detailed in Chapter 21 of this book.

The Quality System Implementation Process as presented here is also designed to be the foundation of a Journey to Excellence and part of a continual improvement process.

Quality Management System implementation, although a simple concept, is not easy to achieve. It requires commitment by management and the provision of adequate resources. Initially, it may cause "pain" to the organization and may also cause a predictable set of employee and management reactions until "buy in" is achieved.

These reactions will test senior management's commitment, resolve, and patience. Adverse reactions should be expected, but can be overcome rather rapidly. To do so, senior management will have to "walk the talk" and will have to be very consistent in their actions. This is why the implementation of an ISO 9001:2000 Quality Management System begins with the decision and commitment of senior management, as discussed in Chapter 1.

Either in advance of this senior management decision, or closely following it, comes the ISO 9001 Quality System Foundation training, as presented in Chapters 2 and 3. This training should include those personnel within the organization who are or will be responsible for the implementation of the system.

Establishment of the organization's quality-related committees is covered in Chapter 4, the next logical implementation step.

The internal high level self-assessment of Chapter 5 will provide a baseline for planning the remainder of the Implementation Process, which begins with Chapter 6.

I suggest that the reader complete Chapters 1 through 4 prior to completing the self-assessment contained in Chapter 5. The self-assessment results indicate which chapters of this book apply to the specific organization's needs. This is particularly helpful if a Quality Management System has already been partially or fully installed.

The remaining chapters cover those Implementation Process steps as shown on the Process Map. It is suggested that the entire map be studied and modified as necessary to be established as the specific organization's Implementation Process Map.

In reading the map, Figures I-1 through I-4 read from the top downward following the arrows. When an arrow flows from the right of an implementation logic box, follow through those steps sequentially before returning to the box and proceeding to the next box.

Chapter references are provided for each box. Here detailed information can be obtained concerning its contents.

So, let's get on with the journey, remembering what Will Rogers said: "Even if you are on the right track, you will get run over if you stand still."

Enjoy!

Raymond J. Murphy
Spring, Texas

Chapter 1

Management Commitment

OBJECTIVES OF MANAGEMENT COMMITMENT

"*Management commitment leads the quality process*." This statement has been repeated over and over by almost every quality expert in the world. There have been countless articles published on the subject and numerous books written. Of course, the reason for this attention is that the statement is true—and it is vital to the success of any Quality, Environmental, or Safety Management System; Malcolm Baldrige National Quality Award initiative; or equivalent initiative.

The major reason these management systems fail is lack of management commitment. Another reason is the failure to establish a solid systems and process foundation based on an effective and proven model, such as the ISO 9000 (or equivalent) standard. In fact, many of the Malcolm Baldrige National Quality Award initiatives fail because of this reason—the organization has not established a solid systems and process foundation.

In its pure sense, "commitment" describes a deep-seated mental or emotional state that is reflected in consistent patterns of behavior. Commitment leaves no room for compromise. Because quality also leaves no room for compromise, the "commitment" involved in the implementation of an ISO 9000-based Quality Management System has to be real and honest. It must define a set of values and priorities and a pattern of positive action.

When management becomes committed, in the true sense, to quality, meaningful change begins. The following shows a sincere commitment of management:

- Implementation of a plan for continual improvement.
- Formation of problem-solving teams to tackle chronic problems. These teams are cross-functional and involve various disciplines (corrective action teams or opportunity for improvement teams).
- Use of measurement to indicate problem areas and to control processes.
- Dismantling of barriers between departments in order to work together for a common solution.
- Perceptive listening to suggestions for improvement from people doing their jobs.
- The prompt implementation of improvement suggestions accepted by management.
- Provisions for the proper tools made available to all employees so that they may do their best work, including the allowance of time to do the job right and the recognition of quality work.
- The commitment of resources to improve processes in all functions of the business.

1

Section 5.1 of the ISO 9001:2000 Standard states that top management shall provide evidence of its commitment to the development and implementation of the quality management system, and to continually improve its effectiveness by

a) communicating to the organization the importance of meeting customer as well as statutory and regulatory requirements,

b) establishing the quality policy,

c) ensuring that quality objectives are established,

d) conducting management reviews, and

e) ensuring the availability of resources.

Management commitment has long been recognized as an unstated necessity for the overall success of a Quality Management System, Environmental Management System, or Safety Management System. The revised IS0 9001:2000 Standard now contains some of the requirements relative to management responsibility and commitment that support and recognize the importance of management commitment. Also, the ISO 14001 Standard, Paragraph A.4.1 makes statements such as "This commitment should begin at the highest levels of management." Likewise, the Malcolm Baldrige National Quality Award Criteria have always recognized the importance of management commitment.

Quality Management

Quality is based on a set of fundamental management concepts that all managers must understand, embrace, and enthusiastically practice. The philosophy is simple: it says that *quality is a key in every organization and must be managed for success in every area of the organization.* In other words:

> *Management = planning, organization, control, and measurement*

Therefore, quality cannot be left to chance. Quality must be as carefully and prudently managed as the organization's finances.

There is a difference between managing processes, as described above, and managing people. People do not like to be managed, and quality does not support the managing of people. People want to and should be led.

An interesting message published in the *Wall Street Journal* by United Technologies Corporation in 1984 says it very well:

> *Let's get rid of management.*
> *People don't want to be managed.*
> *They want to be led.*
> *Whoever heard of a World manager?*
> *World leader, yes.*
> > *Educational leader.*
> > *Political leader.*
> > *Religious leader.*
> > *Scout leader.*

Business leader.
They lead.
They don't manage.
The carrot always wins over the stick.
Ask your horse.
You can lead your horse to water, but you can't manage him to drink.
If you want to manage somebody, manage yourself.
Do that well and you'll be ready to stop managing and start leading.

Employee management, leadership, and overall Quality Management System Implementation might be characterized by a decreasing amount of employee management coupled with a corresponding increase in employee empowerment. This would also correspond to the transition to managing processes and leading people—a Quality System objective.

Every employee should be able to find and solve problems on his or her own and absorb and create new approaches, new ideas. This is what an effective Quality Management System does, and it does so through the establishment of a solid system within which the employee can operate. This system is not driven by management-created fear, but by leadership, which is best characterized by the following quote:

A leader is best when people barely know he exists, not so good when people obey and acclaim him, worse when they despise him. But of a good leader who talks little, when his work is done, his aim fulfilled, they will say "we did it ourselves."
—Cho/Hey

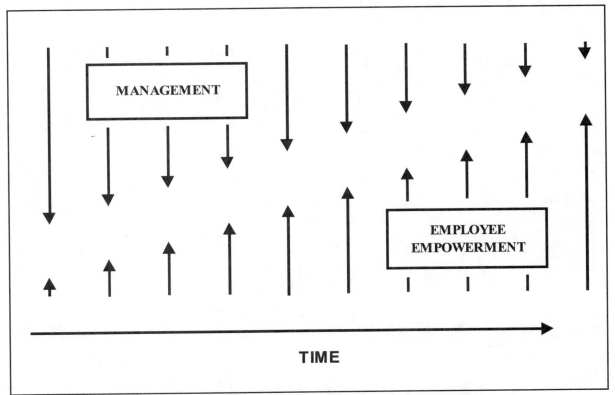

Figure 1-1. Quality Management System Implementation

Conclusion

As Tom Peters so aptly states,

You are either a quality fanatic or you are not in favor of quality.

There are a number of additional requirements in the ISO 9000 Standard which refer to management responsibility, but which are not repeated here. There are similar statements and requirements in both the ISO 14001 and ISO 18000 Standards. It is sufficient to say that the ultimate responsibility for quality resides with management, and that management must ensure continuing effectiveness of the Quality Management System to meet objectives.

Because only management can make such change happen, management commitment is mandatory. Little or nothing will happen until this is achieved.

Chapter 2

Overview of the ISO 9000 Standards

INTERNATIONAL ORGANIZATION FOR STANDARDIZATION (ISO)

The International Organization for Standardization (ISO) is an international organization whose members are the national standards bodies of some 90-plus countries (one from each country). ISO is a nongovernmental organization (NGO) that facilitates the development of global consensus on international standards. The standards are voluntary in nature.

In 1979, the British Standards Institute (BSI) submitted a formal proposal to ISO that a new technical committee should be formed to prepare international standards on quality assurance techniques and practices.

The new technical committee was approved and given the number ISO/TC 176, titled Quality Assurance. Twenty member countries became active participants and fourteen countries became observing members. Today there are over 50 participating members and a lesser number of observing members.

The ISO/TC 176 embarked on the idea of making generic Quality Management Standards for worldwide application, using UK BS-5750 Standards and Canadian CSA Z 299 10 Series Standards as the primary base. One could say that BS-5750 and CSA Z 299 were the "mother" and "father" of the ISO 9000 Standards, but only if it is understood that the offspring has now become the "parent."

The ISO 9000 concept is that certain generic characteristics of management practice can be usefully standardized, giving mutual benefit to producers and users alike. The first editions of these standards (ISO 9000 to 9004) were completed in 1986, published in early 1987, revised and published again in 1994, and again in 2000. After issue, the ISO 9000 Standards became the most widespread in the industry, with the most rapid adoption by the international standards community and the greatest sales of any ISO Standard in existence.

Effects of ISO 9000

What has happened since the ISO 9000 Standards became available?

1. They have been adopted without change as national standards in almost every country, including all of the European Community (EC), Japan, and the United States.
2. They have the highest worldwide awareness of any standard.

d-party assessment and registration services exist for recognizing conform-
to ISO 9000 Standards in most of the more than 70 countries that recognize the
tandard.

...y organizations have come to the conclusion that quality and business improvement has been a result of implementation of the ISO 9000 standard. In addition,
public, customer, and supplier perception has improved as a result of meeting the
requirements of ISO 9000 or better.

5. Many nationally and internationally recognized product certification systems have
   incorporated the ISO 9000 Standards as a first-phase requirement for approval to
   use their mark.

6. A multitude of companies and organizations, both large and small, have initiated
   vigorous company programs to implement the ISO 9000 Standards at their operation sites.

7. Numerous governmental purchasers have made ISO 9000 registration (or its equivalent) a requirement for their large contract suppliers, who have in turn have passed
   the requirement on to their suppliers.

Why have the ISO 9000 Standards had such a major, worldwide impact?

1. The ISO 9000 Standards are simply tools used to achieve the broad objective of
   continual improvement, which is actively pursued at all levels in today's society.

2. Businesses and organizations in every sector have shifted their emphasis to the
   quality side of the quality/price equation because they believe that doing so is absolutely necessary to remain competitive in today's global markets. The push for
   quality and client satisfaction continues to be at an all-time high.

Companies that have successfully implemented an ISO 9000-based Quality Management
System are being pleasantly surprised with reduced costs, reduced products/service cycle
times, improved customer relationships, improved employee enthusiasm, innovation, and
morale.

It's worth the effort.

ISO 9000 Methods

How does the ISO 9000 Quality Management System accomplish all of this? It doesn't—*you*
accomplish it through the following:

- Writing down what you do (procedures and work instructions)

- Doing what you write down (production and service provision)

- Providing visible evidence that you are doing that which you have written down
  (quality records)

- Identifying errors and opportunities for improving what you do (internal audits,
  management review, continual improvement)

- Applying corrective action to prevent future errors and to improve what you do or
  modify what you have written down.

The ISO 9001:2000 Quality Management System provides a formalized and disciplined means of accomplishing this effort. Positive outputs result from the effort—and yes, it does require some faith to stay with the process until the results begin to pull you through.

The ISO 9001:2000 Quality Management System Standard includes such topics as:

Document control	Planning
Management responsibility and commitment	Management review
Customer focus	Resource management
Quality Policy	Work environment
Product realization	Purchasing
Production and service provision	Monitoring and measurement
Analysis of data	Improvement

A Different Perspective of Quality

It's beneficial to start this discussion with a simple definition of "quality." The term *quality* has been used and abused in so many ways that it is on the verge of losing (or has already lost) all meaning. I personally dislike the term quality and look forward to the day when quality simply becomes the way we do business and live our lives, so that the term no longer has to be a standard by which things are measured.

A number of the more popular definitions of quality are associated with various quality gurus:

> *Conformance to requirements*
> —*Philip Crosby*

> *Fitness for use*
> —*J. M. Juran*

> *Exceeding customers' expectations through continuous improvement of processes*
> —*W. Edwards Deming*

For the purposes of ISO 9000:

Quality is not what we do; it is the way we do things.

Until now, management generally focused on who was at fault when an error occurred—finding the guilty party and punishing him or her through reprimands or through negative performance reviews. In reality, a person does not plan to make a mistake or error, so why do they occur? According to W. Edwards Deming's "85-15" rule, 85 percent of what goes wrong is caused by the system; only 15 percent is caused by the individual. Thus, a person makes a mistake or error because the system allows that person to do so. Logic then dictates that if we can control the system and the work processes, we can control the quality.

This gives rise to a very simple approach of how to achieve quality which is the essence of the ISO 9000 Standard requirements.

Quality is the result of controlled processes.

If the process is correct and controlled, then the output of that process is more likely to be correct. The ISO 9000 Quality System is, therefore, based on controlling the work processes and the metrics associated with those processes to ensure that they are in "control."

Process, primary work process, and work process are all terms we must understand in order to fully appreciate the simplistic power of this definition of quality.

Quality is the way we do things.

CONCLUSION

Quality is not what we do, it is the way we do things. Eighty-five percent of what goes wrong is the cause of the system; only fifteen percent is the cause of the individual (Deming). Therefore, a person makes a mistake or error because the system allows that person to do so. Quality, then, is the result of controlled processes.

ISO created the 9001 Standard to provide guidance on controlling work processes. Successfully implementing an ISO 9001:2000 Quality Management System will reduce costs, improve customer relationships and strengthen employee morale.

Chapter 3

Objectives and Awareness

OBJECTIVES OF A QUALITY MANAGEMENT SYSTEM

The ISO 9001:2000 International Standard states the Quality Management System—Requirements, as noted on the title page of the standard. This title is a revision from the 1994 issue of the standard in that it no longer includes the term "Quality assurance."

The Introduction of the ISO 9001 International Standard further states:

> *This International Standard promotes the adoption of a process approach when developing, implementing and improving the effectiveness of a quality management system, to enhance customer satisfaction by meeting customer requirements.*
>
> *An activity using resources, and managed in order to enable the transformation of inputs into outputs, can be considered a process. Often the output from one process directly forms the input to the next.*
>
> *The application of a system of processes within an organization, together with the identification and interactions of these processes, and their management, can be referred to as the "process approach."*

The ISO 9001:2000 Based Quality Management System requirements focus on control of the Work Processes (as stated in Chapter 2 and Chapter 11).

Quality is the result of controlled processes.

The concept is that if the process is controlled, then the quality of the output is also controlled. The Quality Management System accomplishes this control by requiring written operating procedures and work instructions for processes that affect quality and by requiring adherence to them.

The ISO 9001:2000 International Standard emphasizes prevention and corrective action related to errors (called non-conformances). These non-conformances occur and are found while operating according to the written procedures and work instructions and result in corrective and preventive actions. By having a Quality Management System, the customer is therefore offered consistent products and services that meet specified requirements. The revised ISO 9001:2000 Quality Management System now includes the requirement for continual improvement of the processes responsible for producing these products and services.

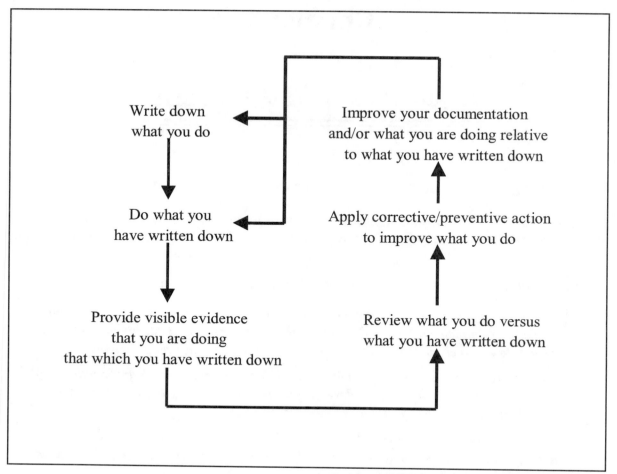

Figure 3-1. A Simplistic Interpretation of ISO 9001

The Quality Management System itself is comprised of a Quality System Manual and a limited number of Quality System Procedures. These Quality System Procedures are overarching—they set the overall framework for the operating procedures, e.g., service delivery procedures and work instructions. The content of the operating procedures and work instructions is owned by those responsible for the associated work and must adequately represent "what you do."

If the work performed is not in accordance with the content of the operating procedures, it is not that the Quality Management System has failed, nor that the Quality Management System does not work. Instead, the failure is evidence that employees are not following the requirements of their operating procedures. The appropriate correction might therefore be a change in the associated procedure, more training, or personnel discipline. If a change in the procedure is required, then it involves changing the Quality Management System documentation and re-issuing in a controlled manner. The Quality Management System is also involved in internal audits of the operations procedures and processes, i.e., "are they being followed?"

It is easy to become confused by the preceding material, and it takes some getting familiar with the terminology and the intent of the ISO 9000 International Standard in order to minimize this confusion.

> *For the purposes of this book, the Quality System is simply that which is defined in the Quality Management System Manual and the Quality Management System procedures coupled with methods for assuring compliance and improvement.*

QUALITY SYSTEM AWARENESS TRAINING

Once the Quality Management System has been established and the Mission Statement, Quality Policy, Quality Goals, and Quality Plan have been developed, it is important to make everyone within the organization aware of it. This is generally accomplished through a planned presentation made to all employees.

The quality awareness presentation should be designed to cover "where we are," "where we are going," "how we are going to get there," and "what is our involvement." The presentation averages about three hours in duration and may include handouts and an applicable video. The quality awareness material is company specific and should be made a part of the new hire orientation program.

The ISO 9001:2000 Standard does not require a quality awareness presentation, but experience shows that it is a necessity for everyone to have a common understanding of the Quality Management System for the implementation efforts to succeed with a minimum of effort.

A typical quality awareness training index might include:

1. A welcome and an introduction
2. The Mission Statement, including quality policies and goals
3. A definition of quality
5. A definition of cycle time (as applicable)
6. A presentation of the organization's quality structure
7. A description of the organization's Quality Management System
8. A review of "where are we now" and "what comes next"
9. A plan for continual improvement
10. A video on quality (approximately 25 minutes in length is recommended)

The quality awareness presentation is usually the first exposure of the employee to the Quality Management System and therefore must be well conceived and presented because it sets the stage for success. A senior management representative should participate in each of the sessions.

CONCLUSION

The Quality Management System requires operations to have a method of providing products/services that consistently meet specified requirements. This is accomplished through requiring operations procedures/work instructions, training, and resource allocation. The Quality Management System also requires independent audits of operations for compliance with the respective procedures/work instructions, noting variations as non-conformances.

In summary, the normal management functions of operations should include, if they do not already:

- Problem identification
- Prioritization
- Corrective action
- Measurement
- Follow-up
- Verification
- Process improvement
- Continual improvement

The Quality Management System provides overarching procedures that define how to write operations procedures/work instructions, how to format requirements, methods for change, and controlled distribution, but do not define procedural content.

Chapter 4

Steering Committees

IMPORTANCE OF STEERING COMMITTEES

It is critical to success that senior management is actively involved in the continuing integration of quality into management systems and processes. It is equally critical to success that senior management is involved in the continuing maintenance of quality relative to management systems and processes. This is most easily accomplished through the formation of a steering committee, made up of senior management, which represents all major functions within the company.

This steering committee (refer to Figure 4-1) is generally named the Quality Steering Committee (QSC) or Continuous (or Continual) Improvement Steering Committee (CISC), as desired. ABS—a company used to demonstrate applied examples throughout this book—began with QSCs and altered the name to CISCs after four years to better reflect the changing role of the steering committee from quality to continuous (continual) improvement.

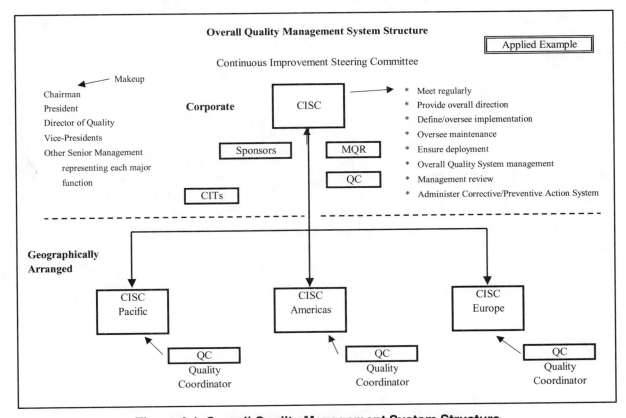

Figure 4-1. Overall Quality Management System Structure

(The difference between continuous and continual improvement is that "continual" represents a trend of improvements that may be interspersed by periods of no improvement whereas "continuous" represents a non-interrupted trend.)

For smaller organizations, one may not have a separate committee, but manage the Quality Management System as a part of regular management staff meetings. These meetings accomplish the same purpose so long as they include the Quality Management System as a regular agenda item.

The CISC, QSC, or staff meetings, as the case may be, is responsible for the Quality Management System's overall direction and management, for the integration of quality, and for the associated maintenance of the Quality Management System in the organization's operational management systems and processes. Keep in mind that direction and management of the Quality Management System and integration of quality into Operational Management Systems are not the same thing.

The CISC (or equivalent) is also responsible for successful implementation and continued maintenance of the Quality Management System, which includes the following tasks:

- Establish guidelines and priorities for operation of the Quality Management System.
- Assure that all employees are appropriately trained and aware of the Quality Management System requirements.
- Address major quality and cycle-time issues.
- Form Corrective Action Teams on critical quality matters/issues as deemed necessary.
- Resolve issues forwarded to the CISC from within the organization or from customers.
- Ensure that internal audits are performed and that follow-up actions resulting from those audits are accomplished.
- Review external audit findings and associated follow-up actions.
- Establish an environment of continual improvement throughout the organization.

The CISC, like all quality-specific teams, is a consensus group. A consensus group is one in which all participants are equal, regardless of title or position within the organization. A consensus group arrives at a decision that each member can live with and support—as compared with an autocratic group, where the leader makes the decision, or with a democratic group, where the group votes and the majority vote is accepted as the decision. A consensus group focuses on agreement rather than on disagreement.

Management Review

The CISC also performs the Management Review requirement as called for in the ISO 9001:2000 Standard, Section 5.6.

> **Top management shall review the organization's quality management system, at planned intervals, to ensure its continuing suitability, adequacy, and effectiveness. This review shall include assessing opportunities for improvement and the need for changes to the quality management system, including the quality policy and quality objectives. Records from management reviews shall be maintained.**

Steering Committee Guidelines

Each steering committee and standing Continual Improvement Team (CIT), as explained below, should develop a charter and publish a listing of membership.

Meetings must occur on a regular basis with consideration of the following meeting guidelines.

1. Start and finish the meeting on time.
2. Establish and complete the planned agenda.
3. Keep discussions relevant.
4. Do not let the Quality Management System meeting (or that portion of the staff meeting relating to the Quality Management System) become a staff meeting.
5. Publish meeting minutes within three (3) working days.
6. De-emphasize status or rank.
7. Do not turn the meetings into problem-solving sessions; direct problems to the appropriate people or teams for solution.
8. Strive for consensus decisions and stronger commitment to those decisions by all members.
9. Allow only one person to speak at a time; eliminate side conversations.
10. Generate different views and suggestions.
11. Don't criticize.
12. Encourage participation, but don't force it.
13. Critique each meeting as a regular agenda item and apply corrective action at the next meeting.

Each CISC should have an appointed chairperson who is responsible for agenda preparation and for facilitating the meeting. The Management System Representative may be the appointed person. If the meetings are a part of regular staff meetings, the portion dedicated to the Quality Management System should have its own agenda.

If there are unit or division CISCs below the top level CISC, they should have a sponsor who resides on the top level CISC. The same is true for CITs (Continual Improvement Teams) or CATs (Corrective Action Teams), each having a sponsor residing on the chartering group.

Continual Improvement Teams

Continual Improvement Teams (CITs) manage parts of the Quality System on behalf of the CISC. Each CIT has a sponsor who is a member of the CISC. The sponsor participates in the selection of a chairperson and the CIT membership. Consideration should be given to the following standing (permanent) CITs:

Communications CIT (C-CIT): This CIT is responsible for internal communications related to quality awareness, and for administering the employee quality recognition programs, if there are any (see paragraph 5.5.3 of the ISO 9001:2000 Standard). An example of one C-CIT Charter includes the following responsibilities:

- Impart an ongoing awareness of the continual improvement process.

- Encourage participation in the organization's continual improvement process.

- Develop and administer programs that acknowledge participation and achievement in the continual improvement process.

- Cultivate an environment that encourages two-way communication.

- Nurture a commitment to the organization's continual improvement process.

Human Resource CIT (HR-CIT): An example of the HR-CIT Charter might include the following:

- Provide each employee with a clear understanding of the organization's personnel policies, programs, and procedures and the role of the Human Resources Department in its implementation.

- Develop and administer policies, programs, and procedures that meet the needs of employees and their families while being cost effective.

- Provide a support role between management and employees that encourages communication and participation in an open environment.

- Ensure that all policies, programs, and procedures are designed and administered in an equitable manner to all employees in accordance with all local, state, and federal rules and laws.

- Develop and administer a Training and Career Development Plan that will achieve quality and consistency throughout the organization and enhance the level of personnel development of employees.

Finance CIT (F-CIT): An example of the F-CIT Charter might include the following:

- Provide leadership, guidance, direction, education, and monitoring of the continual improvement system related to financial matters on behalf of the CISC or equivalent.

- Assist all employees in determining and tracking work process measurements.

Information Management Systems CIT (IMS-CIT) or equivalent: An example of the IMS-CIT Charter might include the following:

- Encourage within IMS a commitment to quality and continuous improvement in the organization's work processes.

- Foster the development of a thorough understanding of the company's Quality Management System and continual improvement process among all IMS employees.

- Ensure IMS work processes adhere to the organization's Quality Management System.

- Manage the IMS related portion of the Corrective and Preventive Action System.

Work Environment and Safety CIT (WES-CIT): This CIT is generally more associated with a manufacturing organization and deals with the general work environment and safety, as stated in its name. The makeup is flexible and the charter is flexible. Some organizations have monthly inspections by the team members with rewards and/or recognition for those areas meeting the developed requirements.

Customer Satisfaction CIT (CS-CIT): This CIT deals with a focus on customer satisfaction and the analysis of customer complaints, surveys, customer communications, etc.

Operations CIT (OP-CIT): Depending on the size and complexity of the organization, this CIT would coordinate operations-related items and manage the Corrective and Preventive Action System associated with operations. Normally, it is made up of the managers of each the operation departments.

Training CIT (T-CIT): This CIT is responsible for the training aspect of the company and is flexible in makeup and charter.

As should be evident, the CITs lend themselves to a Total Quality Management process with elements within them that enhance an ISO 9001:2000 Quality Management System and in integrating quality into management systems in general. If the company is implementing an ISO 9001:2000 Quality Management System as a part of a Total Quality Management System or process, then it is very important to establish the quality structure that encompasses them both. Although the ISO 9001:2000 Standard does not require the establishment of CISCs, QSCs, or CITs, it does imply that there is a quality structure.

If the quality structure is a multi-unit one, then the establishment of a Quality Council should be a consideration. The Quality Council would have the responsibility to coordinate among the various CISCs and to set policy and strategy relative to quality. The Quality Council is usually comprised of the chairpersons of each of the CISCs and selected executive management. The Quality Council would generally meet quarterly.

Of course, any structure within any company is highly dependent upon the size and geographical arrangement of that company and should be adjusted accordingly.

What is presented here may seem quite complex and may seem to apply to larger organizations more than to smaller organizations; however, the functions mentioned within the CISC and CIT charters should be considered independent of who has the responsibility for such.

The bottom line is to keep the quality organizational structure *as simple as possible* but to ensure that the structure meets the needs of the Quality System and its requirements.

Sponsor Responsibilities

The following are examples of responsibilities that might be assigned to the sponsor of a Continuous Improvement Steering Committee (CISC), Continual Improvement Team (CIT), or Corrective Action Team (CAT):

1. Each CISC, CIT, and CAT will have a sponsor assigned by the originating function who resides on that originating function.

2. The sponsor assists in selection of the team chairperson and team members, as necessary and when appropriate.

3. The sponsor assists in the establishment of the team charter, if not already established by the originating function that chartered the team or committee.

4. The sponsor assists in removing any barriers that might interfere with the team's performance of its charter

5. The sponsor monitors the status of the assigned team or committee and reports that status to the respective originating function that chartered the team or committee.

6. The sponsor of CITs and CATs will not normally attend all meetings.

7. Closeout report presentations are coordinated through the respective sponsor.

8. The sponsor is not to interfere in the CIT or CAT operation except to provide guidance and assistance as necessary.

9. CISC sponsors are normally the highest-ranking individuals of the respective organization represented by the CISC.

CONCLUSION

The formation of a Steering Committee is one method of ensuring continuous involvement of management in the quality improvement process. This committee, called either the Quality Steering Committee (QSC) or Continuous (or Continual) Improvement Steering Committee (CISC), is responsible for the direction and control of the Quality Management System, for the integration of quality, and for the associated maintenance of the Quality Management System in the organization's operational management systems and processes.

Chapter 5

Self Assessment

SELF-ASSESSMENT GUIDELINES

Some companies and organizations avoid self-assessments because of a sense of inadequacy or of not really wanting to know the present status of their respective Quality Management System, or for a number of unexplained reasons. However, self-assessment is an effective tool for establishing a baseline with which to compare later status and is a real learning experience that speeds up the implementation process.

Provided in this chapter is a model self-assessment that is coupled with a unique method of rating and prioritizing needs. The method may be adapted and customized to assess almost any organizational area or function. In addition, a complete self-assessment versus the ISO 9001:2000 Standard is provided, the results of which are cross-referenced to the Standard. In other words, the self-assessment is based on a series of questions for each element of the ISO 9001:2000 Standard, which includes two viewpoints, "current implementation status" and "perceived importance" of the element. The results are expressed in numerical form and prioritized based on implementation need. The information can then be converted into an Action Plan relative to the Quality Management System.

From this self-assessment, one can determine the company or organization Quality Management System implementation needs, which can then be used to develop a Quality Management System Implementation Plan (see Chapter 6).

It is suggested that each member of the management team making up the Management Staff, Quality Steering Committee, or equivalent quality system structure complete the assessment questionnaire. The results should then be analyzed, averaged, and compiled using the "Needs Assessment Listing—Ranked by Need" form. The results of this effort can then be used in the development of the Quality Management System Implementation Plan and in the determination of priorities of effort.

In addition, each specific section of the self-assessment should be individually analyzed to determine the individual element implementation needs or commitment as noted in Columns A and B of the form. Any Column A element of less than 4 indicates an implementation need for that element. Any Column B element of less than 4 indicates a lack of commitment or understanding of that element's importance.

It is suggested that this self-assessment be completed annually for the first two years of the implementation process. It is also noted that the format may be adapted for other use within the company or organization.

CONCLUSION

Self-assessment is a vital tool for establishing an initial status with which to compare later status assessments. Self-assessment is also an integral learning experience which facilitates the implementation process. A self-assessment questionnaire, to be completed by each member of management making up the quality structure, should be based on the ISO 9001:2000 Standard.

Needs Assessment Inventory

In your view, with what success is this being achieved in your company?	4 Quality Management System 4.1 General Requirements	In your view, how important is this item?

Instructions: Read the assessment question/statement and circle your response in Column A and B; total column A and enter in the marked box. If an item does not apply enter a 5 in each column.

5 4 3 2 1 | | 5 4 3 2 1

Column A / **Column B**

Column A		Column B
5 4 3 2 1	1. Has the organization established, implemented and does it maintain a quality management system?	5 4 3 2 1
5 4 3 2 1	2. Does the organization continually improve the effectiveness of the quality management system?	5 4 3 2 1
5 4 3 2 1	3. Has the organization identified the processes needed for the quality management system and their application throughout the organization?	5 4 3 2 1
5 4 3 2 1	4. Has the organization determined the sequence and interaction of these processes.	5 4 3 2 1
5 4 3 2 1	5. Has the organization determined the criteria and methods needed to ensure that both the operation and control of these processes are effective?	5 4 3 2 1
5 4 3 2 1	6. Does the organization ensure the availability of resources and information necessary to support the operation and monitoring of these processes?	5 4 3 2 1
5 4 3 2 1	7. Does the organization monitor, measure and analyze these processes?	5 4 3 2 1
5 4 3 2 1	8. Does the organization implement actions necessary to achieve planned results and continual improvement of these processes?	5 4 3 2 1
5 4 3 2 1	9. Has the organization identified the control of any outsourced processes to ensure conformity with requirements? If no processes are outsourced, mark a "5."	5 4 3 2 1

Sum Column A   Difference

45 − [ ] = [ ]

Any A Item of < 4 reflects a need in that category.

00-09 = Excellent
10-18 = Needs Work
19-27 = Strong Need
28-50 = Very Strong Need

Any B Item of < 4 reflects a need for improved commitment in that category.

Needs Assessment Inventory

In your view, with what success is this being achieved in your company?	**4 Quality Management System** **4.2 Documentation Requirements** Instructions: Read the assessment question/statement and circle your response in Column A and B; total column A and enter in the marked box. If an item does not apply enter a 5 in each column.	In your view, how important is this item?
5 4 3 2 1		5 4 3 2 1
Column A		Column B
5 4 3 2 1	1. Does the quality management system documentation include a Quality Policy and Quality Objectives?	5 4 3 2 1
5 4 3 2 1	2. Does the organization have a quality manual that includes the scope of the quality management system?	5 4 3 2 1
5 4 3 2 1	3. Does the quality manual include or reference documented procedures established for the QMS?	5 4 3 2 1
5 4 3 2 1	4. Does the quality manual include a description of the interaction between the processes of the QMS?	5 4 3 2 1
5 4 3 2 1	5. Are documents required by the quality management system controlled?	5 4 3 2 1
	6. Is there a documented procedure established to define the controls needed:	
5 4 3 2 1	a) to approve documents prior to issue	5 4 3 2 1
5 4 3 2 1	b) to review and update as necessary and re-approve	5 4 3 2 1
5 4 3 2 1	c) to ensure that changes and current revision status are identified.	5 4 3 2 1
5 4 3 2 1	d) to ensure that relevant and applicable versions are available at points of use.	5 4 3 2 1
5 4 3 2 1	e) to ensure that documents remain legible and readily identifiable.	5 4 3 2 1
5 4 3 2 1	f) to ensure that document of external origin are identified and their distribution controlled.	5 4 3 2 1
5 4 3 2 1	g) to prevent unintended use of obsolete documents.	5 4 3 2 1
5 4 3 2 1	7. Does the quality management system documentation include the identification and control of records?	5 4 3 2 1
5 4 3 2 1	8. Does the quality management system documentation include documents needed by the organization to ensure the effective planning, operation and control of its processes?	5 4 3 2 1

Summation A   Difference

70 − ☐ = ☐

Any A Item of < 4 reflects a need in that category.	00-14 = Excellent 15-28 = Needs Work 29-42 = Strong Need 43-70 = Very Strong Need	Any B Item of < 4 reflects a need for improved commitment in that category.

Needs Assessment Inventory

In your view, with what success is this being achieved in your company? 5 4 3 2 1 Column A	**5 Management Responsibility** Instructions: Read the assessment question/statement and circle your response in Column A and B; total column A and enter in the marked box. If an item does not apply enter a 5 in each column.	In your view, how important is this item? 5 4 3 2 1 Column B
	Management Commitment (5.1)	
5 4 3 2 1	1. Does Top Management communicate to the organization the importance of meeting customer as well as statutory and regulatory requirements?	5 4 3 2 1
5 4 3 2 1	2. Has Top Management ensured the establishment of Quality Objectives?	5 4 3 2 1
5 4 3 2 1	3. Does Top Management conduct regular Management Reviews of the Quality Management System?	5 4 3 2 1
5 4 3 2 1	4. Does Top Management ensure the availability of resources?	5 4 3 2 1
	Customer Focus (5.2)	
5 4 3 2 1	5. Has Top Management ensured that customer requirements are determined and are met with the aim of enhancing customer satisfaction.	5 4 3 2 1
	Quality Policy (5.3)	
5 4 3 2 1	6. Has Top Management established a Quality Policy?	5 4 3 2 1
5 4 3 2 1	7. Is the Quality Policy appropriate to the organization?	5 4 3 2 1
5 4 3 2 1	8. Does the Quality Policy include a commitment to comply with requirements and continually improve the effectiveness of the Quality Management System?	5 4 3 2 1
5 4 3 2 1	9. Does the Quality Policy provide a framework for establishing and reviewing Quality Objectives?	5 4 3 2 1
5 4 3 2 1	10. Is the Quality Policy communicated and understood within the organization?	5 4 3 2 1
5 4 3 2 1	11. Is the Quality Policy reviewed for continuing suitability?	5 4 3 2 1

Summation A   Difference

55 − ☐ = ☐

Any A Item of < 4 reflects a need in that category.

00-11 = Excellent
12-22 = Needs Work
23-33 = Strong Need
34-55 = Very Strong Need

Any B Item of < 4 reflects a need for improved commitment in that category.

Needs Assessment Inventory

In your view, with what success is this being achieved in your company? 5 4 3 2 1 Column A	**5.4 Planning** **5.5 Responsibility, Authority and Communication** Instructions: Read the assessment question/statement and circle your response in Column A and B; total column A and enter in the marked box. If an item does not apply enter a 5 in each column.	In your view, how important is this item? 5 4 3 2 1 Column B
	Quality Objectives (5.4.1)	
5 4 3 2 1	1. Has Top Management ensured that quality objectives and product related objectives have been established at relevant functions and levels within the organization?	5 4 3 2 1
5 4 3 2 1	2 Are the quality objectives measureable and consistent with the quality policy?	5 4 3 2 1
	Quality Management System Planning (5.4.2)	
5 4 3 2 1	3. Has the planning of the QMS been carried out in order to meet the quality objectives?	5 4 3 2 1
5 4 3 2 1	4. Has the planning of the QMS been carried out in order to meet the general requirements of Section 4.1?	5 4 3 2 1
5 4 3 2 1	5. Is the integrity of the QMS maintained when changes to the system are planned and implemented?	5 4 3 2 1
	Responsibility and authority (5.5.1)	
5 4 3 2 1	6. Are responsibilities and authorities defined and communicated within the organization?	5 4 3 2 1
	Management representative (5.5.2)	
5 4 3 2 1	7. Has a member of the management who, irrespective of other responsibilities, been appointed as Management Quality Representative (MQR)?	5 4 3 2 1
5 4 3 2 1	8. Does the MQR ensure that the processes needed for the Quality Management System (QMS) are established, implemented and maintained?	5 4 3 2 1
5 4 3 2 1	9. Does the MQR report to top management on the performance of the QMS and any need of improvement?	5 4 3 2 1
5 4 3 2 1	10. Does the MQR ensure the promotion of awareness of customer requirements throughout the organization?	5 4 3 2 1
	Internal Communications (5.5.3)	
5 4 3 2 1	11. Have communications processes been established within the organization regarding the QMS?	5 4 3 2 1

Summation A Difference

$$55 - \boxed{} = \boxed{}$$

Any A Item of < 4 reflects a need in that category.

00-11 = Excellent
12-22 = Needs Work
23-33 = Strong Need
34-55 = Very Strong Need

Any B Item of < 4 reflects a need for improved commitment in that category.

Needs Assessment Inventory

In your view, with what success is this being achieved in your company?	5.6 Management Review	In your view, how important is this item?
5 4 3 2 1	Instructions: Read the assessment question/statement and circle your response in Column A and B; total column A and enter in the marked box. If an item does not apply enter a 5 in each column.	5 4 3 2 1
Column A		Column B

Column A	5.6 Management Review	Column B
	General (5.6.1)	
5 4 3 2 1	1. Does Top Management review the QMS at planned intervals to ensure its continuing suitability, adequacy and effectiveness?	5 4 3 2 1
5 4 3 2 1	2 Does this review include assessing opportunities for improvement and the need to change the QMS?	5 4 3 2 1
	Review Input (5.6.2)	
	3. Does the input to management review include:	
5 4 3 2 1	a) results of audits?	5 4 3 2 1
5 4 3 2 1	b) customer feedback?	5 4 3 2 1
5 4 3 2 1	c) process performance and product conformity?	5 4 3 2 1
5 4 3 2 1	d) status of preventive and corrective action?	5 4 3 2 1
5 4 3 2 1	e) follow-up actions from previous reviews?	5 4 3 2 1
5 4 3 2 1	f) changes that could affect the QMS?	5 4 3 2 1
5 4 3 2 1	g) recommendations for improvement?	5 4 3 2 1
	Review Outputs (5.6.3)	
	4. Does the output of the management review include:	
5 4 3 2 1	a) improvement of the effectiveness of the QMS and its processes?	5 4 3 2 1
5 4 3 2 1	b) improvement of product related to customer requirements?	5 4 3 2 1
5 4 3 2 1	c) resource needs?	5 4 3 2 1

Summation A   Difference

$$\boxed{60} - \boxed{} = \boxed{}$$

00-12 = Excellent
13-24 = Needs Work
25-36 = Strong Need
36-60 = Very Strong Need

Any A Item of < 4 reflects a need in that category.

Any B Item of < 4 reflects a need for improved commitment in that category.

Needs Assessment Inventory

In your view, with what success is this being achieved in your company?	**6 Resource Requirements** Instructions: Read the assessment question/statement and circle your response in Column A and B; total column A and enter in the marked box. If an item does not apply enter a 5 in each column.	In your view, how important is this item?
5 4 3 2 1 Column A		5 4 3 2 1 Column B
	Provision of Resources (6.1)	
	1. Has the organization determined and does it provide the resources needed:	
5 4 3 2 1	a) to implement and maintain the QMS and continually improve its effectiveness	5 4 3 2 1
5 4 3 2 1	b) to enhance customer satisfaction by meeting customer requirements?	5 4 3 2 1
	Human Resources (6.2)	
5 4 3 2 1	2. Are personnel performing work affecting product quality competent on the basis of appropriate education, training, skills and experience?	5 4 3 2 1
	3 Does the organization:	
5 4 3 2 1	a) provide training or other action to satisfy competence needs?	5 4 3 2 1
5 4 3 2 1	b) evaluate the effectiveness of the actions taken relative to personnel competence?	5 4 3 2 1
5 4 3 2 1	c) ensure that its personnel are aware of the relevance and importance of their activities and how they contribute to the achievement of quality objectives?	5 4 3 2 1
5 4 3 2 1	d) maintain appropriate records of education, training, skills and experience?	5 4 3 2 1
	Infrastructure (6.3)	
	4. To ensure conformity to product requirements, does the organization:	
5 4 3 2 1	a) provide buildings, workspace and associated utilities needed to achieve conformity?	5 4 3 2 1
5 4 3 2 1	b) provide the necessary process equipment?	5 4 3 2 1
5 4 3 2 1	c) provide the necessary supporting services?	5 4 3 2 1
	Work Environment (6.4)	
5 4 3 2 1	5. Has the organization determined and does it manage the work environment needed to achieve conformity to product requirements?	5 4 3 2 1

Summation A   Difference

$$\boxed{55} - \boxed{} = \boxed{}$$

Any A Item of < 4 reflects a need in that category.

00-11 = Excellent
12-22 = Needs Work
23-33 = Strong Need
34-55 = Very Strong Need

Any B Item of < 4 reflects a need for improved commitment in that category.

Needs Assessment Inventory

In your view, with what success is this being achieved in your company?	7 Product Realization 7.1 Planning of Product Realization Instructions: Read the assessment question/statement and circle your response in Column A and B; total column A and enter in the marked box. If an item does not apply enter a 5 in each column.	In your view, how important is this item?
5 4 3 2 1		5 4 3 2 1
Column A		Column B
5 4 3 2 1	1. Has the organization planned and developed the processes needed for product realization?	5 4 3 2 1
5 4 3 2 1	2. Is the planning of product realization consistent with the requirements of the other processes of the QMS?	5 4 3 2 1
	3. In planning product realization, has the organization determined:	
5 4 3 2 1	a) the quality objectives and requirements for the product?	5 4 3 2 1
5 4 3 2 1	b) the need to establish processes, documents, and provide resources specific to the product?	5 4 3 2 1
5 4 3 2 1	c) the required verification, validation, monitoring, inspection and test activities specific to the product and the criteria for product acceptance?	5 4 3 2 1
5 4 3 2 1	d) the records needed to provide evidence that the realization process and resulting product meet requirements?	5 4 3 2 1

Summation A   Difference

30 — ⬚ = ⬚

| 00-06 = Excellent |
| 07-12 = Needs Work |
| 13-18 = Strong Need |
| 19-30 = Very Strong Need |

Any A Item of < 4 reflects a need in that category.

Any B Item of < 4 reflects a need for improved commitment in that category.

Needs Assessment Inventory

In your view, with what success is this being achieved in your company?	7 Product Realization 7.2 Customer Related Processes Instructions: Read the assessment question/statement and circle your response in Column A and B; total column A and enter in the marked box. If an item does not apply enter a 5 in each column.	In your view, how important is this item?
5 4 3 2 1 Column A		5 4 3 2 1 Column B
	Determination of requirements related to the product (7.2.1)	
	1. Has the organization determined:	
5 4 3 2 1	a) the requirements specified by the customer, including delivery and post delivery activities?	5 4 3 2 1
5 4 3 2 1	b) the requirements not stated but necessary for specified or intended use, where known?	5 4 3 2 1
5 4 3 2 1	c) statutory and regulatory requirements related to the product?	5 4 3 2 1
5 4 3 2 1	d) additional organization determined requirements?	5 4 3 2 1
	Review of requirements related to the product (7.2.2)	
5 4 3 2 1	2. Does the organization review the requirements related to the product prior to the commitment to supply it?	5 4 3 2 1
	3. Does the organization ensure that:	
5 4 3 2 1	a) the product requirements are defined?	5 4 3 2 1
5 4 3 2 1	b) the contract or order requirements differing from those previously expressed are resolved?	5 4 3 2 1
5 4 3 2 1	c) the organization has the ability to meet the defined requirements?	5 4 3 2 1
5 4 3 2 1	4. Are records of the results of the review and actions arising out of the review maintained?	5 4 3 2 1
5 4 3 2 1	5. Where there is no documented statement of requirement does the organization confirm the requirements?	5 4 3 2 1
5 4 3 2 1	6. Where product requirements are changed, are amendments made and personnel advised?	5 4 3 2 1
	Customer Communication (7.2.3)	
	7. Does the organization determine and implement arrangements for communicating with customers related to:	
5 4 3 2 1	a) product information?	5 4 3 2 1
5 4 3 2 1	b) enquiries, contracts or order handling?	5 4 3 2 1
5 4 3 2 1	c) customer feedback, including customer complaints?	5 4 3 2 1

Summation A   Difference

$$\boxed{70} - \boxed{} = \boxed{}$$

Any A Item of < 4 reflects a need in that category.

00-14 = Excellent
15-28 = Needs Work
29-42 = Strong Need
43-70 = Very Strong Need

Any B Item of < 4 reflects a need for improved commitment in that category.

Needs Assessment Inventory

In your view, with what success is this being achieved in your company?	7 Product Realization 7.3 Design and Development Planning and Inputs	In your view, how important is this item?

Instructions: Read the assessment question/statement and circle your in Column A and B; total column A and enter the marked box. If an item does not enter a 5 in each column.

Column A		Column B
5 4 3 2 1		5 4 3 2 1

Column A		Column B
	Design and Development Planning (7.3.1)	
5 4 3 2 1	1. Does the organization plan and control the design and development of product?	5 4 3 2 1
	2. In the design and development planning, does the organization determine:	
5 4 3 2 1	a) the design and development stages?	5 4 3 2 1
5 4 3 2 1	b) the review, verification and validation that are appropriate to each design and development stage?	5 4 3 2 1
5 4 3 2 1	c) the responsibilities and authorities for design and development?	5 4 3 2 1
5 4 3 2 1	3. Does the organization manage the interfaces between different groups involved in design and development to ensure effective communication and assignments?	5 4 3 2 1
5 4 3 2 1	4. Is the planning output updated as the design and development progresses?	5 4 3 2 1
	Design and Development Inputs (7.3.2)	
5 4 3 2 1	5. Are inputs related to product requirements determined and records maintained?	5 4 3 2 1
	6. Do the Design and Development Inputs include:	
5 4 3 2 1	a) functional and performance requirements?	5 4 3 2 1
5 4 3 2 1	b) applicable statutory and regulatory requirements?	5 4 3 2 1
5 4 3 2 1	c) information derived from previous similar designs, where applicable?	5 4 3 2 1
5 4 3 2 1	d) other essential requirements?	5 4 3 2 1
5 4 3 2 1	7. Are inputs reviewed for adequacy, conflict and completeness?	5 4 3 2 1

Summation A   Difference

$$\boxed{60} - \boxed{} = \boxed{}$$

00-12 = Excellent
13-24 = Needs Work
25-36 = Strong Need
37-60 = Very Strong Need

Any A Item of < 4 reflects a need in that category.

Any B Item of < 4 reflects a need for improved commitment in that category.

Needs Assessment Inventory

In your view, with what success is this being achieved in your company?	7 Product Realization 7.3 Design and Development Outputs, Review, Verification, Validation & Changes Instructions: Read the assessment question/statement and circle your response in Column A and B; total column A and enter in the marked box. If an item does not apply enter a 5 in each column.	In your view, how important is this item?
5 4 3 2 1 Column A		5 4 3 2 1 Column B
	Design and Development Outputs (7.3.3)	
5 4 3 2 1	1. Are the outputs of design and development provided in a form that enables verification against the input?	5 4 3 2 1
	2. Do the design and development outputs:	
5 4 3 2 1	a) meet the input requirements.	5 4 3 2 1
5 4 3 2 1	b) provide appropriate information for purchasing, production and for service provision?	5 4 3 2 1
5 4 3 2 1	c) contain or reference product acceptance criteria?	5 4 3 2 1
5 4 3 2 1	d) specify the characteristics of the product that are essential for its safe and proper use?	5 4 3 2 1
	Design and Development Review (7.3.4)	
5 4 3 2 1	3. Are systematic reviews of design and development done at suitable stages in accordance with the plan?	5 4 3 2 1
5 4 3 2 1	4. Are reviews done to evaluate the ability of the results to meet requirements?	5 4 3 2 1
5 4 3 2 1	5. Are reviews done to identify any problems and propose necessary action?	5 4 3 2 1
5 4 3 2 1	6. Do participants in design reviews include representatives of functions concerned with the design and development stages being reviewed?	5 4 3 2 1
5 4 3 2 1	7. Are the results of reviews and any necessary actions documented and maintained?	5 4 3 2 1
	Design and Review Verification (7.3.5)	
5 4 3 2 1	8. Is verification performed to ensure that the design and development outputs have met the input requirements? Are the results documented?	5 4 3 2 1
	Design and Development Validation (7.3.6)	
5 4 3 2 1	9. Is validation performed to ensure that the resulting product is capable of meeting the specified requirements? Are the results documented?	5 4 3 2 1
	Control of Design and Development Changes (7.3.7)	
5 4 3 2 1	10. Are changes identified and records maintained?	5 4 3 2 1

Summation A   Difference

$$ \boxed{65} - \boxed{} = \boxed{} $$

Any A Item of < 4 reflects a need in that category.

00-13 = Excellent
14-26 = Needs Work
27-39 = Strong Need
40-65 = Very Strong Need

Any B Item of < 4 reflects a need for improved commitment in that category.

Needs Assessment Inventory

In your view, with what success is this being achieved in your company?	**7 Product Realization** **7.4 Purchasing** Instructions: Read the assessment question/statement and circle your response in Column A and B; total column A and enter in the marked box. If an item does not apply enter a 5 in each column.	In your view, how important is this item?
5 4 3 2 1		5 4 3 2 1
Column A		Column B
	Purchasing Process (7.4.1)	
5 4 3 2 1	1. Does the organization ensure that the purchased product conforms to specified purchase requirements?	5 4 3 2 1
5 4 3 2 1	2. Does the organization evaluate and select suppliers based on their ability to supply product in accordance with the organization's requirements?	5 4 3 2 1
	Purchasing Information (7.4.2)	
	3. Does the purchasing information describe the product, including where appropriate:	
5 4 3 2 1	a) requirements for approval?	5 4 3 2 1
5 4 3 2 1	b) requirements for qualification of personnel?	5 4 3 2 1
5 4 3 2 1	c) quality management system requirements?	5 4 3 2 1
	Verification of purchased product (7.4.3)	
5 4 3 2 1	4. Has the organization established and implemented inspection or other activities necessary for ensuring that purchased product meets specified purchase requirements?	5 4 3 2 1
5 4 3 2 1	5. When the organization or its customer intends to perform verification at the supplier's premises, are the intended verification arrangements and method of product release in the purchasing information stated?	5 4 3 2 1

Any A Item of < 4 reflects a need in that category.

Summation A   Difference

$$ \boxed{35} - \boxed{} = \boxed{} $$

00-07 = Excellent
08-14 = Needs Work
15-22 = Strong Need
23-35 = Very Strong Need

Any B Item of < 4 reflects a need for improved commitment in that category.

Needs Assessment Inventory

In your view, with what success is this being achieved in your company?	7 Product Realization 7.5 Production and Service Provision Instructions: Read the assessment question/statement and circle your response in Column A and B; total column A and enter in the marked box. If an item does not apply enter a 5 in each column.	In your view, how important is this item?
5 4 3 2 1 Column A		5 4 3 2 1 Column B
	Control of production and service provision (7.5.1)	
	1. Does the organization plan and carry out production and service under controlled conditions, including:	
5 4 3 2 1	a) the availability of information that describes the characteristics of the product?	5 4 3 2 1
5 4 3 2 1	b) the availability of work instructions, as necessary?	5 4 3 2 1
5 4 3 2 1	c) the use of suitable equipment?	5 4 3 2 1
5 4 3 2 1	d) the availability and use of monitoring and measuring equipment?	5 4 3 2 1
5 4 3 2 1	e) the implementation of monitoring and measurement equipment?	5 4 3 2 1
5 4 3 2 1	f) the implementation of release, delivery and post-delivery activities?	5 4 3 2 1
	Validation of processes for production & service provision	
5 4 3 2 1	2. Does the organization validate any processes for production and service provision where the resulting output cannot be verified by subsequent monitoring or measurement?	5 4 3 2 1
5 4 3 2 1	3. Does the validation demonstrate the ability of these processes to achieve planned results?	5 4 3 2 1
	4. Has the organization established arrangements for these processes, as applicable:	
5 4 3 2 1	a) defined criteria for review and approval?	5 4 3 2 1
5 4 3 2 1	b) approval of equipment and qualification of personnel?	5 4 3 2 1
5 4 3 2 1	c) use of specific methods and procedures?	5 4 3 2 1
5 4 3 2 1	d) requirements for records?	5 4 3 2 1
5 4 3 2 1	e) revalidation?	5 4 3 2 1

Summation A   Difference

$$\boxed{65} - \boxed{} = \boxed{}$$

Any A Item of < 4 reflects a need in that category.

00-13 = Excellent
14-26 = Needs Work
27-39 = Strong Need
40-65 = Very Strong Need

Any B Item of < 4 reflects a need for improved commitment in that category.

Needs Assessment Inventory

In your view, with what success is this being achieved in your company?	7 Product Realization 7.5 Production and Service Provision (continued) Instructions: Read the assessment question/statement and circle your in Column A and B; total column A and enter the marked box. If an item does not enter a 5 in each column.	In your view, how important is this item?
5 4 3 2 1		5 4 3 2 1
Column A		Column B
	Identification and Traceability (7.5.3)	
5 4 3 2 1	1. Is the product identified by suitable means throughout the production process (where appropriate)?	5 4 3 2 1
5 4 3 2 1	2. Does the organization identify the product status with respect to monitoring and measurement requirements?	5 4 3 2 1
5 4 3 2 1	3. Where traceability is a requirement, does the organization control and record the unique identification of the product?	5 4 3 2 1
	Customer Property (7.5.4)	
5 4 3 2 1	4. Does the organization identify, verify, protect and safeguard customer property provided for use of incorporation into the product?	5 4 3 2 1
5 4 3 2 1	5. If any customer property is lost, damaged or otherwise found to be unsuitable for use, is this reported to the customer and are records maintained?	5 4 3 2 1
	7.5.5 Preservation of Product (7.5.5)	
5 4 3 2 1	6. Does the organization preserve the conformity of product during internal processing and delivery to the intended destination?	5 4 3 2 1
5 4 3 2 1	7. Does the preservation include identification, handling, packaging, storage and protection?	5 4 3 2 1

Summation A   Difference

| 35 | − | | = | |

Any A Item of < 4
reflects a need
in that category.

00-07 = Excellent
08-14 = Needs Work
15-22 = Strong Need
22-35 = Very Strong Need

Any B Item of < 4
reflects a need for
improved
in that category.

Needs Assessment Inventory

In your view, with what success is this being achieved in your company?	**7 Product Realization** **7.6 Control of Monitoring and Measuring Devices** Instructions: Read the assessment question/statement and circle your response in Column A and B; total column A and enter in the marked box. If an item does not apply enter a 5 in each column.	In your view, how important is this item?
5 4 3 2 1		5 4 3 2 1
Column A		Column B
5 4 3 2 1	1. Has the organization determined the monitoring and measurement to be undertaken and the devices needed to provide evidence of conformity of product to determined requirements?	5 4 3 2 1
5 4 3 2 1	2. Has the organization established processes to ensure that monitoring and measuring equipment can be carried out and are carried out in a manner that is consistent with the monitoring and measurement requirements?	5 4 3 2 1
	3. Where necessary to validate results, is the measuring equipment:	
5 4 3 2 1	a) calibrated or verified at specified intervals, or prior to use, against measurement standards traceable to international or national standards?	5 4 3 2 1
5 4 3 2 1	b) where no such standard exists, is the basis used for calibration or verification recorded?	5 4 3 2 1
5 4 3 2 1	c) adjusted or re-adjusted as necessary?	5 4 3 2 1
5 4 3 2 1	d) identified to enable the calibration status to be determined?	5 4 3 2 1
5 4 3 2 1	e) safeguarded from adjustments that would invalidate the measurement result?	5 4 3 2 1
5 4 3 2 1	f) protected from damage and deterioration during handling, maintenance and storage?	5 4 3 2 1
5 4 3 2 1	4. Does the organization assess and record the validity of the previous measuring results when the equipment is found not to conform to requirements?	5 4 3 2 1
5 4 3 2 1	5. Are records of the results of calibration and verification maintained?	5 4 3 2 1
5 4 3 2 1	6. When used, is the ability of computer software to satisfy the intended application confirmed prior to use and reconfirmed as necessary?	5 4 3 2 1

Summation A   Difference

$$\boxed{45} - \boxed{} = \boxed{}$$

Any A Item of < 4 reflects a need in that category.	00-09 = Excellent 10-18 = Needs Work 19-27 = Strong Need 28-45 = Very Strong Need	Any B Item of < 4 reflects a need for improved commitment in that category.

Needs Assessment Inventory

In your view, with what success is this being achieved in your company?	**8 Measurement, Analysis and Improvement** Instructions: Read the assessment question/statement and circle your response in Column A and B; total column A and enter in the marked box. If an item does not apply enter a 5 in each column.	In your view, how important is this item?
5 4 3 2 1		5 4 3 2 1
Column A		Column B

	General (8.1)	
	1. Has the organization planned and implemented the monitoring, measurement, analysis and improvement processes needed to:	
5 4 3 2 1	a) demonstrate conformity of the product?	5 4 3 2 1
5 4 3 2 1	b) ensure conformity of the quality management system?	5 4 3 2 1
5 4 3 2 1	c) continually improve the effectiveness of the quality management system?	5 4 3 2 1
	Monitoring and Measurement (8.2)	
	Customer Satisfaction (8.2.1)	
5 4 3 2 1	2. Does the organization monitor information relating to customer perception as to whether customer requirements have been met?	5 4 3 2 1
5 4 3 2 1	3. Have the methods for obtaining and using customer satisfaction information been determined?	5 4 3 2 1
	Monitoring and Measurement of Processes (8.2.3)	
5 4 3 2 1	4. Does the organization monitor and measure the quality management system processes?	5 4 3 2 1
5 4 3 2 1	5. Does the monitoring and measures of processes demonstrate the ability of the processes to achieve planned results?	5 4 3 2 1
5 4 3 2 1	6. When planned results are not achieved, does the organization take corrective and preventive action?	5 4 3 2 1
	Monitoring and Measurement of Product (8.2.4)	
5 4 3 2 1	7. Does the organization monitor and measure the characteristics of the product to verify that product requirements have been met at appropriate stages?	5 4 3 2 1
5 4 3 2 1	8. Is evidence of product conformity with the acceptance criteria maintained including records indicating the person(s) authorizing release of product?	5 4 3 2 1

Summation A   Difference

$$ \boxed{50} \; - \; \boxed{} \; = \; \boxed{} $$

| 00-10 = Excellent |
| 11-20 = Needs Work |
| 21-30 = Strong Need |
| 31-50 = Very Strong Need |

Any A Item of < 4 reflects a need in that category.

Any B Item of < 4 reflects a need for improved commitment in that category.

Needs Assessment Inventory

In your view, with what success is this being achieved in your company?	8.2 Monitoring and Measurement (continued) Instructions: Read the assessment question/statement and circle your response in Column A and B; total column A and enter in the marked box. If and item does not apply enter a 5 in each column.	In your view, how important is this item?
5 4 3 2 1 Column A		5 4 3 2 1 Column B
	Internal Audit (8.2.2)	
5 4 3 2 1	1. Does the organization conduct internal audits at planned intervals?	5 4 3 2 1
	2. Do the audits determine whether the quality management system:	
5 4 3 2 1	a) conforms to the planned arrangements to the requirements of the Quality Management System established by the organization?	5 4 3 2 1
5 4 3 2 1	b) is effectively implemented and maintained?	5 4 3 2 1
5 4 3 2 1	3. Is the audit program planned, taking into consideration the status and importance of the processes and areas to be audited, as well as the results of previous audits?	5 4 3 2 1
5 4 3 2 1	4. Are the audit criteria, scope, frequency and methods defined?	5 4 3 2 1
5 4 3 2 1	5. Does the selection of auditors and conduct of audits ensure the objectivity and impartiality of the audit process?	5 4 3 2 1
5 4 3 2 1	6. Is there a documented procedure which includes the responsibilities and requirements for planning and conducting audits, and for reporting results and maintaining records for internal audits?	5 4 3 2 1
5 4 3 2 1	7. Does management responsible for the area being audited ensure that actions are taken in a timely manner to eliminate detected nonconformities and their causes?	5 4 3 2 1
5 4 3 2 1	8. Do follow-up activities include the verification of the actions taken and the reporting of verification results?	5 4 3 2 1

Summation A Difference

45 — ☐ = ☐

Any A Item of < 4 reflects a need in that category.

00-09 = Excellent
10-18 = Needs Work
19-27 = Strong Need
28-45 = Very Strong Need

Any B Item of < 4 reflects a need for improved commitment in that category.

Needs Assessment Inventory

In your view, with what success is this being achieved in your company?	8.3 Control of Nonconforming Product	In your view, how important is this item?

Instructions: Read the assessment question/statement and circle your response in Column A and B; total column A and enter in the marked box. If and item does not apply enter a 5 in each column.

Column A		Column B
5 4 3 2 1		5 4 3 2 1

Column A	Question	Column B
5 4 3 2 1	1. Does the organization ensure that product that does not conform to product requirements is identified and controlled to prevent its unintended use or delivery?	5 4 3 2 1
5 4 3 2 1	2. Does the organization have a documented procedure that defines the controls and related responsibilities and authorities for dealing with nonconforming product?	5 4 3 2 1
	3. Does the organization deal with nonconforming product by one or more of the following ways:	
5 4 3 2 1	a) by taking action to eliminate the detected nonconformity?	5 4 3 2 1
5 4 3 2 1	b) by authorizing its use, release or acceptance under concession by a relevant authority and, where applicable, by the customer?	5 4 3 2 1
5 4 3 2 1	c) by taking action to preclude its original intended use or application?	5 4 3 2 1
5 4 3 2 1	4. Are records of the nature of nonconformities and any subsequent actions taken, including concessions obtained, maintained?	5 4 3 2 1
5 4 3 2 1	5. Is nonconforming product re-verified to demonstrate conformity to the requirements?	5 4 3 2 1
5 4 3 2 1	6. When nonconforming product is detected after delivery or use has started, does the organization take action appropriate to the effects, or potential effects of the nonconformity?	5 4 3 2 1

Summation A   Difference

$$40 - \boxed{} = \boxed{}$$

00-08 = Excellent
09-16 = Needs Work
17-24 = Strong Need
25-40 = Very Strong Need

Any A Item of < 4 reflects a need in that category.

Any B Item of < 4 reflects a need for improved commitment in that category.

Needs Assessment Inventory

In your view, with what success is this being achieved in your company?	8.4 Analysis of Data	In your view, how important is this item?
5 4 3 2 1	Instructions: Read the assessment question/statement and circle your response in Column A and B; total column A and enter in the marked box. If and item does not apply enter a 5 in each column.	5 4 3 2 1
Column A		Column B
5 4 3 2 1	1. Does the organization determine, collect and analyze appropriate data to demonstrate the suitability and effectiveness of the quality management system and to evaluate where continual improvement of the effectiveness of the quality management system can be made?	5 4 3 2 1
5 4 3 2 1	2. Does the data include that generated as a result of monitoring and measurement and from other relevant sources?	5 4 3 2 1
	3. Does the analysis of data provide information relating to:	
5 4 3 2 1	a) customer satisfaction?	5 4 3 2 1
5 4 3 2 1	b) conformity to product requirements?	5 4 3 2 1
5 4 3 2 1	c) characteristics and trends of processes and products including opportunities for preventive action?	5 4 3 2 1
5 4 3 2 1	d) suppliers?	5 4 3 2 1

Summation A   Difference

$$30 \ - \ \boxed{} \ = \ \boxed{}$$

Any A Item of < 4
reflects a need
in that category.

| 00-06 = Excellent |
| 07-12 = Needs Work |
| 13-18 = Strong Need |
| 19-30 = Very Strong Need |

Any B Item of < 4
reflects a need for
improved commitment
in that category.

Needs Assessment Inventory

In your view, with what success is this being achieved in your company?	8.5 Improvement	In your view, how important is this item?
5 4 3 2 1	Instructions: Read the assessment question/statement and circle your response in Column A and B; total column A and enter in the marked box. If and item does not apply enter a 5 in each column.	5 4 3 2 1
Column A		Column B

Continual Improvement (8.5.1)

5 4 3 2 1	1. Does the organization continually improve the effectiveness of the quality management system through the use of the quality policy, quality objectives, audit results, analysis of data, preventive actions and management review?	5 4 3 2 1

Corrective Action (8.5.2)

5 4 3 2 1	2. Does the organization take action to eliminate the cause of nonconformities in order to prevent recurrence?	5 4 3 2 1
5 4 3 2 1	3. Does the organization have a documented procedure to define the requirements for:	5 4 3 2 1
5 4 3 2 1	a) reviewing nonconformities (including customer complaints)?	5 4 3 2 1
5 4 3 2 1	b) determining the causes of nonconformities?	5 4 3 2 1
5 4 3 2 1	c) evaluating the need for action to ensure that nonconformities do not recur?	5 4 3 2 1
5 4 3 2 1	d) determining and implementing action needed?	5 4 3 2 1
5 4 3 2 1	e) records of results of action taken?	5 4 3 2 1
5 4 3 2 1	f) reviewing corrective action taken?	5 4 3 2 1

Preventive Action (8.5.3)

5 4 3 2 1	4. Does the organization determine the action to eliminate the causes of potential nonconformities in order to prevent their occurrence?	5 4 3 2 1
	5. Does the organization have a documented procedure to define the requirements for:	
5 4 3 2 1	a) determining the potential nonconformities and their causes?	5 4 3 2 1
5 4 3 2 1	b) evaluating the need for action to prevent occurrence of nonconformities?	5 4 3 2 1
5 4 3 2 1	c) determining and implementing action needed?	5 4 3 2 1
5 4 3 2 1	d) records of results of action taken?	5 4 3 2 1
5 4 3 2 1	e) reviewing preventive action taken?	5 4 3 2 1

Summation A   Difference

$$70 - \boxed{} = \boxed{}$$

Any A Item of < 4 reflects a need in that category.

00-14 = Excellent
15-28 = Needs Work
29-42 = Strong Need
43-70 = Very Strong Need

Any B Item of < 4 reflects a need for improved commitment in that category.

Needs Assessment Listing		Ranked by Need		
Complete this Needs Assessment by listing the self-assessment numbers contained in the Block marked "Difference" of each section. Then rank in order of magnitude, the largest number (greatest need) first and the smallest number last.				
Section	Difference	Rank	Comments	
4 Quality Management System				
4.1 General Requirements				
4.2 Documentation Requirements				
5 Management Responsibility				
5.1-5.3 Management Commitment, Customer Focus, Quality Policy				
5.4 Planning &				
5.5 Responsibility, Authority, Communication				
5.6 Management Review				
6 Resource Requirements				
6.1-6.4 Provision of Resources, Human Resources Infrastructure & Work Environment				
7 Product Realization				
7.1 Planning of Product Realization				
7.2 Customer Related Processes				
7.3 Design and Development Planning and Inputs				
7.3 Design and Development Outputs, Review, Verification, Validation and Changes				
7.4 Purchasing				
7.5 Production and Service Provision, Control, and Validation				
7.5 Identification & Traceability, Customer Property & Preservation of Product				
7.6 Control of Monitoring and Measuring Devices				
8 Measurement, Analysis and Improvement				
8.1-8.2 General & Monitoring and Measurement				
8.2.2 Internal Audit				
8.3 Control of Nonconforming Product				
8.4 Analysis of Data				
8.5 Improvement				

Chapter 6

Developing an Implementation Plan

IMPORTANCE OF PLANNING

Before launching into a Quality Management System effort of the magnitude required within most organizations, one should put together an overview of a plan. Planning should be done even before the hiring of any quality-specific personnel so as to fit the right person(s) with the requirements as well as to determine the need for such personnel.

Planning is one of the most difficult tasks an organization has to perform. In the process of planning, many members of the organization will have the sense that "we aren't getting the work done that is so evidently in need of doing. Why don't we just get on with it?" This mindset is precisely why so many organizations work at addressing short-term rather than long-term issues, and symptoms rather than root causes of organizational problems.

Planning is tedious, hard work, but nothing an organization does can prove more beneficial than the time spent in planning. Planning allows an organization to ensure that each action adds a step in the journey towards accomplishing its mission. It is planning that allows an organization to have a sense of control over its endeavors and to know that success in that endeavor is attainable.

Planning, without question, is the most important factor that determines the cost, speed, and effectiveness of a Quality Management System and, therefore, the success of installation and implementation.

There is no substitute for good planning!

If you fail to plan, you plan to fail.

IDENTIFYING ELEMENTS OF THE PLAN

The planning elements for implementing an ISO 9001:2000 Quality Management System may vary depending on the status of the organization relative to their quality journey. It should also be noted that the implementation of an ISO 9001:2000 Quality Management System is one step or phase of the larger implementation of an organization's "Journey to Performance Excellence" (see Chapter 18).

Determination of the needed plan elements may wait until after the initial self-assessment is completed and the results are analyzed. The needed plan elements may be determined through a "brainstorming" process, by using a typical shopping list developed for a complete journey plus any customized elements required by the specific organization.

Typical Shopping List of ISO 9001:2000 Quality Management System Plan Elements

- Audits and Pre-assessments of the existing system and implemented system
- Development of an organization Mission Statement
- Quality Policy development and distribution
- Establishing Quality System goals and objectives
- Quality System Structure determination
- Quality Management System Manual Development
- Determination and development of Quality Management System Procedures
- Determination of any Organization-wide Policies and Procedures
- Operating Procedures determination
- Operating Work Process Instructions/Checklists determination
- Determination of types of training required for each procedure or work instruction
- Determination and listing of the Primary Work Processes
- Determination of the baseline training requirements for each listed process
- Determination of personnel categories associated with each process
- Development of a Title Matrix associated with each personnel category
- Position Descriptions preparation
- Delegation of Authority method and preparation
- Organization Chart development or update
- Determination of special training requirements associated with procedures/work instructions
- Comparison of each employee against the procedure requirements
- Document the personnel qualifications associated with each operating procedure/work instruction
- Determination and development of training courses as may be needed
- Preparation of New Hire Plan to assimilate personnel into work processes

Presentation of the ISO 9001:2000 Implementation Plan and overall schedule might look like what is shown in Figure 6-1.

ARRANGEMENT OF PLAN ELEMENTS

After having determined the plan elements listing, elements should be arranged and numbered by priority. They do not have to be in a sequence-of-occurrence order. Tied to each plan element are the tasks associated with that element and the corresponding schedule for each. Configuration of the elements, tasks, and schedule into a project schedule (as illustrated in Figure 6.1) allows good visibility and tracking by senior management. One should be cautioned, however, not to make the schedule too detailed or complex, such that one manages the schedule and its presentation rather than the plan elements.

The plan element and schedule presentation should show the relationship between the various tasks of each element, and should have a timeline showing status on a monthly basis. A monthly report would include this timeline as well as a written status of each plan element, including actions in process and the responsibility for such.

In the following chapters of this book, each of the listed plan elements is presented in detail.

CONCLUSION

The preparation of an appropriate Quality Management System Development and Implementation Plan is a key success step. Without it, one may stumble through a less than cost-effective approach. It is also important that the plan be maintained, updated, and modified as necessary to accurately reflect the actual deployment status.

Plan Element	Month 1	Month 2	Month 3	Month 4	Month 5	Month 6	Month 7	Month 8	Month 9	Month 10	Month 11	Month 12	Month 13	Month 14	Month 15
1. Audits/Assessments	Status Audit				X...Develop Internal Audit Procedures & Checklists...X				Develop Schedule	Select/Qualify Internal Auditors		Internal Audit	Correct Findings	Registrar Pre-Assessment	Registrar Audit
2. Mission Statement Development and Distribution		Drafts Reviewed	Final Approved	X......Distribution....X											
3. Quality Policy Development and Distribution		Drafts Reviewed	Final Approved	X......Distribution....X											
4. Determine Quality System Objectives and Goals		Assignment Made	Draft Reviewed	Final Approved											
5. Establish Quality System Structure	Define Structure	Finalize Structure													
7. Quality Management System Manual		QSM Draft Prepared		QSM Reviewed/Modified and Approved		QSM Distribution		X........QSM Training.............X				QSM Registrar Submittal	Adjust Re-Issue		
8. Quality Management System Procedures		Define List	X........Draft/Review/Approve/Issue........X					X..Quality System Procedure Implementation..X and Training				Registrar Submittal	Adjust Re-Issue		
9. Organization-wide Policies and Procedures		Define List	Finalize List & number		X.......Draft/Review/Approve/Issue.......X				X....... Organization-wide and Operating Procedure.......X Implementation and Training						
10. Operation Procedures			Define List	Finalize List & number	X...Draft/Review/Approve/Issue.......X				X.... Operation Procedures Implementation/Training.......X						
11. Operation Work Instructions and associated Check Lists			Define List	Finalize List & number	X...Draft/Review/Approve/Issue.......X				X.... Operation .Work Instructions...........X Implementation and Training						
12. Training - Determination of Types Required associated with each Procedure					Determine Types										
13. Determination of Primary Work Processes		Define and Finalize List													
14. Determine Baseline Training Requirements for each Listed Work Process		Inputs Received	Consolidate Inputs	Issue List	Final Reqmt's Approved										
15. Determine Personnel Categories associated with each Work Process		Inputs Received	Consolidate Inputs	Issue List	Final List Approved	X....Prepare Job Descriptions......X									
16. Determine any Special or Mandatory Training Requirements				Inputs Received	Consolidate Inputs	Issue List	Final Reqmt's Approved								
17. Compare Each Person against Requirements					Compare w/ Reqmt's			Compare w/ Special	X..Incorporate in Training Budget/Plan..X						
18. Training - Documentation			Determine Record Keeping Requirements		Establish Method	Implement Training Documentation Method						X.........Update Training Records.........X			
19. Training - Develop Courses as may be necessary					X....Develop Training Courses (In-House or Outside)...X										
20. Prepare New Hire Training Plan for each Personnel Category					X.........Develop New Hire Training Plan/Method.........X										

Figure 6-1. ISO 9001:2000 Implementation Plan/Overall Schedule

Chapter 7

The Quality Policy

IMPORTANCE OF THE QUALITY POLICY

ISO 8402 paragraph 3.4 defines the quality policy as:

> *The overall quality intentions and direction of an organization as regards to quality, as formally expressed by top management.*

It is important to note that the Quality Policy forms one element of the corporate policy and is authorized by top management. ISO 9001:2000 paragraph 5.1 states:

> *Top management shall provide evidence of its commitment to the development and implementation of the quality management system and continually improving its effectiveness by b) establishing the quality policy and c) ensuring that quality objectives are established*

ISO 9001:2000 paragraph 5.3 states:

> *Top management shall ensure that the quality policy:*
>
> *a)   is appropriate to the purpose of the organization,*
>
> *b)   includes a commitment to comply with requirements and continually improve the effectiveness of the quality management system,*
>
> *c)   provides a framework for establishing and reviewing quality objectives,*
>
> *d)   is communicated and understood within the organization, and*
>
> *e)   is reviewed for continuing suitability.*

The Quality Policy is the first section of a company's Quality System Manual and, in conjunction with the company's values, principles, mission, and vision, should capture the essence of the organization. The quality policy defines the organization's existence ("what we do") and essence ("what we are").

The main purpose of the quality policy is to make clear where management stands on quality, and to make known where the company is headed. If management does not establish a formal policy, then the personnel will select their own—on an individual basis. It is vital that one clear quality policy is established and that each member of operating management understands and agrees with this policy, and more importantly—implements it.

Elements of the Quality Policy

The *Values and Principles Statement* of an organization denotes the "who I am" and sets the "culture" resulting from the organization's background. The *Mission Statement* of an organization denotes "why we exist," and ties into the value-added and primary work processes. The Mission Statement should consider factors such as: outputs, customers, processes, inputs, and suppliers.

The *Vision Statement* denotes "how we wish to exist" and includes such considerations as:

- How we treat each other
- How we treat customers
- How we maintain health, environment, and safety
- How we help our community and nation
- How we grow our business

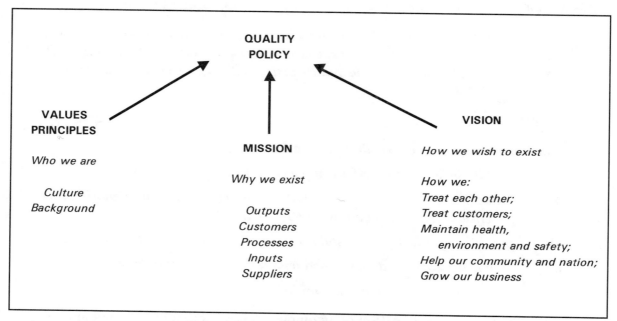

Figure 7-1. Quality Policy Development

These four elements—values, principles, mission, and vision—feed the Quality Policy, which then becomes the vehicle for communicating "the overall quality intentions and direction of the organization" to the organization. The steps to develop a Quality Policy are clear and relate directly to the above-listed elements.

QUALITY POLICY DEVELOPMENT STEPS

Step One—Code of Ethics

Step One is the development and distribution of a document containing the organization's values and principles. This document is generally the organization's Code of Ethics and is given to and understood by each employee.

Development of a Code of Ethics is a very personal organizational matter. The Code of Ethics should be kept simple, easy to read, and easy to understand.

The Code of Ethics might address such items as:

- Integrity
- Credibility
- Confidentiality of information
- Compliance with laws and regulations
- Services—manner offered
- Conflicts of interest

The organization's background and culture help determine the "who I am" of the organization, which is encompassed by the Code of Ethics.

The senior manager or staff should develop the Code of Ethics for the organization, if it does not already exist. If it does exist, it may need to be reviewed and updated to reflect any changes.

Distribution methods of the Code of Ethics may include:

- Directly to each employee
- As a part of the quality system manual
- Through group meetings

Step Two—Mission Statement

Step Two is the development and distribution of a Mission Statement.

A Mission Statement is a clear, concise affirmation (50 words or less) of the unique reason or purpose for the existence and efforts of the organization.

Developing a Mission Statement may be a rather lengthy process but it is the foundation statement for the work of the organization and, therefore, significant time and effort should be given to its development.

One of the values of keeping a Mission Statement to fifty (50) words or less is to make it possible for employees to remember the mission of the organization as they plan their day-to-day work.

The Mission Statement should reflect the values that drive the organization.

The Mission Statement should answer the following questions:

- What business are we in?
- Who are our customers?
- How do we want our customers to know us?

The Mission Statement should be clear, short, and include more than one task. It should be something everyone can easily understand and remember, and it should be hung on the wall.

Remember that the Mission Statement should not describe any activities unless the activities are an intricate part of the *mission* of the organization.

Mission Statement example:

> *The mission of the American Bureau of Shipping is to serve the public interest as well as the needs of our clients by promoting the security of life, property and the natural environment primarily through the development and verification of standards for the design, construction, and operational maintenance of marine-related facilities.*

The Mission Statement may be displayed in any manner desired. Some possibilities include:

- On business cards (reverse side)
- As a wall display in conference rooms
- As a wall display in individual offices
- In all proposals/literature
- In the Quality System Manual

Distribution of the Mission Statement may be delegated to a Communications Continuous Improvement Team (C-CIT) or another designated team or individual.

Note: Some ISO 9000 auditors have suggested that there be some method to ensure that any displayed or distributed Mission Statement is the latest version. Although the ISO Standard does not require this, it could be accomplished by having the Statement signed and dated as a part of the original document. Or, if it is included in the Quality System Manual, ensure that distributed copies are the same.

Step Three—Vision Statement

Step Three is the development and sharing of the vision of the organization. Presentation of the organization's Vision Statement can take almost any form and be called by a number of different names, so long as it shares the "how we wish to exist" message.

Typical subjects addressed in a Vision Statement include:

- Teamwork
- Organizational effectiveness
- Leadership
- Commitment
- Innovation
- Communications

When preparing the Vision Statement, consider the "how we wish to exist" listing shown in Figure 7-1.

The vision is perhaps best developed by senior management.

Step Four—Preparation and Setup

Step Four is the actual preparation of the Quality Policy guidelines. The quality policy should:

1. Be short and to the point.
2. Contain the name of the company.

The quality policy should not:

1. Be a treatise on the "economics of quality."
2. Have a number in it.
3. Indicate any method of deviating from it.
4. Delegate the responsibility for evaluating performance to the policy.
5. Be hidden in a book reserved for executive personnel only. It should be stated and publicized until everyone knows, understands, and believes it.

DISPLAY AND DISTRIBUTION OF THE QUALITY POLICY

The Quality Policy may be displayed in any manner desired. Some possibilities include:
- On business cards (reverse side)
- On wall displays in conference rooms
- On wall displays in individual offices
- In all proposals/sales literature

- Within the Quality System Manual (not an option—it *must* be contained here)
- On the inside cover of all manuals
- Network computer screens when logging onto the system each day

Distribution of the Quality Policy may be delegated to a Communications Quality Improvement Team (C-QIT) or another designated team or individual.

Some ISO 9000 auditors have required that there be some method to ensure that any distributed or displayed Quality Policy is the latest version. Although the ISO 9000 Standard does not require this, distributed copies must be the same as that which is contained in the Quality System Manual.

Sample Quality Policy

The Quality Policy of the American Bureau of Shipping is a combined quality and environmental policy, meeting the requirements of both the ISO 9001:2000 Standard and the ISO 14001 Standard.

> *It is the policy of the American Bureau of Shipping to be responsive to the individual and collective needs of our clients as well as those of the public at large, to provide quality services in support of our mission and to provide our services consistent with international standards developed to avoid, reduce or control pollution to the environment.*
>
> *All of our client commitments, supporting actions, and services delivered must be recognized as expressions of quality.*
>
> *We pledge to monitor our performance as an on-going activity and to strive for continuous improvement.*
>
> *We commit to operate consistent with applicable environmental legislation and regulations and to provide a framework for establishing and reviewing quality and environmental objectives and targets.*

CONCLUSION

The organization's values and principles, mission, and vision are key inputs in the development of the organization's Quality Policy. The Values and Principles Statement of an organization denotes the "who I am" and sets the "culture" resulting from the organization's background. The Mission Statement of an organization denotes "why we exist" and ties into the value-added and primary work process. The Vision Statement of an organization denotes "how we wish to exist."

The Quality Policy is a clear statement of where management stands on quality. Management's responsibility is to ensure that the Quality Policy is understood, implemented, and maintained at all levels of the organization.

Using the Mission Statement, Vision Statement, and other organizational characteristics to prepare the Quality Policy is the first step in the quality system implementation plan. The documents must be consistent as to their content and meaning, and they must be displayed and understood by all personnel within the organization. Figure 7-2 represents Step One.

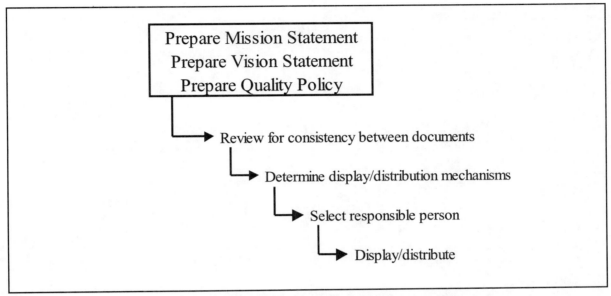

Figure 7-2. Quality System Implementation Plan—Step One

Chapter 8

Configuration of the Quality Management System

DOCUMENTATION STRUCTURE AND RELATIONSHIPS

The Quality System Manual (QSM) is defined as "a high level document that adequately describes the organization's Quality Management System." The QSM section makeup is depicted in the Table of Contents of the QSM. Figures 8-1 and 8-2 define the relationship of the ISO 9000 major elements to each other. The generic version of this figure (without the QSM Section Listing and the Quality System Procedure Listings) can be customized for each company or organization and used as a Quality System Implementation training tool (see Chapter 9).

As detailed in Chapter 7, the Quality Policy input drivers include the company values and principles, mission, and vision. The Quality Policy itself is the main driver of the QSM and is contained in the first section of the QSM, as shown in Chapter 9. Additional QSM drivers include the ISO 9001:2000 standard requirements and the organization's Quality Objectives.

An overall Quality Management System description of one or two pages for use in proposals and customer distribution in lieu of the entire QSM is of benefit. This document is a condensed description of the Quality Management System. It is not considered a controlled document.

The QSM is considered the highest level, or Level 1 (see Figure 8-3), of the Quality Management System documentation structure. The ISO 9000:2001 Standard states in paragraph 4.2.2, relative to the Quality Manual:

The organization shall establish and maintain a quality manual that includes

- The scope of the quality management system, including details of and justification for any exclusions,
- The documented procedures established for the quality management system, or reference to them, and
- A description of the interaction between the processes of the quality management system.

Level 2 of this structure is the Quality System Procedures. The Quality System Procedures are documentation that details the requirements and controlling factors applicable to the entire organization. These procedures are referenced by name in the QSM (for those that the selected ISO 9001 Standard requires) and they in turn reference a specific QSM section. A typical Quality System Procedure partial listing is depicted in Figure 8-1 and can be customized, as discussed in Chapter 10.

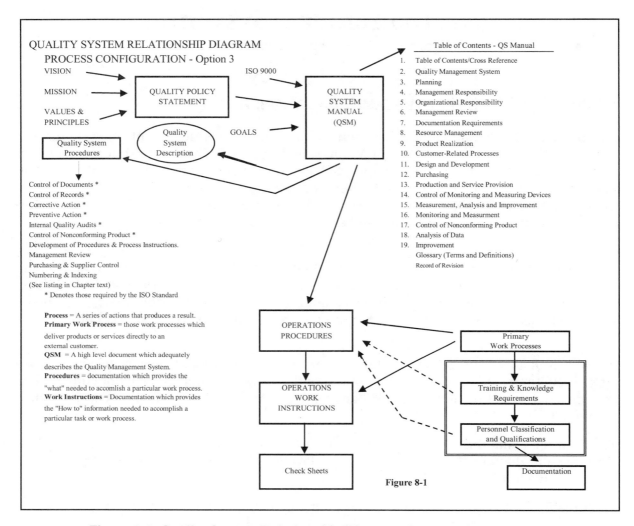

Figure 8-1: Quality System Relationship Diagram, Option 3 Configuration

The next step in the Quality System Relationship Diagram is *not* to develop the Quality System and Operations Procedures. Many companies and organizations immediately execute this step and cause themselves a great deal of re-work and complication as a result. Instead, determine the organization's Primary Work Processes, as discussed in Chapter 11; list and group these procedures in accordance with their respective categories, as explained in the text of that chapter.

Following the Primary Work Process listing is the determination of the Associated Training and Knowledge Requirement (Chapter 12) and Personnel Classifications and Qualifications for each (Chapter 13).

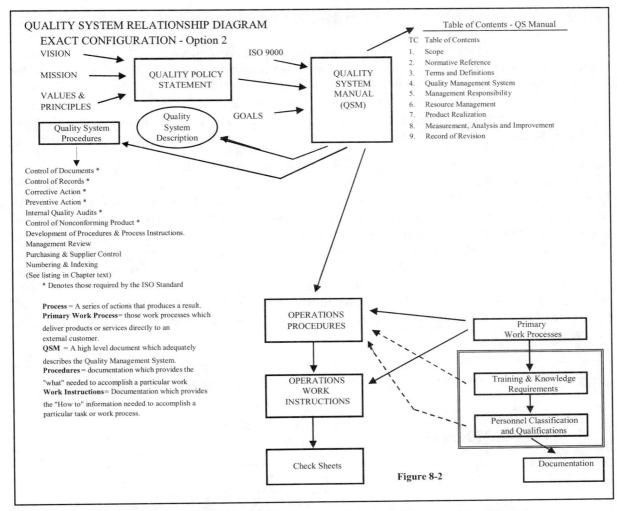

Figure 8-2: Quality System Relationship Diagram, Option 2 Configuration

The output of this effort will be the simplest grouping of the resulting Procedures and Work Instructions, which encompass all of the Primary Work Processes.

A few organizations choose *not* to go this route, electing to concentrate on a product-oriented system rather than a process-oriented system (see Chapter 11). When doing so, however, remember that the ISO 9001 Standard is a process-oriented standard, not a product-oriented standard.

The Organization-wide Policies and Procedures (if the organization has such) are Level 3 documents. Level 4 documents are the Operations Procedures and Level 5 documents are the associated Work Instructions. Check Sheets are actually a part of the Work Instructions as detailed in Chapter 15 and are a Level 6 document.

QUALITY SYSTEM MANUAL (QSM) CONFIGURATION AND STRUCTURE

Deciding on the configuration and structure of the QSM is significant in the development of a Quality Management System that meets both the requirements of ISO 9001 as well as the needs of the organization. There is no one prescribed configuration for the QSM, but there are three viable configuration options from which one might choose. Before deciding which best suits the needs of your organization, it is important to understand the concept of the QSM and basis of each configuration option.

Clause 4.2.2(a) of the ISO 9001 Standard (stated above) requires the QSM to cover the scope of the Quality Management System, including any justifications for exclusions. The QSM, therefore, should be a reflection of the ISO 9001 Standard used to establish the structure upon which the organization's Quality Management System is based. For most organizations, the QSM should be generic and straightforward in its presentation, and cover only those requirements (the what) of the ISO Standard that are applicable to the Quality Management System with regard to the organization's product or service. The Quality Management System, in turn, supports the QSM and clearly defines the processes, methods, and/or systems in place by which the requirements are implemented to achieve product realization and continual improvement. A typical Quality Management System structure is illustrated below.

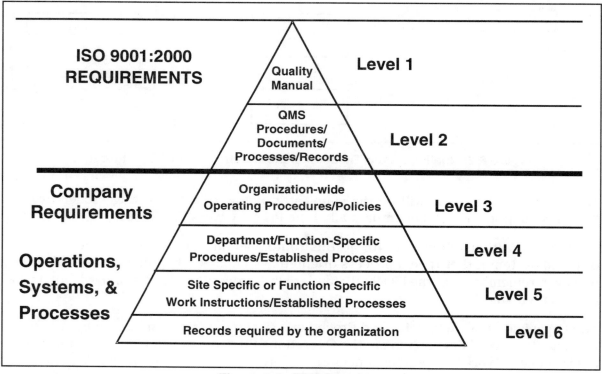

Figure 8-3. QSM Structure

The depth of the Quality Management System documentation (i.e., the number of levels) is dependent upon the size of the company and the complexity of its documentation. Very small organizations can satisfactorily implement a Quality Management System with only two levels of documentation. Although Clause 4.2.2(b) of the ISO 9001:2000 Standard allows Quality Management System procedures to be included in the Quality manual, it is generally best not to include any prescriptive requirements of the company's Quality Management System in the quality manual itself. The quality manual should simply state what is required to happen and reference the level 2 supporting procedures and/or processes. In other words, the QSM should function as a road map for the Quality Management System documentation and processes.

QSM MANUAL CONFIGURATION OPTIONS

In order to determine which of the configuration options presented here you want to use you should review the description of each option before deciding. The following provides a brief overview of the three configuration options.

Configuration Option 1

Organizations that are currently ISO 9000:1994 certified may want to consider this first option. Most organizations that are currently certified to the ISO 9000:1994 Standard customized and structured their ISO 9001:1994 quality manual according to the structure and numbering of the 1994 Standard. This provided a quality manual that was user-friendly for persons both inside and outside the organization. The ISO 9001:2000 Standard has been completely restructured, however, and attempting to maintain a 20-element structure based on the 1994 Standard may cause confusion. Many of the 1994 requirements have been retained in the 2000 Standard, but have been repositioned and retitled. Since the users of your current quality manual and quality system are accustomed to its current structure, however, this option revises your manual by using its existing configuration and overlaying the requirements of the 2000 Standard across the quality manual. The text within each section of your 1994 version quality manual is modified as necessary to add the new requirements, including changes in terminology. Proper training within the organization to the new requirements should enable the users to maintain conformance to the quality manual and the supporting Quality Management System procedures.

Configuration Option 2

For the same reasons that quality manuals were configured to the 20 basic elements of the 1994 Standard, this option configures the Quality System Manual exactly like the ISO 9001:2000 Standard arrangement. There are several advantages for using this configuration, including:

1. It provides a quality manual that is user-friendly for employees as well as all other interested parties when comparing it to the actual standard.

2. This configuration makes it easier to demonstrate that the supporting Quality Management System documentation meets the requirements of the Standard.

3. This option will provide organizations that are considering certification to other management systems, such as ISO 14000 and ISO 18000, a quality manual whose configuration is more in alignment with those standards.

Developing a new quality manual under this option will require training of personnel to familiarize them with the new structure. The disadvantage of Option 2 is that it places so much information into only five manual sections that they become long and somewhat cumbersome as can be seen in Sections 7 and 8 of the following QSM Index.

The following outline of Option 2 demonstrates that the sections follow the ISO 9001:2000 Standard exactly (the numbers in parenthesis are the corresponding element numbers of the 1994 Standard).

QSM Section	QSM Section Contents and Reference
0	Introduction
1	Scope & TOC (1)
2	Normative Reference (2)
3	Terms and Definitions (3)
4	**Quality Management System**
	4.1 General Requirements (4.2.1)
	4.2 Documentation Requirements
	4.2.1 General (4.2.2)
	4.2.2 Quality Manual (4.2.1)
	4.2.3 Control of Documents (4.5)
	4.2.4 Control of Records (4.16)
5	**Management Responsibility**
	5.1 Management Commitment (4.1.1)
	5.2 Customer Focus (4.3.2)
	5.3 Quality Policy (4.1.1)
	5.4 Planning
	5.4.1 Quality Objectives (4.1.1)
	5.4.2 QMS Planning (4.2.3)
	5.5 Responsibility, Authority and Communications
	5.5.1 Responsibility and Authority (4.1.2.1)
	5.5.2 Management Representative (4.1.2.3)
	5.5.3 Internal Communication (new)
	5.6 Management Review
	5.6.1 General (4.1.3)
	5.6.2 Input (new)
	5.6.3 Output (new)
6	**Resource Management**
	6.1 Provision of Resources (4.1.2.2)
	6.2 Human Resources
	6.2.1 General (4.1.2.2)
	6.2.2 Competence, Awareness and Training (4.18)

Configuration Option 3

This option meets the requirements of ISO 9001:2000 by maintaining a 20-section configuration. The reconfigured ISO 9001:2000 Standard has consolidated the elements of the ISO 9000:1994 Standard into five sections, but has not removed the elements themselves. Therefore, the various clauses are regrouped within the 20-section configuration to present the requirements in a manner that maintains the "process approach" of the ISO 9001:2000 Standard. This configuration necessitates a cross-reference matrix that shows the relationship between the organization's Quality Management System and the ISO 9001:2000 standard.

This author recommends the Option 3 configuration. Therefore, one of the manuals included in the Appendix is configured with Option 3. Based on this configuration, it is a very simple matter to convert to Option 2 by simply cutting and pasting into the appropriate Option 2-configuration section listed above.

The following outline of Option 3 demonstrates that the sections are configured in a process orientation. (The numbers in brackets are the corresponding ISO 9001:2000 element numbers; the numbers in parenthesis are the corresponding element numbers of the 1994 Standard.)

QSM Section	QSM Section Contents and Reference
1	**Table of Contents and Cross-reference**
2	**Quality Management System**
	[1.0] Scope (1.0)
	[4.1] General Requirements (4.2.1)
	[5.3] Quality Policy (4.1.1)
	[5.4.1] Quality Objectives (4.1.1)
3	**Planning [5.4]**
	[5.4.2] Quality Management System (4.2.3)
4	**Management Responsibility [5.0]**
	[5.1] Management Commitment (4.1.1)
	[5.2] Customer Focus (4.3.2)
	[5.5.3] Internal Communication (new)
5	**Organizational Responsibility**
	[5.5.1] Responsibility and Authority (4.1.2.1)
	[5.5.2] Management Representative (4.1.2.3)
6	**Management Review [5.6]**
	[5.6.1] General (4.1.3)
	[5.6.2] Review Input (new)
	[5.6.3] Review Output (new)
7	**Documentation Requirements [4.2]**
	[4.2.1] General (4.2.2)
	[4.2.2] Quality Manual (4.2.1)
	[4.2.3] Control of Documents (4.5)
	[4.2.4] Control of Records (4.16)
	Structure (4.2.1 - optional)

CONCLUSION

The configuration of the Quality Management System and the relationship of the various component parts must be realized before the actual preparation of the QSM. Determination of the QSM arrangement and selection of the approach prior to the beginning of the writing of the Manual will save rework.

The following chapters carry the Quality System Implementation through the details of preparing each of the elements shown on the Quality System Relationship Diagram. It is a guide to assist in maintaining the proper relationship between the Quality System elements and as a very useful training tool during and after implementation. Keep it updated as you progress through the implementation process.

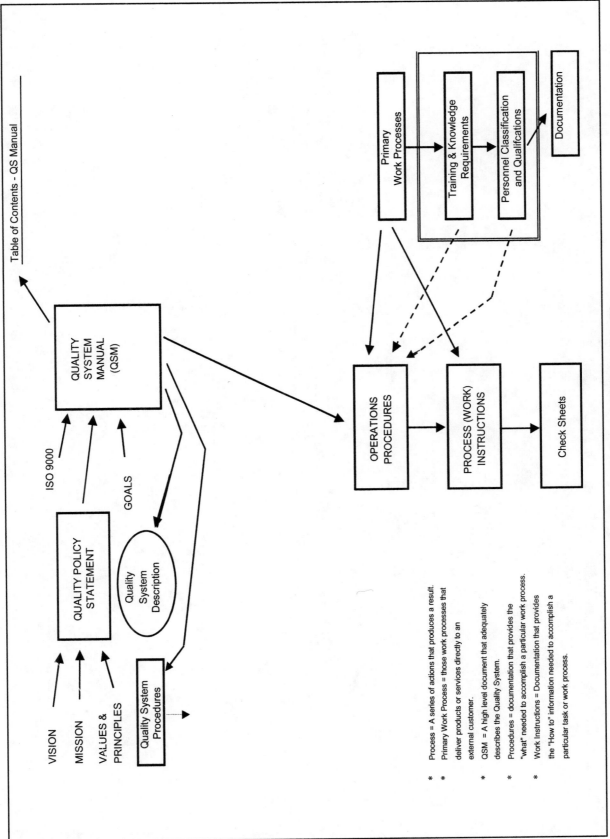

Figure 8-4. Quality System Relationship Diagram

Chapter 9

Quality System Manual

QUALITY SYSTEM MANUAL PREPARATION

Companies or organizations in the process of implementing or planning to implement an ISO 9001:2000 Quality Management System need a document that describes the system in a way suitable for presentation to the ISO 9000 auditor, to customers, and for internal use. Such a document is generally called a Quality System Manual (QSM).

A Quality System Manual needs to demonstrate for the reader that the Quality System is complete with regard to the requirements of the ISO 9001:2000 Standard.

Some organizations get carried away in the preparation of a QSM, making it so complex and full of information and references that its purpose is completely missed. The QSM should be kept *simple*. There is neither a need nor a requirement to make it other than a simple, high-level document that adequately describes the Quality Management System and its requirements to its readers.

Remember that the QSM is the outside person's entry document into your organization's Quality Management System.

Although the 1987 ISO 9000 Standard implied but did not specifically require a QSM, the 1994 revision to the ISO 9000 Standard and the updated ISO 9001:2000 revision specifically require a Quality System Manual.

Assessment

An ISO 9000 auditor will examine your organization's QSM against the ISO 9001:2000 requirements, verify that all of the requirements are met, and audit your organization against your own QSM. Therefore, it is necessary to make the QSM as "auditor friendly" as possible and as close as possible to the ISO 9001 Standard arrangement of content headings. Doing so allows a great deal of standardization between QSMs of all companies. A proper QSM can be completed within one week after the Mission Statement, Quality Policy, Quality Objectives, and Quality Organizational Structure have been determined.

The QSM must describe, at all times, the Quality Management System as it currently exists. When changes are made within the system, appropriate changes must be made to the QSM immediately.

Caution: The QSM is the top level, controlling document. Therefore, one must be careful of the "tail wagging the dog" syndrome, and compare any proposed changes within the Quality Management System with the QSM requirements and the effects of those changes on the QSM. Remember that the QSM represents the ISO 9001:2000 Standard requirements and must maintain that representation.

Distribution and Control

The QSM must be widely available to company personnel. Managers at all levels must understand the Quality System Manual requirements with which they must comply and for which they are responsible. Familiarization can be obtained through reading the material, in-house training sessions, participation in periodic review meetings, and in teaching staff.

The QSM should provide a "broad brush" description of how quality is managed (not a detailed set of instructions), and should reference the next level of documentation, which is the Quality Management System Procedures. The QSM is a "controlled document."

A simple approach to the development of a QSM is presented in the following process steps. Remember, there is no required way and, with the differences between organizations, there are innumerable ways that requirements can be met.

If your organization already has a QSM, do not scrap it. Simply compare it to the ISO 9001 requirements or to the process steps listed here, noting the deficiencies and upgrading as necessary. Refer to the Options listed in Chapter 8 of this book.

An ISO 9001:2000 QSM described as Option 3 and one described as Option 2 in Chapter 8 have been included in the Appendix. Option 3 is laid out in a Process Configuration and Option 2 in the exact format of the Standard.

As in any endeavor associated with the implementation of a Quality Management System, planning the task of writing the QSM is important for success. A part of this planning is the selection of the person, team, or task group that will be responsible for the QSM production process and for the QSM maintenance and distribution.

Foundation Material

Another part of the preparation phase of a QSM is obtaining the QSM foundation material (developed in Chapter 7):

- Mission Statement
- Quality Policy
- Code of Ethics
- Quality Objectives

Finally, before launching into the writing process, decide upon the QSM format and structure, considering such items as:

- Cover page design
- Packaging of the QSM
- Determination of QSM sections to be included
- Each QSM section page header
- A standardized page layout

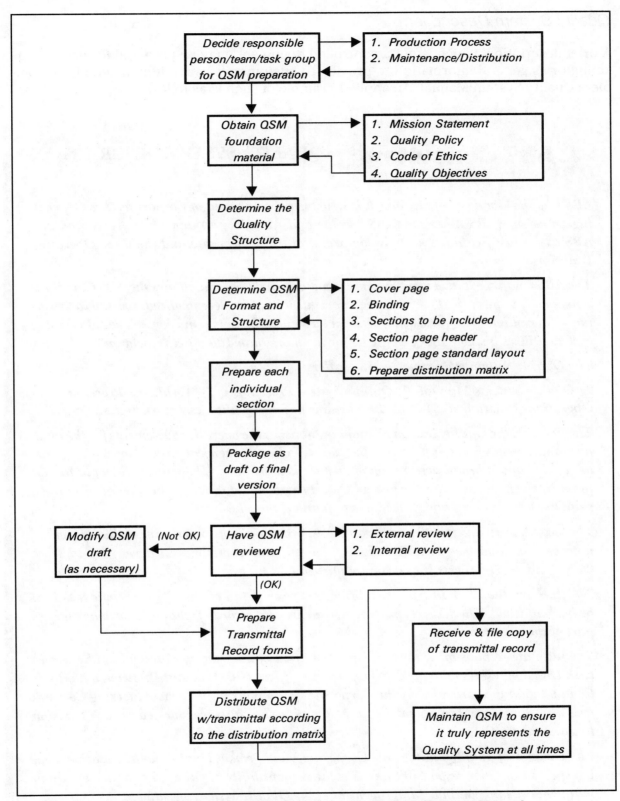

Figure 9-1: The Development Process of a Quality System Manual

Quality System Description

A brief description, which is not a controlled document, may be prepared for use in marketing or as general information to provide to customers or suppliers in lieu of the complete Quality System Manual. An applied example of such is as follows:

☰ABS Consulting   QUALITY SYSTEM DESCRIPTION

ABS is a worldwide company which is structurally comprised of Corporate, three Operating Divisions (ABS Americas, ABS Europe and ABS Pacific) and affiliated companies. ABS as a Classification Society is comprised of ABS Corporate and the three Operating Divisions.

The ABS Quality Management System is modular in design and allows the ABS Classification Society to meet the ISO 9001 requirements within its decentralized, worldwide structure while maintaining consistency between the structural units (Divisions). The ABS Quality System utilizes a single ISO Certificate for the more than 100 offices worldwide.

The Quality System is documented in six tiers:

1) Quality Systems Manual, 2) Quality System Procedures, 3) Worldwide Procedures, 4) Operations Procedures, 5) Work Instructions and 6) Quality Records/Check sheets.

The first tier, the Quality System Manual, establishes the overall requirements for the quality management system. It provides the Quality Policy, the general philosophy with regards to quality, and a broad description of "what" is to be done. The Quality System Manual provides the framework for the overall Quality System and provides the top down controls, standards, consistency and procedures to maintain a cohesive system.

The second, third and fourth tiers, Procedures, provide a more descriptive outline of "what" is to be done and also "who", "where," "when" and sometimes in a very broad sense "how" that work process is to be accomplished.

The fifth tier, the Work Instructions, provide explicit detail of "how" the specific task is to be accomplished. Check sheets provide a sequence and record of what is to be done and are part of the sixth tier.

The ultimate responsibility for the implementation of the Quality Management System in each Division resides with the Chief Operating Officer (COO) of that Division, with direction and guidance provided by the Corporate Continuous Improvement Steering Committee. A Continuous Improvement Steering Committee has also been formed in each Division to assist the COO.

The Director of Total Quality is the Corporate Management Quality Representative who, irrespective of other responsibilities, has the responsibility to ensure the implementation, maintenance and continued improvement of the Quality System worldwide.

QSM Section Development

The layout of each QSM section should be consistent, including the paragraph numbering method. Paragraph numbering should be sequential with sub-paragraphs also numbered. It is suggested that QSM section paragraphs of each section be the same, except for content, i.e., *Purpose, Reference Documents, Definitions, QMS Requirements, Responsibilities, and Records* respectively.

Although there is no set requirement for section titles or groupings within the QSM, the following list is suggested as being logical, user friendly, and process oriented as applied to any organization. This is Option 3 as discussed in Chapter 8. An Option 2 listing is also provided, should the organization choose that configuration (see Chapter 8 Options). Obviously, the presentation sequence is determined by each organization; but it is strongly suggested that this sequence be given very careful consideration. Whether the Glossary and Record of Revision are in the front or back of the manual makes no difference, though the back makes a more presentable package.

Sufficient material is presented here to prepare a QSM that will not only meet the ISO requirements but also be very serviceable and user friendly.

All ISO 9001 categories are required to be addressed even though they do not literally apply. This is done as described in the ISO 9001:2000 Standard in Section 1.2.

Where exclusions are made, claims of conformity to this International Standard are not acceptable unless these exclusions are limited to requirements within Clause 7, and such exclusions do not affect the organization's ability, or responsibility, to provide product that meets customer and applicable regulatory requirements.

In addition, avail yourself of several good examples of Quality System Manuals. Most companies will not mind if you use their QSM as a benchmark, but be sure to ask permission. There are also a number of books containing, in my opinion, poor examples of Quality System Manuals. Your best option is to use a real case example.

The QSM Sections do not have to match the literal headings of the ISO 9001-2000 Standard. An example would be 17, Control of Nonconforming Product, which is necessary for a manufacturing organization but may not be for a service organization. In such a case, this section may be titled Client Supplied Product and Materials, which may be only drawings or information or product. However, all of the ISO 9001:2000 Sections must be addressed—as may be shown by a cross-reference index when the sections do not match exactly.

QSM Sections Listing—Option 3- Process Focused Configuration

Cross-referenced to ISO 9001

QSM Sections Listing—Option 2 – ISO 9001:2000 Exact Configuration

Cross-referenced to ISO 9001

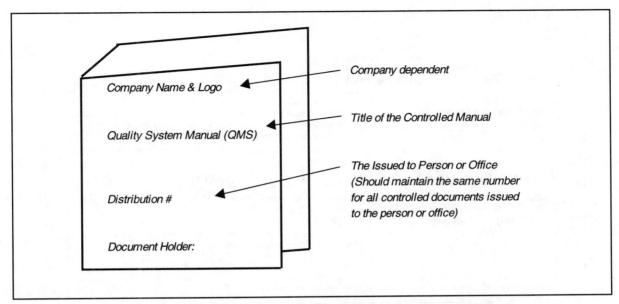

Figure 9-2. Cover and Packaging of Quality Safety Manual

Cover and Packaging for Hardcopy Distribution

The cover page (reference Figure 9-2) for hardcopy distribution should be insertable and changeable, allowing for easy update. A specific color might help identify the QSM (such as blue or green). A three-ring binder packaging is most convenient. Using a case bound or spiral binding does not allow for easy individual section updates (a necessity).

Obviously, electronic distribution would be most cost effective, saving all of the associated hardcopy distribution costs.

Standard Page Header

The QSM consists of a number of individually controlled sections (21 for Option 3 and 9 for Option 2). Each page of each section must be consistent in the use of the header and in terms of its format. Each section of the QSM needs to be individually controlled, carrying its own section revision level.

Determination of the specific QSM format (i.e., standard header information, footer information, and general presentation arrangement) is under the control of the individual organization or company (reference Figure 9-3).

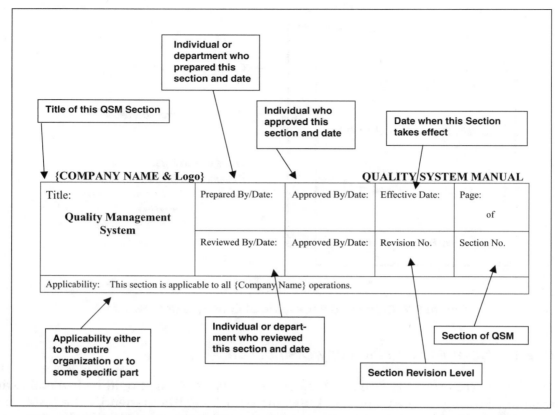

Figure 9-3. Typical Standardized Heading Format for the Quality System Manual

Foreword/Certification

The Foreword/Certification does not normally carry a QSM section number and is located first in the manual. Typical Foreword/Certification content is shown in Figure 9-4. An applied example is also shown on the following below.

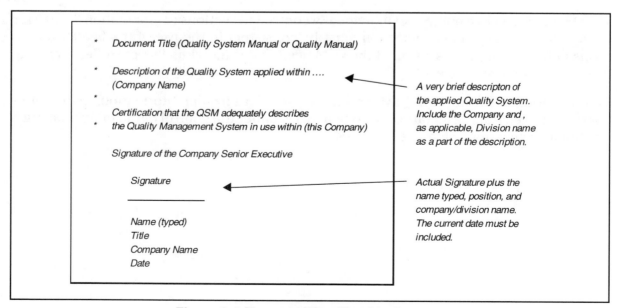

Figure 9-4. Foreword/Certification Content

What makes the example below so exemplary is that it begins with the key objectives and emphasis and commitment to quality within the organization, covers the overall layout of the system, and provides the reasons for its implementation. Customer commitment is included as well. Finally, the senior manager or authority signs the Foreword.

ABS Quality System Manual Foreword/Certification – Example

One of the key objectives of "ABS 2000" is to instill an emphasis on quality and quality management in all aspects of ABS activities. Our goals are to totally integrate quality into everything we do and to enable ABS to become a model of quality management for other companies to follow. The foundation for this effort is the establishment of the quality system as described in this manual throughout ABS and its affiliated companies.

The Quality System Manual describes the ABS Quality Management System as defined by the International Association of Classification Societies (IACS) and the International Organization for Standardization (ISO). It is designed to meet all aspects of both IACS and ISO 9001 requirements with ABS's decentralized, worldwide structure while maintaining consistency between the structural units (Divisions).

The ABS Quality Management System will serve as a means of ensuring that ABS services conform to requirements through the preparation and effective implementation of procedures and work instructions as well as through concentration on quality education program for all our employees that includes team effectiveness, problem solving skills, and the identification of quality parameters for all of our activities.

Our goal is to instill in all ABS employees a common focus on client satisfaction and to forge and maintain an identification with the important words: safety and quality; with safety defining what we do and quality defining how we do it.

The Quality System Manual shall be distributed and maintained on a controlled copy basis.

 **ABS Consulting**

Frank J. Iarossi
Chairman & CEO
22 June 2000

Table of Contents—Cross Reference

This section of the QSM is normally Section 1 and must be updated every time any of the other sections are updated.

{COMPANY NAME & Logo}			QUALITY SYSTEM MANUAL		
Title: Table of Contents	Prepared By/Date:	Approved By/Date:	Effective Date:	Page: of	
	Reviewed By/Date:	Approved By/Date:	Revision No.	Section No. 1	
Applicability: This section is applicable to all *{Company Name}* operations.					

Section Number	Section Title	ISO 9001:2000 Reference	Page No.	Revision No./Date

Figure 9-5. Cross Referenced Table of Contents

The Cross Reference Table is applied wherever there may be confusion relative to the sections of the Quality System Manual and the ISO 9001:2000 Standard. Its purpose is to demonstrate that all elements of the ISO Standard have been addressed and to show within the QSM where those elements are addressed.

QUALITY SYSTEM MANUAL OPTIONS

The Appendix contains two complete generic Quality System Manuals with customization instructions for use in the development of an organization's own QSM. Option 2 and 3 are described in the text of Chapter 8. The first QSM presented in the Appendix is in accordance with Option 3, and the second with Option 2. In this way, the reader may choose the configuration that best fits their organizational direction.

The approach to prepare your organization's own QSM using either of these Options is to superimpose your processes over the generic version, being sure that all elements are addressed. In addition, one must add the references to supporting Quality System Procedures in each section of the QSM.

CONCLUSION

The Quality System Manual is perhaps the most important document of an organization's Quality Management System. It is the outside person's entry document into the organization.

The Appendix presents two template options for the preparation of a Quality System Manual which will meet the requirements of the ISO 9001:2000 Standard. Both options have been thoroughly examined by an ISO 9000 Registrar.

Once an organization has completed their QSM, it can be sent to the chosen Registrar, along with the six required quality system procedures for a desk study. A desk study usually requires about 2-days of the Registrar's time and, of course, charges. The required procedures are:

> Control of documents
>
> Control of records
>
> Control of nonconforming product
>
> Internal audits
>
> Corrective action
>
> Preventive action

Some additional interesting information relative to the ISO 9001:2000 Standard, which one can take into consideration when preparing their respective QSM, includes:

Customer Satisfaction appears twenty-one times in the new revision. It only appeared once in the 1994 version.

Infrastructure includes maintenance.

Customer Satisfaction uses "Customer Perception."

Internal Audit shifted responsibility of "effective implementation" from auditors to top management.

"Analysis of Data" asks the question "How is the QMS working?"

Continual improvement is mandated.

"Corrective Action" means "Don't make the same mistakes."

"Preventive Action" means "Don't make the first mistake."

Chapter 10

Quality System Procedures

RELATIONSHIP OF THE QUALITY SYSTEM PROCEDURES TO THE QUALITY MANAGEMENT SYSTEM

The Quality System Procedures are those that directly support the Quality System Manual of Chapter 9 and that are considered to be applicable to all operations and support functions. All procedures other than those designated as Quality System Procedures are *operating procedures*, **NOT** Quality System Procedures. There is often confusion over this issue, in that all procedures are sometimes mistakenly considered as Quality System Procedures.

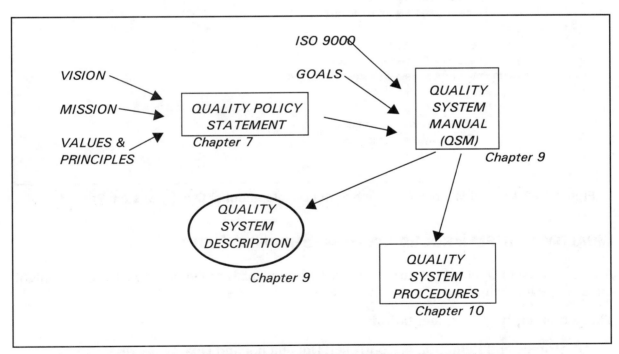

Figure 10-1. Quality System Relationship Diagram Segment

Where do the Quality System Procedures fit into the Quality System? How does one determine which ones to develop? What is their preparation method? Which are the key Quality System Procedures? Where does one start in their development? These are just a few of the questions that cross one's mind relative to the Quality System Procedures. It appears to be an overwhelming task, but is not when approached in a logical manner.

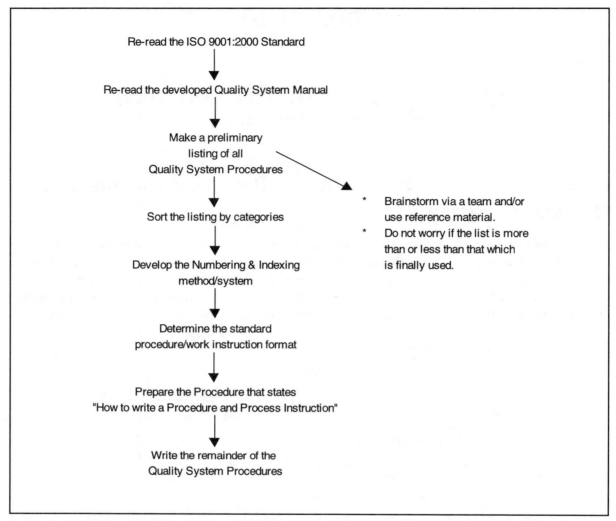

Figure 10-2. Logical Manner Approach to the Development of Quality System Procedures

QUALITY SYSTEM PROCEDURES—A SHOPPING LIST

A shopping list of Quality System Procedures grouped into implementation categories might include the following:

Those that apply to documentation:

- Storage and Retention of Controlled Documents and Quality Records
- Control of Documents *(Required)*
- Control of Records *(Required)*
- Numbering and Indexing
- Development of Operating Procedures and Work Instructions (Process Instructions)
- File Management and File Retention
- Correspondence Control

Those that apply to work control or process control:

- Contract Review (may be an organization-wide procedure, level 3)
- Design Control
- Product/Project Identification and Traceability
- Process Control and Checklists
- Handling, Storage, Packaging, Preservation, and Delivery
- Control of Customer Supplied Product (may be part of Purchasing Procedure)

Those that apply to quality control:

- Inspection and Testing
- Control of Inspection, Measuring, and Test Equipment
- Inspection and Test Status
- Control of Nonconforming Product *(Required)*

Those that are training related:

- Training and Development
- Human Resources

Those that apply to corrective and preventive action:

- Corrective Action *(Required – may be combined with Preventive Action)*
- Preventive Action *(Required – may be combined with Corrective Action)*
- Customer Feedback or Customer Satisfaction
- Nonconformance Reporting

Those that apply to the Quality System Improvement:

- Internal Quality Audit *(Required)*
- Internal Auditor Certification
- Statistical Techniques
- Management Review
- Continual Improvement
- Measurement, Analysis, and Improvement

Those that apply to supplier control:

- Subcontracted Technical Personnel
- Supplier Assessment and Control
- Purchasing

Those that are independent:

- Confidentiality

The following text provides some insight and details for each of the listed Quality System Procedures. The choice of use is determined by the amount of detail provided in the Quality System Manual (QSM). In general, the better choice is to keep the QSM at a high level, supplemented by the Quality System Procedures. Together, these two documents, the QSM and the Quality System Procedures must completely define the Quality Management System in accordance with the ISO 9001:2000 Standard.

DEVELOPING THE NUMBERING AND INDEXING SYSTEM

The primary task is selecting an appropriate Numbering and Indexing System for all documentation required by the Quality Management System. There are five basic types of documents to which the Numbering and Indexing must apply: Quality System Procedures, Operating Procedures, Work Instructions, Quality Records, and Position Descriptions. For the purpose of establishing a numbering system, the documents are grouped together into levels, not associated with the Quality System Structure levels of documents. These groupings include the top-level processes, the categories of work within those processes, the procedures for the respective categories, and the work instructions associated with the respective procedures.

Procedures state "what the requirements are." Work Instructions state "how the work is done" and are subservient to procedures. Quality Records are the documentation or visible evidence of the work having been done and are defined within each respective Procedure or Work Instruction. A Check Sheet is an example of a Quality Record. Position Descriptions are generally "stand alone" documents.

Procedures are Numbering and Indexing Level 3 documents, as shown in Figure 10-3, and are associated with either a primary or supporting work process. Procedures are generally grouped together with other procedures into categories of processes. These categories are considered Level 2 documents in respect to the Numbering and Indexing System. The processes themselves are Level 1—the top level associated with the Numbering and Indexing System presented here.

The first step is to define a Numbering System that will encompass all of the top-level work functions, the categories of work within those work functions, the associated Work Process Procedures, and the Work Instructions associated with each of the procedures. The Level 1 work functions might include Engineering, Manufacturing, Research and Development, Finance, Information Management, Human Resources, Legal, Office Services, Business Development (Sales/Marketing), etc. Within each work function of Level 1, there are a number of work categories. For example, within the Level 1 work function of manufacturing, the following work categories might be found: Shipping, Receiving, Production, Systems Test, Quality Control, and Process Control.

For each of the work categories, there is at least one procedure and could be as many as 99. For each procedure, there may be from 0 to 999 directly associated work instructions.

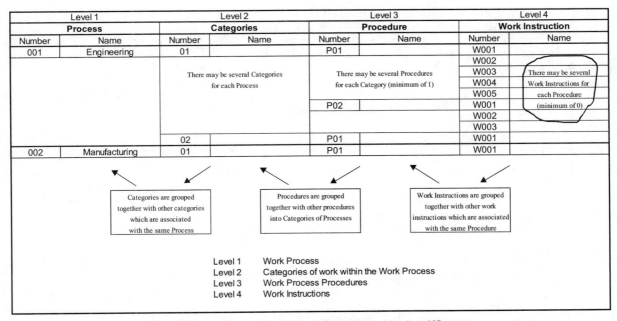

Level 1		Level 2		Level 3		Level 4	
Process		**Categories**		**Procedure**		**Work Instruction**	
Number	Name	Number	Name	Number	Name	Number	Name
001	Engineering	01		P01		W001	
						W002	
			There may be several Categories for each Process		There may be several Procedures for each Category (minimum of 1)	W003	There may be several
						W004	Work Instructions for
						W005	each Procedure
				P02		W001	(minimum of 0)
						W002	
						W003	
		02		P01		W001	
002	Manufacturing	01		P01		W001	

Categories are grouped together with other categories which are associated with the same Process

Procedures are grouped together with other procedures into Categories of Processes

Work Instructions are grouped together with other work instructions which are associated with the same Procedure

Level 1   Work Process
Level 2   Categories of work within the Work Process
Level 3   Work Process Procedures
Level 4   Work Instructions

Figure 10-3. Numbering and Indexing Method/System

Sample formats for each basic type of document for which the Numbering and Indexing must apply are shown in Figures 10-4 through 10-7. Of course, the intent of these samples is to aid in the development of one's own system. In so doing, one should keep in mind the following key principles:

The numbering system must be kept simple in its approach and configuration such that it is not difficult to understand and use, but is meaningful to the organization. The numbering system must also be such that it is easily computerized in such a manner that it will allow for sorting by selected fields.

The number must be placed on each page of each document and must be "stand-alone," in that it refers upward to its associated document, but is unique in itself. The numbers should not refer downward to subservient documents but need to refer upward to the document to which it is subservient. This is easily accomplished as noted in the Figures 10-4 through 10-7.

A number of documents may be Quality Records, but do not need to have a Quality Record Number applied if they contain the contract or project identification number in an obvious location. The project or contract number becomes the Quality Record Number.

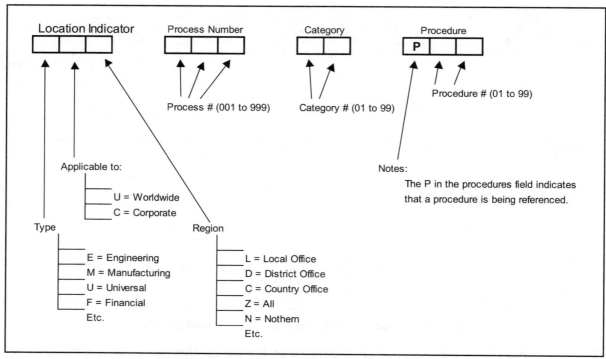

Figure 10-4. Printed Number on Procedure—Sample Format

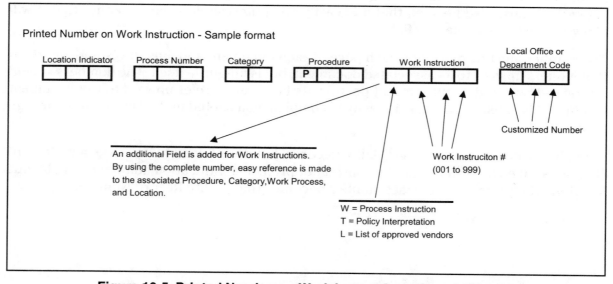

Figure 10-5. Printed Number on Work Instruction—Sample Format

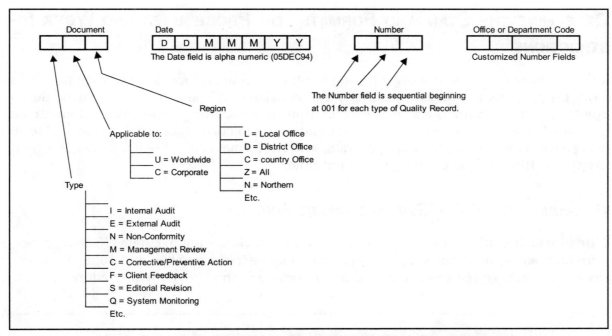

Figure 10-6. Printed Number on Quality Records—Sample Format

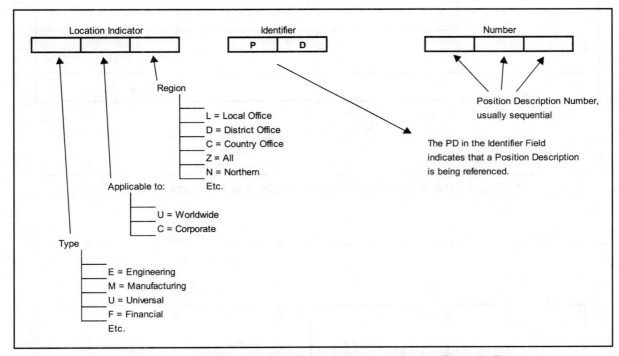

Figure 10-7. Printed Number on Position Descriptions—Sample Format

Determine the Standard Formats for Procedures and Work Instructions

It is important for the entire organization to utilize a standard format for Procedures and Work Instructions in order to ensure overall consistency. These formats must be developed prior to initiating the writing/preparation process. Doing otherwise will create an uncontrollable situation, which is difficult and costly to correct. Creating a standard form using a word processing software program, with the formats already established, is a great assist in getting the job done right the first time.

Procedure Title Block—Sample Standard Format

Title block: The title block should contain the title, revision number, date effective, procedure number, name of the Preparer, approver's name, page number, and volume number (as applicable). The title block should be printed on each page of the procedure.

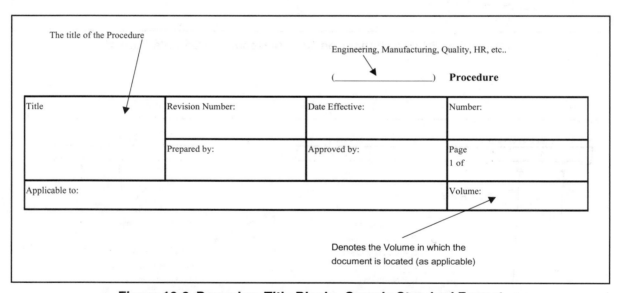

Figure 10-8. Procedure Title Block—Sample Standard Format

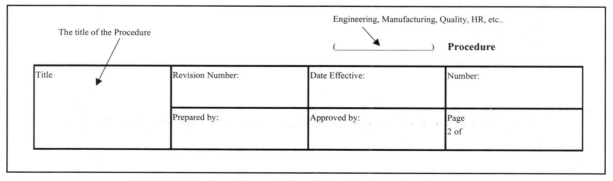

Figure 10-9. Procedure Title Block for Subsequent Pages

Work Instruction Title Block—Sample Standard Format

Title Block: The title block should contain the title, revision number, date, work instruction number, name of the preparer, approver's name, page number, and volume number. The title block should be printed on each page of the Work Instruction.

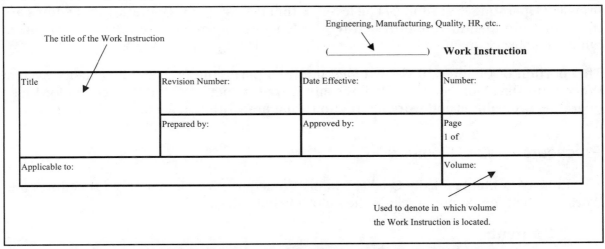

Figure 10-10. Work Instruction Title Block—Sample Standard Format

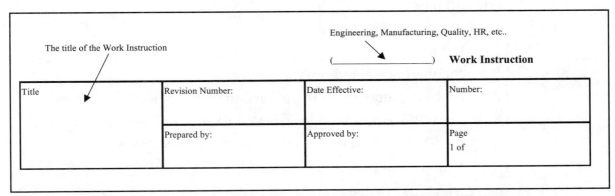

Figure 10-11. Work Instruction Title Block for Subsequent Sections

DEVELOPMENT OF PROCEDURES AND WORK INSTRUCTIONS - STANDARDIZED CONTENT

Once the standard title blocks have been determined, the content categories for both procedures and work instructions must be standardized. This Quality System Procedure should state the requirements that govern the format, development, revision, control, and approval of Operating Procedures at all levels within the company. Operating Procedures are those that are identified and owned by the function to which they relate (i.e., finance, human resources, manufacturing, engineering, marketing, quality, etc.).

This portion of Chapter 10 is sectioned into two parts, the first for the Quality System Procedure "Development of Procedures and Work Instructions" and the second for those operating procedures and work instructions that are written in accordance with it.

Procedure Table of Contents

The Table of Contents for the Quality System Procedure "Development of Procedures and Work Instructions" should include the following considerations:

Contents

1.0   References

2.0   Scope

3.0   Responsibility

4.0   Description of the Procedure

    4.1   Definitions

    4.2   Numbering and Indexing

    4.3   New Procedure or Work Instruction Development and Review

    4.4   Local Procedure/Work Instruction Change or Development

    4.5   Revisions to Issued Procedures or Work Instructions

    4.6   Content and Format Requirements

5.0   Training and Knowledge

6.0   Quality Records

7.0   Confidentiality

8.0   Revision History

    Figures (1, 2, ...)

    Check Sheets

    Attachments (A, B,.....)

Explanation of Each Section of the Contents for the Quality System Procedure

1.0   References

All references directly associated with the Quality System Procedure or Work Instruction are listed in this section. When referencing a document, always indicate the number and index and include complete title of the referenced document. The reference must be directly to the document containing the needed information. Never reference a document that references another document for the necessary information.

Examples of references:

      1.1   Quality System Manual, Section 8, Volume 1.

      1.2   Quality System Procedure, (title), (number), (other, as appropriate).

2.0   Scope

This section should state the scope of this specific procedure in a clear, concise manner and should address the extent of the subject matter covered.

Example of a typical Scope Statement:

This procedure addresses the initiation, development, revision and approval of Quality System and operating procedures at all levels within [company name]. Operating procedures include those identified by the function to which they relate (e.g., Engineering Procedures/Work Instructions, Manufacturing Procedures/Work Instructions, Quality System Procedures, etc.).

3.0   Description of the Procedure

    3.1   Definitions

        All definitions that are necessary for fully understanding this procedure and the terminology used within the procedure that are not standard should be included here. Examples of typical definitions are listed below.

        Procedure—defines what work is to be done and the responsibility for such work

        Work Instruction (Process Instruction)—describes how to perform work categorically defined in a related procedure

        Local Procedure/Work Instruction—deals solely with an office/department

        Organization-wide Procedure/Policies—those that are applicable to all offices/departments throughout the company

    3.2   Numbering and Indexing

        Included here is a statement that requires all procedures to be numbered and indexed in accordance with the Quality System Procedure, Numbering and Indexing (procedure number).

Example of a typical Statement:

Procedures and Work Instructions are numbered and indexed in accordance with the Quality System Procedure, Numbering and Indexing, QSZ-999-99-P03 Vol. 2.

3.3   New Procedure or Work Instruction Development and Review

This section addresses the development, review, and approval requirements for operations-related procedures generated within the company. Perhaps the best way to demonstrate this section is by the use of a flowchart with accompanying words, as necessary, included in this section of the procedure.

See Figure 10-1, New Procedure or Work Instruction Development Flow Diagram as an example.

3.3.1   New Procedure Development Worksheet

Consideration should be given to the use of a worksheet for gathering the necessary data and information for the preparation of the respective document. The worksheet of Attachment A can be used for determining the knowledge requirements needed to perform the tasks associated with the document to be prepared. This is different from the training requirements, which is a listing of those skills that can be taught providing one has the basic knowledge as listed. The applicability (to what does the document apply) and the purpose of the procedure/work instruction should also be stated. The next major consideration is to outline (list) the process steps in the space provided. The completed worksheet will provide a good basis for the final document preparation.

An example of the contents of this section might include:

Prior to creating a new procedure/work instruction, a work process analysis should be performed to determine the following as they relate to the process under consideration.

- Applicability (which locations/offices/departments are affected)
- Scope (objective)
- Primary steps, components, and deliverables
- Knowledge requirements
- Training requirements

The Procedure/Work Instruction Development Worksheet (Attachment A), process mapping, or other analysis tools may be used to conduct the Work Process Analysis. This analysis is a working document and will not become a part of the procedure/work instruction.

Date:	Applicability:
Division/Region/Office/Department:	
Procedure/Process Instruction Title:	Purpose:
Knowledge Requirements:	
	Procedure Outline (primary steps, components, deliverables)
Training Requirements:	
	Related Procedure(s):
	Related Work Instruction(s):

Development of Procedures and Work Instructions, QSZ-999-99-P07   Attachment A - Revision 0   Page 1 of 1

Figure 10-12. Procedure and Process Instruction Development Worksheet

3.3.2 New Procedure/Work Instruction Development

The development and review steps for a new procedure or work instruction should be listed here. Also, a flow diagram showing the document development steps may be included in a referenced figure located just prior to the attachments at the end of the document.

An example of the contents of this section might include:

See Figure 1, New Procedure or Work Instruction Development Flow Diagram.

1. *The originator initiates a New Procedure/Work Instruction Review and Approval Tracking Sheet (Attachment C), which accompanies the Procedure/Work Instruction throughout the review and approval process.*

2. *The Work Process Analysis, if utilized, and the Tracking Sheet shall be forwarded to the person responsible for the work process and approval (the Corporate Responsible Person). See Section 1 of the Tracking Sheet.*

3. *If approved, the Procedure and Work Instruction Worksheet shall be used to develop the Procedure/Work Instruction.*

3.3.3 New Procedure/Work Instruction Review

The review requirements for a new procedure or work instruction should be stated in this section. One should also include a new Procedure Tracking Sheet to ensure that all requirements are met. This Tracking Sheet ensures that the responsible personnel have reviewed and approved the new document and provides evidence to an auditor that it has been done.

The person responsible for the process associated with the new procedure/work instruction may choose to assign a team or an individual to develop the document.

A matrix may be included that indicates by function the persons responsible for the various processes or product lines.

3.3.4 Developer of Procedure/Work Instruction

This section provides instructions to the developer of the document stating the format to be followed is stated in the Quality System requirements. This section also states how the developer is to proceed after completion as exampled below.

1. *The person (team) assigned to the development of the procedure/work instruction utilizes all necessary inputs and resources to develop the draft of the document in accordance with the requirements. The format is to follow the Quality System requirements.*

2. *Upon completion of development, the developer signs and dates the tracking sheet in the appropriate location (Section 3). The developed document and associated tracking sheet are returned to the responsible person.*

3.3.5 Responsible Person Final Review

This section states the requirements for the final review by the person responsible for the associated process/product line. It also includes the instructions for the final sign-off of the associated Tracking Sheet.

3.3.6 Company Quality Organization Review and Processing for all Procedures/Work Instructions

The final review will be the quality organization within the company. This may be a single person who is responsible for ensuring that the form, fit, and function of the document is in order. This person/organization is also the one who is responsible for the controlled distribution of the generated document.

3.4   Local Procedure/Work Instruction Change or Development

When a procedure has been determined to be only locally applicable, the development, change, and review requirements and the process for review must be stated here.

3.5   Revisions to Issued Procedures/Work Instructions

There are several reasons for revising issued procedures/work instructions that need to be detailed here.

3.5.1 Editorial Revisions

A simple method of addressing editorial revisions to procedures needs to be established with a simple initiating form. This method should be detailed here.

Editorial revisions are typos, grammatical errors, incorrect numbering, and editorial inconsistencies in the Quality System Procedures or Work Instructions.

3.5.2 Substantive Revisions

A method of initiating and effecting changes to procedures or work instructions that are not editorial in nature needs to be established and detailed here. A tracking sheet to both initiate and track the changes through the process is the document that is normally used as a Quality Record for resulting procedure changes. Both procedures and work instructions that are applicable to the entire organization and those that are locally applicable need to be included.

3.5.3 Management Directed Revisions

Senior management may, at their discretion, make substantive changes to the procedures. The method for so doing should be described here.

3.6   Contents and Format Requirements

It is recommended that the contents of each operating procedure or work instruction be as indicated below. However, what is presented may be modified to fit the company requirements or those of the current operation.

Development of Operating Procedures and Work Instructions—Contents Described

The following describes the contents of the operating procedures and refers to Paragraph 3.6 content and format requirements of the Quality System Procedure, "Development of Procedures and Work Instructions."

The contents of each procedure or process instruction shall be as indicated below, in the order presented.

Title Block

A Title Block is required on all pages of the body of the Quality Procedure or Work Instruction. The required format and elements of a first page Title Block are shown at the top of Page 1 of this procedure. The Title Block for the second and subsequent pages is formatted as appears at the top of this page. In both cases, replace the words "Quality System Procedure" with the words "Procedure" or "Work Instruction," preceded by the function to which it belongs, such as Finance, Human Resources, Engineering, etc.

Note: The designation above the Title Block should not be "Quality System Procedure" except for the Quality System Procedures themselves. For those procedures that are operating procedures, the designation should carry the respective function name (e.g., Engineering Procedure for procedures related to engineering matters, etc.). (See figure 10.8 for an example of a Title Block.)

Table of Contents

A Table of Contents is required. It lists major section headings and subheadings, with associated starting page numbers. Important tables and figures, with their associated starting page numbers, may also be listed. Use the Table of Contents of Page 1 of this procedure as an example.

List of Check Sheets

A list of work instructions is required. List process-related work instructions that are attached to the Quality Procedure or Work Instruction in alphabetical order by work instruction letter, with associated revision numbers and dates. If there are no work instructions, state "None."

List of Attachments

A list of attachments is required. When attachments are present, list attachments in alphabetical order by attachment letter, with associated revision numbers and dates. If there are no attachments, state "None."

List of References

All references directly associated with the procedure shall be listed in this section. When referencing a document, the number and index shall always be indicated and the complete title included. Directly reference the document containing the needed information.

Scope

This section is required if the scope or objective is not explicit in the title of the Quality Procedure or Work Instruction. The scope makes clear, up front, limits to the applicability of a procedure or work instruction—for example, specific limitations on who may perform a process or task, or specific limitations on the range of equipment or circumstances under which a procedure or work instruction applies.

Responsibility

This section is required when technical, administrative, or managerial oversight responsibilities are not clear from the text of the Quality Procedure/Work Instruction, or go beyond those described in position descriptions, the Quality System Manual, or parent procedure in the case of a work instruction. If included, this section identifies personnel categories responsible for the work described in the document and designates managerial oversight responsibilities.

Description of the Procedure or Work Instruction

This section shall describe in a clear, concise manner what is to be done or how it is to be done. The description shall follow a logical sequence in order to achieve the objectives. The description may be in the form of logic flow diagrams coupled with text or text alone.

Training and Knowledge

This section is conditionally required. It may detail training and knowledge requirements, or may refer to training and knowledge requirements prescribed in related documents.

If a process requires specific training and certification, a corresponding training form must be developed and referenced here. The Training Form may be a part of the procedure as it applies to all work instructions subservient to that procedure. This section may also describe cross-qualification for multiple processes, for example: "Certification in this procedure also qualifies the employee to perform..."

Quality Records

This section is required when records generated in compliance with a procedure or work instruction are auditable under the Quality System.

Files

This section identifies external or internal records other than controlled documents and Quality Records. This section may not appear in all Quality Procedures or Work Instructions.

Confidentiality

This section is required only if confidentiality requirements exceed the requirements of Quality System Procedure, Confidentiality, (procedure number).

Revision History

This required section provides an abstract of substantive revisions to a procedure or process instruction. Each revised section is referred to by section number and, optionally, by title. Enough detail is provided to make the nature of the change clear to the reader. If revisions are so extensive that line-by-line entries are not practical, the author may summarize the overall nature and/or scope of changes.

Check Sheets

A work instruction may be added to the procedure when the procedure is of sufficient detail that it does not warrant an associated work instruction. This section may not appear in most procedures.

Attachments

Attachments, when included, must carry a "footer" on each page that identifies the name of the procedure, the procedure number, the revision level of the procedure, and the number of pages in the attachment. Attachments of manuals, copyrighted materials, and other documents should be avoided.

4.0 Training and Knowledge

The following is an Example of the text that should be included in this section:

All initiators of new procedures or work instructions or changes to existing procedures or work instructions shall be familiar with the Quality System and the subject of the Quality Procedure or Work Instruction. Individuals who review and approve these documents are to have an understanding of the Quality System Manual and Quality System Procedures, their objectives, and implementation.

5.0 Responsibility

The responsible functions for the development of the various procedures or work instructions should be detailed here.

6.0 Quality Records

The following is an example of the text that should be included in this section:

All approved procedures or work instructions shall appear on the list of approved controlled documents, which is a controlled document and shall be maintained in accordance with Quality System Procedure, Storage and Retention of Controlled Documents, and Quality Records, (procedure number). These procedures and work instructions are to be distributed in accordance with Quality System Procedure, Document Control, (procedure number).

The completed Procedure or Work Instruction Review and Approval Tracking Sheets are Quality Records and act as Check Sheets for this process and shall be maintained in the files with the procedures in accordance with Quality System Procedure, Storage and Retention of Controlled Documents and Quality Records, (procedure number).

7.0   Confidentiality

The following is an example of the text that should be included in this section:

This document shall be controlled by the standard confidentiality policy in the Quality System Procedure, Confidentiality (procedure number).

8.0   Revision History

The revision history of this specific procedure should be included here. Alternately, revisions may be marked in some manner within the text of the procedure (i.e., use of a vertical line on the side of the affected paragraph or the shading of the affected paragraph).

PREPARE REMAINING QUALITY SYSTEM PROCEDURES

After completion of the two key Quality System Procedures—Numbering and Indexing, Development of Procedures and Work Instructions—have them reviewed by a third party as a "sanity" check. The tendency is to make them overly complicated rather than simple. Be sure to have them checked before going further.

Prepare the remaining Quality System Procedures in accordance with those just written. Have them reviewed and revise them as necessary.

One way to help in the preparation task is to obtain some reference examples for the type of operation that closely matches your own—service, manufacturing, etc. Most companies are glad to provide these, sometimes at a cost to offset expenses if the demand is high. It is worth the effort in terms of assurance and time saved. Many companies include access to these procedures on their respective web site.

The Quality System Procedures should be written with the assurance that they describe what is currently being done. It is not necessary to re-engineer the current processes at this time. Remember that the Quality System for this part of the implementation process is simply writing down the overall guideline requirements.

Following the completion of the writing and review tasks, one must determine the following: the distribution list, the person responsible for their control, the printing and packaging method, the acknowledgment of receipt after distribution, training of personnel in the Quality System requirements, and follow-up to ensure compliance. These elements are straightforward and therefore are not addressed here.

CONCLUSION

This chapter should have answered the following Quality System Procedures related questions:

- What are they?
- Where do they fit in the overall management system?

A list was also provided with instructions from which to make a determination of the remaining procedures that will be needed by the organization. The key procedures, their preparation in relationship to numbering and indexing, and the development of procedures and associated work instructions were also presented.

These steps are summarized in Figure 10-13, Quality System Procedure Development.

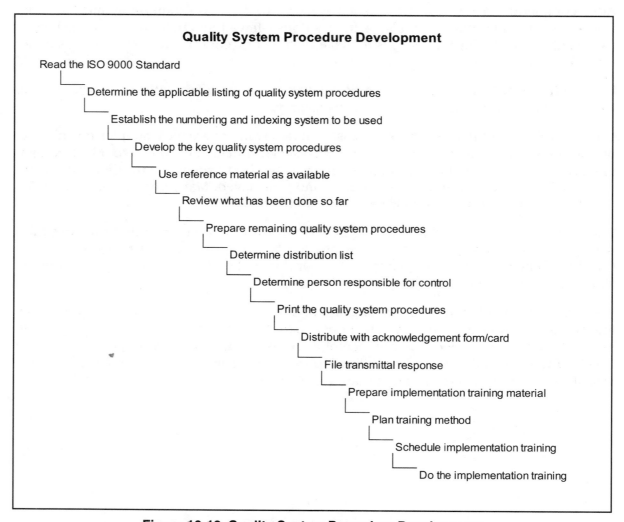

Figure 10-13. Quality System Procedure Development

Work Process Status Matrix	High Level Work Process:						Updated: (DATE)		
Quality System Procedures			Quality System Procedures						
PROCEDURE NAME	PROCEDURE NUMBER	DEVELOPMENT RESPONSIBILITY	PREPARATION STATUS	PROCEDURE REVIEW STATUS	PROCEDURE ISSUE STATUS	PROCEDURE TRAINING STATUS	AUDIT ASSIGNMENT	AUDIT STATUS
Storage and Retention of Controlled Documents and Quality Records	QSZ-999-99-P01	TCD Department	Draft Completed 3/23/94	Completed 3/30/94				

Listing of all Quality System Procedures

Procedure number, assignment, and status maintained until procedure is issued and implemented

Figure 10-14. Sample Procedure Planning and Scheduling Document

Chapter 11

Work Processes

This chapter defines work processes in detail, including the work process model, value-added vs. non-value-added process steps, process-controlling factors, continual improvement of processes, process related management mindset, and fire fighting associated with processes. It is important to understand work processes because the ISO 9001:2000 standard revolves around the control of those processes.

DEFINITION OF WORK PROCESSES

ISO 9001:2000 Quality System implementation, as well as the installment of a Quality Management System, begins with an understanding of the organization's basic Work Processes.

All work is a process—a series of actions that produce a result.

Each of these series of actions can be represented by a process step, which itself produces an intermediate result or output as shown in Figure 11-1.

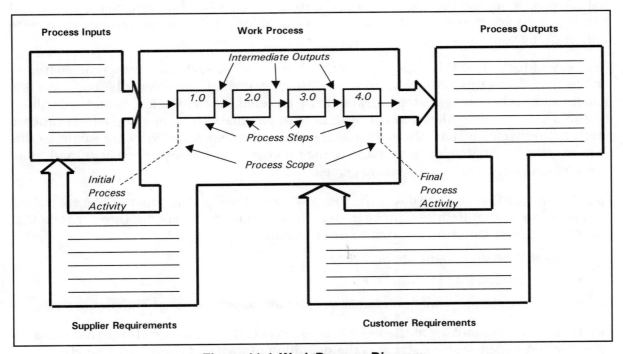

Figure 11-1. Work Process Diagram

The process steps are generally named, numbered, and placed in their respective sequence of occurrence.

The scope of the process is bounded by the initial process activity and the final process activity, selection of which is a choice.

Each process has one or more process outputs and one or more process inputs. There may also be process inputs at any of the intermediate stages.

A process is the work we do to convert process inputs to process outputs.

Actually, everything we do is a process and can be analyzed using process thinking. Getting dressed, eating, swimming, driving a car, designing a control system, delivering a package, writing a check, auditing a system, and writing a book are all names of processes. Each of these processes is comprised of a sequence of steps producing a result.

Work processes are, of course, those processes we do relative to our work. These may include what are called **Primary Work Processes** (those that deliver products or services directly to an external customer) and **Supporting Work Processes** (those that support the Primary Work Process). Chapters 12 and 13 detail the identification of Primary Work Processes.

VALUE ADDED AND NON-VALUE ADDED PROCESS STEPS

Each Work Process contains both **"value added"** process steps and **"non-value added"** process steps as shown in Figure 11-2. Value added process steps are those that are essential for producing the product or service output of the Work Process. Non-value added process steps are those steps that are not essential for producing the product or service output of the work process.

One way of looking at this aspect of a Work Process is through the eyes of the customer and asking, "Does this activity or process step add value?" If the answer is "no," then it is a non-value added process step and should be targeted for elimination. In fact, one objective of a good Quality Management System is to eliminate the non-value added process steps entirely. This is done through challenge questions, such as: "Why are we doing this process step?" "What value does it add to the process?" "Is it really necessary?" and "Who does it serve—the customer or management?"

In process thinking, one considers the item that goes through the process and each thing that happens to that item as a process step. In such thinking, there are three criteria that must be satisfied for a process step to be considered value-added.

- It must be done right the first time
- The customer must care
- There must be a physical change to the item passing through the process

Another method of looking at the Work Processes in this manner (i.e., through the evaluation of value added process steps) is the definition of waste as offered by Cho/Hey.

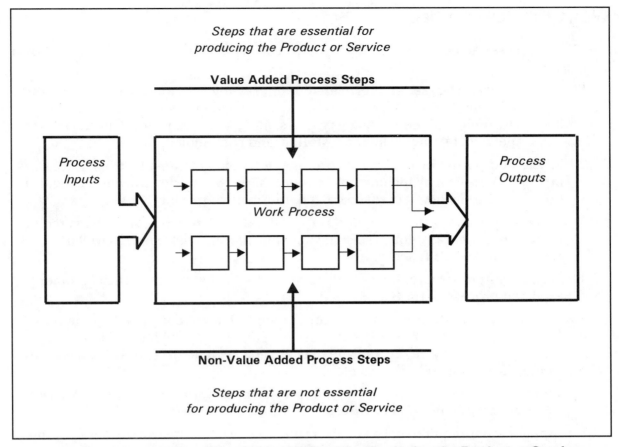

Figure 11-2. Essential and Non-Essential Steps for Producing the Product or Service

Waste equals:

Anything other than the minimum amount of equipment, materials, parts, space, and worker's time which are absolutely essential to add value to the product or service.

Viewing the work processes through this definition of waste has both a positive and a negative aspect. In the negative sense, anything short of meeting the value-added requirements of the Work Processes does not meet the quality requirements of the process and therefore must be eliminated. In the positive sense, anything beyond meeting the value added requirements of the Work Processes may exceed the quality requirements of the process but may still be classified as waste because it expends the organization's resources beyond what is necessary from a process viewpoint. However, there may be marketing or other reasons for those resources; therefore, they must be planned occurrences.

One key Quality System goal and effort is to entirely eliminate negative waste and unplanned positive waste.

This can best be accomplished through the complete understanding of the work processes and ISO 9001:2000 Quality Management System implementation requirements.

WORK PROCESS MODEL

Any Work Process can be represented in a model consisting of nine (9) elements as shown in Figure 11-3.

1. Work processes—A set of interrelated or interacting activities, which transforms inputs into outputs. Work processes are diverse and may include but are not limited to such activities as analyzing, designing, purchasing, measuring, recording, inspecting, testing, delivering, storing, and communicating.

2. Process outputs—the deliverable product or service that results from a work process. Outputs may include but are not limited to reports, drawings, specifications, measurements, records, data and information, product, or services.

3. Process customer—the customer(s) to whom the process output is delivered or for whom the work is done. This may include internal customers as well as external customers (clients).

4. Process output requirements—a description by the customer of the customer expected process outputs.

5. Process inputs—the inputs to the work process that are consumed by the process or that become part of the process output after having had value added. Process inputs may be diverse and may include such items as drawings, specifications, material, and equipment.

6. Suppliers—those who provide inputs (service or material) to the work process. Suppliers may be internal or external to the organization.

7. Supplier input requirements—a description by those in the work process of the expected inputs to be provided by the supplier.

8. Process output feedback—feedback to the customer or from the customer relative to the process outputs, satisfaction, complaints, problems, and improvement opportunities.

9. Process input feedback—feedback to the suppliers or from the suppliers relative to the inputs, satisfaction, complaints, problems, and improvement opportunities.

The ISO 9001 Standard views the work processes inward, through the eyes of the customer and the supplier, as well as outward, towards the customer and the supplier. It also views the process through the factors that control or affect the process quality.

It is estimated that about 60 percent of customer dissatisfaction and supplier problems are a result of poor communications between the customer or supplier and the organization in the area of properly defining and communicating the requirements. The ISO 9001:2000 Standard addresses this in sections and paragraphs 5.4, 5.5, 7.1, 7.2, 7.4, 7.5, and 8.2.

The importance that the ISO 9001 Standard applies to these areas should be obvious. In addition to the communication-related areas that directly affect quality, a number of other process factors control and affect the quality of the outputs(s).

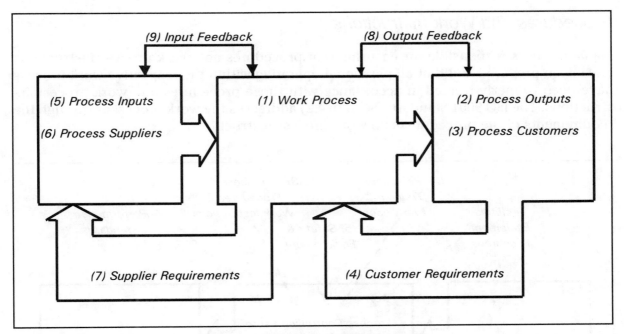

Figure 11-3. Work Process Elements

WORK PROCESS—CONTROLLING FACTORS

Work process controlling factors consist of those factors that are controlled by management and that directly affect the quality of the work process output. These controlling factors are not under the control of personnel within the work process. The controlling factors affect the consistency, content, and integrity of the work processes.

Facilities, Equipment, and Allocated Resources

Management is responsible for providing proper facilities, equipment, and allocated resources in support of the work process. This responsibility includes the work environment, office equipment, and the process required equipment. The ISO 9001 Standard (Section 5.1e & 6.0) addresses work processes through the facilities, equipment, and allocated resource requirements.

Training and Knowledge

Management is responsible for ensuring that the personnel placed into the work process have sufficient knowledge coupled with the necessary training to ensure the quality of the process output. The ISO 9001 Standard (Section 6.2.2) addresses the work processes through the training and knowledge requirements.

Procedures and Work Instructions

Management is responsible for ensuring that procedures and work process instructions have been prepared and that all personnel operating within the respective work process have been properly trained in accordance with those procedures and work process instructions. The ISO 9001 Standard (Section 4.2) addresses the work processes through the requirements of the procedures and work process instructions.

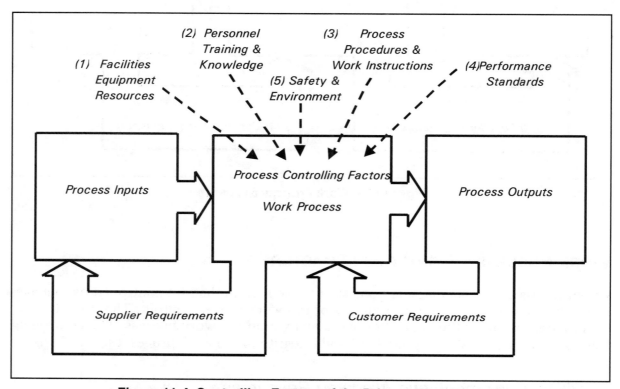

Figure 11-4. Controlling Factors of the Primary Work Process

Performance Standards

Management is responsible for ensuring that management does not negatively affect the work process quality through the imposition of unrealistic cost and schedule requirements onto the processes. Management should also avoid setting other negatively affecting performance standards as well. The ISO 9001 Standard (Section 4.1 & 5.1) addresses the work processes through the requirements and mindset of management. There may be other standards that control the Primary Work Process, as well, such as state, federal, local, etc.

Safety & Environment

Management is responsible for ensuring that the environment wherein the work processes are carried out is safe and secure, such that the environment is void of fear and conducive to the carrying out of the requirements. The ISO 9001 Standard (Section 6.4) looks at the work processes through the requirements of the working environment. In other words, the ISO 9000 Management System Standard looks at the Work Processes and the effect that the work environment has on to the quality of the output of those processes.

The ISO 14000 Environmental Management System Standard looks at the effect that the work process and its associated output has on the natural environment. To this extent, the factors that control quality of the work processes also can effect the environmental aspects of that process. Therefore, it makes sense to consider the environmental effect as a part of the Work Process Model.

Process Continual Improvement

Another way of diagramming the Work Process Model, which includes the process continual improvement cycle, is based on customer feedback, corrective and preventive action results and trending analysis, internal and external audit results and analysis, process measurement and analysis, and management reviews. The diagram is shown in Figure 11-5.

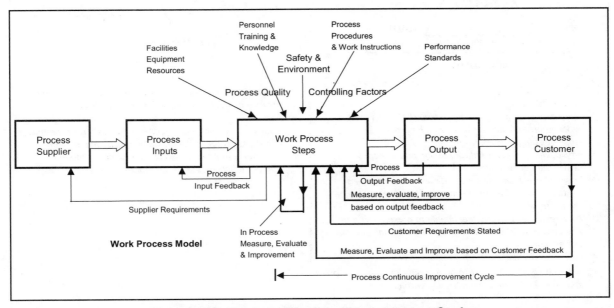

Figure 11-5. Process Continual Improvement Cycle

MANAGEMENT MINDSET

Traditional Management Mindset

The traditional management mindset is represented by a triangle in which the work process, with its associated outputs and inputs, is shown at the base (see Figure 11-6). In this mindset the employees within the processes are generally operating in a "responsive" mode to a management, which carries the responsibility for the processes. As such, most employees serve middle and upper management rather than the customer.

There are a number of effects associated with the traditional mindset that negatively affect quality and that are not compatible with an ISO-based Quality Management System. These effects are listed in Figure 11-6 and should be studied thoroughly.

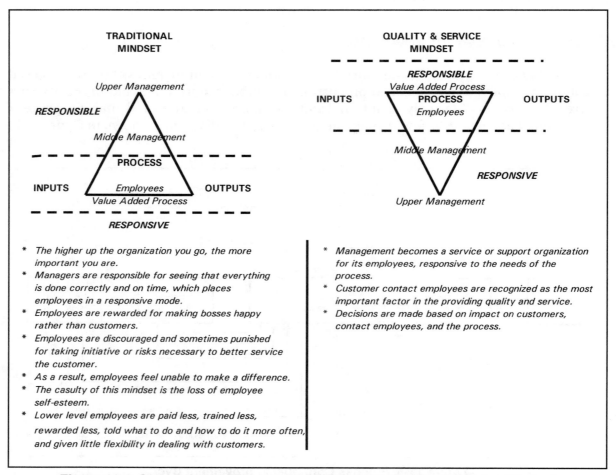

Figure 11-6. Comparison of Traditional Mindset with Quality & Service Mindset

Quality and Service Mindset

The correct management mindset of quality and service turns the traditional triangle over, such that the base—containing the work process, with its associated outputs and inputs—is shown at the top. In this mindset, the employees within the processes are responsible for the quality of their work and management is responsive to the needs of the employees and the process. This arrangement matches the Work Process Model, Figure 11-1, where management is responsive to the needs of the process through the controlling factors. This management mindset also allows a significant reduction in non-value added information (such as paper) and significantly improves employee morale.

CRISES MANAGEMENT OR FIRE FIGHTING

Another aspect affecting the Quality Organizational Mindset is that of fire fighting or crises management.

Many supervisors, managers, and senior managers have been promoted through the ranks to their current position because they were good at "crisis management" or "fire fighting." They run from crisis to crises applying a quick fix, never taking the time to address root causes so as to prevent the same crises from reoccurring.

Personnel become so accustomed to this "fire fighting" mode of operation that it becomes part of the culture and of the individual's job security and personal self esteem. They become fearful and worried if the work environment becomes peaceful or too controlled. This can lead to the point, perhaps, of subconsciously creating crises.

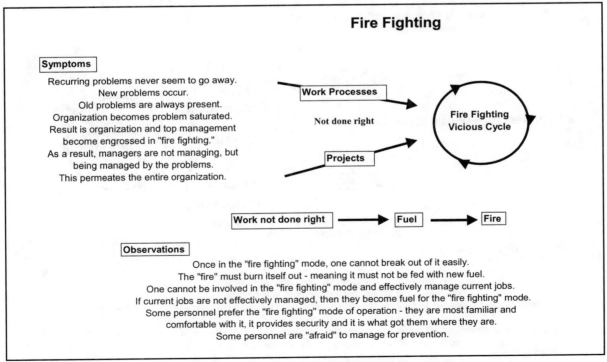

Figure 11-7. Fire-fighting Mode of Operation

The symptoms of such an operation are that recurring problems never seem to go away while new problems occur with the old problems still present.

The organization becomes "problem saturated", resulting in the organization and management (all levels) becoming engrossed in "fire fighting." This permeates the entire organization.

Managers are not managing, but being managed by the problems

A number of observations can be made of such an organization and of individuals within the organization.

Once in the "fire fighting" mode, one cannot break out of it easily.

The "fire" must burn itself out, meaning it must not be fed with new fuel.

One cannot be in the fire fighting mode and effectively manage current projects/jobs/processes.

If current projects/jobs/processes are not effectively managed, then they become fuel for the fire fighting" mode.

Some personnel prefer the "fire fighting" mode of operation. They are most familiar and comfortable with it. It provides security and it is what got them where they are.

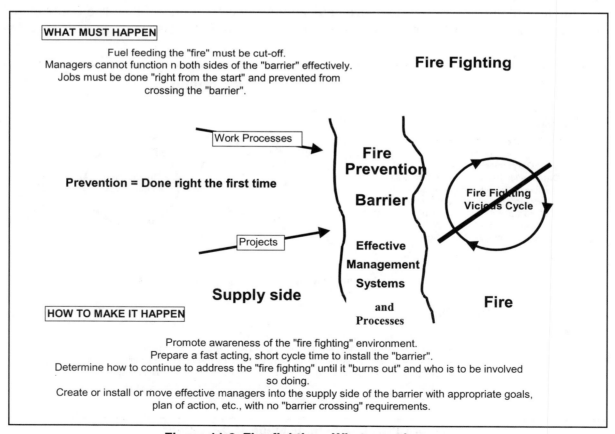

Figure 11-8. Fire-fighting - What must happen

Some personnel are afraid to manage.

What must happen is that the fuel feeding the fire must be "cut off,"creating a "fire prevention barrier.". Managers cannot function on both sides of this "barrier" effectively, as they will be consumed by fire fighting, allowing no time for prevention.

Jobs must be done "right from the start" and prevented from becoming fuel.

"Fire Fighting" is not compatible with an operating ISO 9000 based Management System.

How to make this happen requires patience, time, and effective management systems and processes. Awareness of the "fire fighting" environment must be promoted and a solid ISO 9000 based Quality Management System must be implemented.

CONCLUSION

Management is responsible and should be held accountable for providing proper facilities, equipment, employee training, and employee knowledge of procedures and work process instructions for each Primary and Support Work Process.

Management must not set performance standards that negatively affect the quality of the work process.

Management must provide a working environment needed to obtain the desired work process output, including safety considerations.

Continual Improvement of the Work Process utilizing process measurements, output measurements, and customer satisfaction measurements must be applied.

The ISO 9000 Standard looks at the work processes through these process-controlling factors whereas the ISO 14000 Standard looks at the effect of the work process and its output on the natural environment.

The quality and service mindset turns the traditional mindset triangle over such that the employee within the process is responsible for the process work quality. Management becomes a service or support organization for its employees, responsive to the needs of employees and the process.

Most organizations find themselves caught up in crisis management or fire fighting, where the problems are actually managing the processes. The fire-fighting mode of operation must be eliminated as it is not compatible with the ISO 9001:2000 based Quality Management System or with effective management systems in general.

Chapter 12

Primary Work Processes

This Primary Work Process approach in determining the procedures and work instructions to be written is described in this chapter, which will explain the identification and establishment of primary work processes, determination of associated procedures, work instructions, training and knowledge requirements, and check sheets.

APPROACH

It is often tempting for a company to jump right into writing procedures and work instructions prior to determining which ones need to be written, which often leads to rework and confusion. It is far better to determine which procedures and work instructions are needed to fully describe the work done within the company or organization prior to writing any of them. One method of so doing is through the Primary Work Process approach presented in Figure 12-1, which shows the relationships between work processes and the associated procedures, work instructions, and check sheets.

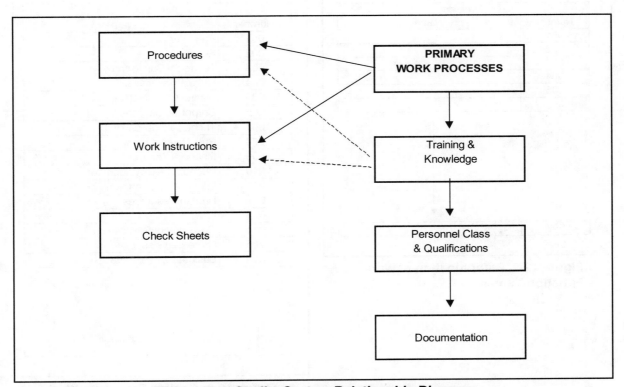

Figure 12-1. Quality System Relationship Diagram

ESTABLISHING PRIMARY WORK PROCESSES

A Primary Work Process (PWP) is one that delivers value-added outputs to a client or external customer (refer to Chapter 8 and Chapter 11 for the definition of "value-added"). By definition, every business has Primary Work Processes, the focus of the ISO 9001:2000 Standard.

Step 1—Determine Top Level Functions

The first step is to determine what are the top level (Level 1) functions performed within the organization or company and to name and number them in accordance with the previously developed "Numbering and Indexing" Quality System Procedure of Chapter 10. This determination can be accomplished in any way that works—individual effort, team effort, etc. Level 1 Function names might include Manufacturing, Engineering, Finance, Sales/Service, etc.

Figure 12-2 is a suggested format for the numbering and naming of the Level 1 functions. Figure 12-3 shows the actual function names for the American Bureau of Shipping as an applied example. The Level 1 Functions are high level and not to be confused with the Primary Work Processes described below.

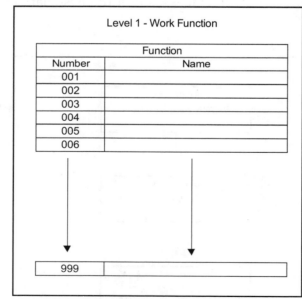

Figure 12-2. Determination of Work Function Names

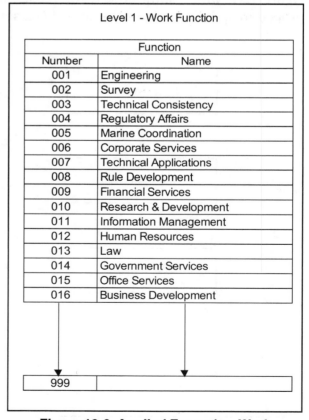

Figure 12-3. Applied Example—Work Functions

Step 2—List Primary Work Processes

The second step is to list all of the Primary Work Processes performed within the organization or company. The determination of the listing may again be through individual effort, team effort, interviews of personnel within each work function, etc. Once the listing is generated, group the listed processes into categories of work within each Level 1 Function and as described in the previously developed Quality System Procedure "Numbering and Indexing" of Chapter 10.

Since several Primary Work Processes may fall into one category of work within a function, the category should carry a name that is appropriate to the grouping. Figure 12-4 is a continuation of a suggested format for displaying the Level 1 Functions and Level 2 Categories together.

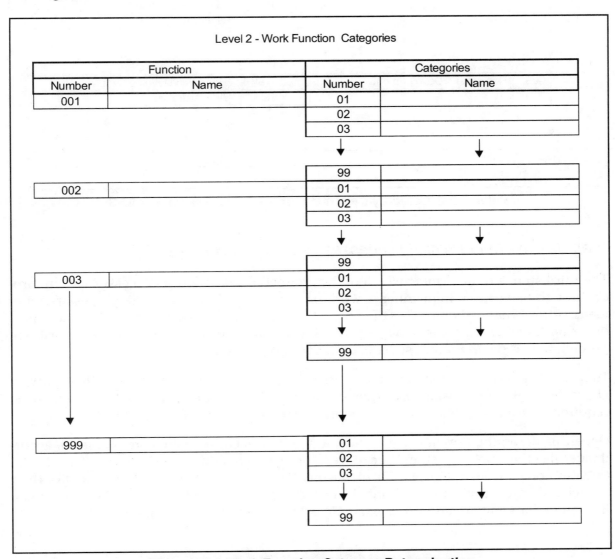

Figure 12-4. Work Function Category Determination

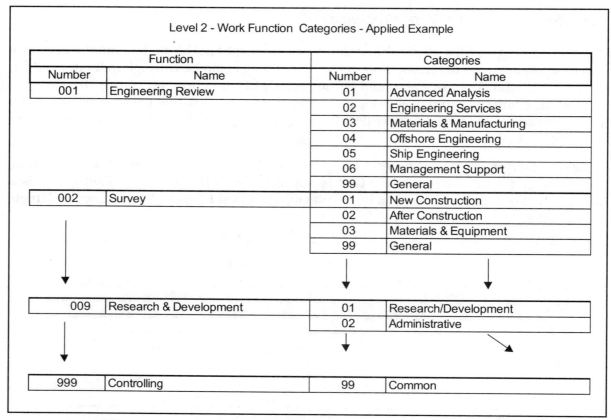

Level 2 - Work Function Categories - Applied Example

Function		Categories	
Number	Name	Number	Name
001	Engineering Review	01	Advanced Analysis
		02	Engineering Services
		03	Materials & Manufacturing
		04	Offshore Engineering
		05	Ship Engineering
		06	Management Support
		99	General
002	Survey	01	New Construction
		02	After Construction
		03	Materials & Equipment
		99	General
009	Research & Development	01	Research/Development
		02	Administrative
999	Controlling	99	Common

Figure 12-5. Category Determination—Applied Example of ABS

Step 3—Determine Which Processes Require Procedures

The third step is to determine which of the grouped Primary Work Processes require procedures to be written. Remember, a work process procedure states the process requirements—the "what is required" of the process; whereas, the associated work instruction(s) describe "how" the work is done. In general, every work process will require at least one procedure and could require several, with an upper limit of 99.

To make this determination, one must determine if not having a procedure will negatively affect the quality or consistency of the output of the associated process. If so, then one is required. The same is true relative to work instructions and check sheets.

Once this determination has been made, assign a procedure name and number in accordance with the Quality System Procedure "Numbering and Indexing." Figure 12-6 is a continuation of a suggested format for displaying the Level 3 Procedures together with their associated categories and functions. Figure 12-7 is the applied example of the American Bureau of Shipping. An additional example is included later in this chapter.

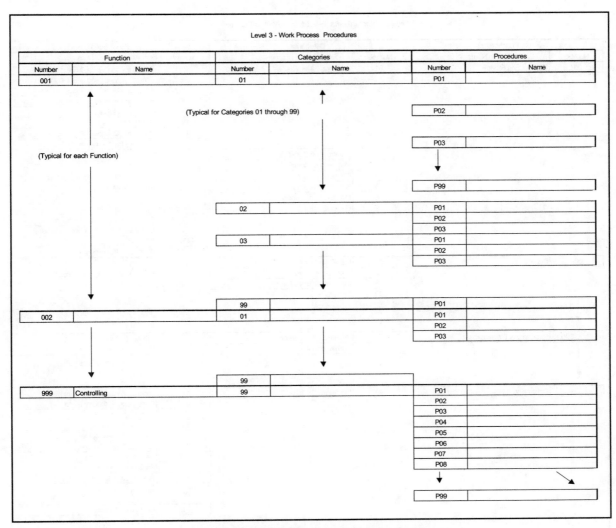

Figure 12-6. Procedure Determination

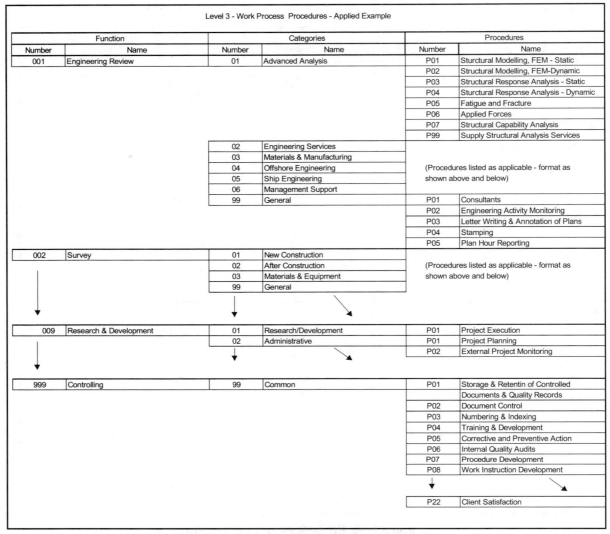

Figure 12-7. Procedure Determination—Applied Example

Step 4—Determine Work Instructions

The fourth step is the determination of the necessary work instructions to support the work process procedures. A procedure does not always require a work instruction, but a work instruction must always be directly associated with a procedure. A procedure may have as many as 999 subservient work instructions; however, the average is perhaps one to four. The written Work Instructions should be named and numbered in accordance with the Quality System Procedure "Numbering and Indexing." It may be that the actual determination of the work processes cannot be done until the procedures are written, or at least outlined as to their content.

Figure 12-8 is a continuation of a suggested format for displaying the Level 4 Work Instructions together with their associated procedures, categories, and processes. The applied example of the American Bureau of Shipping is included later in this chapter.

Function		Categories		Procedures		Work Instruction	
Number	Name	Number	Name	Number	Name	Number	Name
		01		P01		W001	
						W002	
						W00?	
				P02		W001	
(Typical per Function)						W002	
						W00?	
				P03		W001	
						W002	
						W00?	
		02		P01		W001	
						W002	
						W00?	
				P02		W001	
						W002	
						W00?	
				P03		W001	
						W002	
						W00?	
		03		P01		W001	
						W002	
						W00?	
				P02		W001	
						W002	
						W00?	
				P03		W001	
						W002	
						W00?	
		99	General	P01		W001	
						W002	
						W00?	
				P02		W001	
						W002	
						W00?	
				P03		W001	
						W002	
						W00?	

Figure 12-8. Procedure and Work Instruction Listing

TRAINING AND KNOWLEDGE REQUIREMENTS

Training and knowledge are two of the factors that control the quality of the output of the work processes (refer to Chapter 11, Primary Work Processes—Controlling Factors). If someone is placed into the work process without the necessary training, knowledge, or skills to perform the work (competency), then opportunity for error is introduced into that process. Ensuring that employees have the proper training and knowledge to perform their work properly is a management responsibility.

The next step after determining what the work processes are is to determine the necessary training and knowledge requirements for each of the processes. To do so, one might develop a work form similar to the one shown in Figure 12-1 for each process requiring procedures and work instructions. Refer also to Paragraph 3.3.1 of Chapter 10.

TRAINING AND KNOWLEDGE WORKSHEET

The following is a brief description of the various fields and associated terminology of the Training and Knowledge Worksheet.

Procedure Title:	The proposed title of the procedure to be developed.
Applicability:	The work functions for which this procedure will be applicable.
Purpose:	The stated purpose of this procedure.
Procedure Outline:	A "high level" listing of the primary steps, components, and deliverables associated with this procedure.
Related Procedure:	Listing of any related procedure that may be affected or referenced by this proposed procedure.
Related Work Instruction:	Listing of any related work instruction that may be affected or referenced by this proposed procedure.

Date:

Applicability:

Division/Region/Office/Department:

Procedure/Process Instruction Title:

Purpose:

Knowledge Requirements:

Procedure Outline (primary steps, components, deliverables)

Training Requirements:

Related Procedure(s):

Related Work Instruction(s):

Development of Procedures and Work Instructions, QSZ-999-99-P07   Attachment A - Revision 0   Page 1 of 1

Figure 12-9. Training and Knowledge Determination Worksheet

Knowledge Requirements:	Listing/description of the "baseline" knowledge required by those performing the work required by this procedure. Knowledge includes educational background requirements.
Training Requirements:	Listing/description of the necessary training requirements (completed or to be completed) for those performing the work required by this procedure.

Training and Assessment

Consideration needs to be given to the assessment of training needs and the preparation of training courses and materials necessary to ensure that employees are provided with the requisite skills.

In many companies, needs assessment determines the basis for the entire training program. Training needs assessment defines the process for comparing the existing employee skills with the skills currently required and projected to be required in the future. It takes into account employee turnover, budgetary constraints, technological developments, competing market trends, relevant legislation, and the labor market.

Training Plan

A written Training Plan for each office/department should be maintained as a working document and include the results of the Training Needs Assessment. The Training Plan should consider new hire training, on-the-job training, self-administered training, and formal group training provided by both internal and external resources.

On-the-Job Training

On-the-job training is generally preferred when the number of trainees in any one location is small, when a physical skill is involved, and when the material is difficult to communicate except by personal demonstration and participation. The persons providing on-the-job training shall have technical expertise in the skills being taught. The instruction process should consist of, as a minimum:

- Explaining what is to be learned
- Demonstrating how the task is to be performed
- Requiring the trainee to perform the task
- Providing feedback on the trainee's performance
- Follow-up

Group Training

Group training should be performed in the following cases:

- When other than a very small number of employees is involved
- When the purpose is to provide technical information, solve problems, or explain a method or procedure
- When input from several sources, including the trainee, may be required
- When the information or skills do not have to be demonstrated at the trainee's workplace

Self-Administered Training

Self-administered training should be considered for suitable subjects and where extensive hands-on experience is not required. Printed and/or audio-visual materials are possibilities as well as e-training. Some objective measure of performance provided by the trainee is needed to demonstrate progress or proficiency in the targeted areas. Work Instructions can also be used for self-administered training in specific work processes with progress monitored by supervisory personnel.

Budget Provisions for Training

Each manager needs to make suitable provisions in the budget for anticipated department training needs.

Completion of Training Courses

Records need to be maintained and retained of the successful completion of any training course with the respective employee's personnel record updated. If available, the training database of employee vs. training taken should also be updated.

Specific Process Training

When a Quality System Procedure or Work Instruction contains training requirements for specific work, each employee carrying out the process must be trained in accordance with those stated requirements and it must be documented.

Consideration should be given to the documentation of personnel versus the processes for which they are qualified, perhaps in a training database, accessible by all managers making assignments of work.

Additional consideration should be given to developing a specific Quality System procedure for "Training and Development," which addresses all of the issues stated above as well as a procedure or work instruction for "Process Training Certification."

Process Training Certification

Prior to any employee being qualified to carry out any process on an independent basis, the employee needs to be trained in accordance with the specific requirements of the Procedure/Work Instruction for the process being carried out. This process is usually contained in a Quality System Work Instruction or procedure entitled, "Process Training Certification." An example of the scope of such a document would be:

> *This Work Instruction provides information on how training records are completed and what is needed to qualify or decertify an employee for work delineated in a Work Instruction or Procedure, as applicable.*

POSITION DESCRIPTION MANUAL

The Position Description Manual is intended to provide personnel with a basic and comprehensive understanding of the job positions and reporting relationships within the company. The contents should include an introduction, a distribution listing, a job title matrix, and position descriptions for each position within the company.

The Position Description Manual is normally a controlled document that is issued from the Human Resource Department and can easily be done electronically.

The Position Description Manual may be configured into meaningful sections or separate manuals, with consideration given for Support Staff, Professional Staff, and Operating Personnel. Any breakdown of personnel categories that makes sense should be utilized.

DESIGN OF POSITION DESCRIPTIONS

The position descriptions contained in the Position Description Manual(s) should be designed to meet the basic requirements of the company. Outlined in each are the general requirements, skills, and job knowledge needed for each position. Typical contents of a position description include:

Title Block: The title block would only be necessary if issued as a controlled document and would contain the Name of the Position, Revision Number, Date Effective, Position Description Number, Preparer's Name, Approver's Name, and Page Number.

Title: The title associated with the position

Grade: The salary grade(s) associated with the position

General Summary: A brief summary of the position

Principal Duties and Responsibilities: A listing of such by type

Knowledge, Skills, and Abilities Required: A listing of these, including educational requirements and skills

Working Conditions: A description of the working environment

Disclaimer Clause: A disclaimer clause such as stated here might be a consideration:

This position description is not intended, and should not be construed, to be an all inclusive list of responsibilities, skills, efforts, or working conditions associated with the job of the incumbent. It is intended to be an accurate reflection of the principal job elements for making a fair decision regarding the pay structure of the job.

Reporting Relationships: A description of the reporting structure of the position

Revision History: If issued as a controlled document, this is a description of the revisions made to the respective position description.

An example of a Position Description is shown on below.

Title Matrix

The Title Matrix contained in the Position Description Manual is simply a matrix of grades/ levels (not necessarily salary grades or levels) that show all position titles within each grade/level across the entire company. One advantage of having a Title Matrix is to ensure a visible consistency of position titles versus the actual grade/level and associated responsibilities. An example of a Title Matrix is shown in Figure 12-11.

		QUALITY MANAGEMENT	
POSITION DESCRIPTION	**Revision Number:** 1	**Date Effective:** 1 April 1997	**Number:** ACZ-PD-014
Total Quality Management	**Prepared by:**	**Approved by:**	**Page** 1 of 2

Title: Director of Total Quality Management

General Summary

Responsible for the promotion, support, and assurance of continuous improvement in the quality of the management process and the products of the work processes. The purpose is to continuously improve the basic work processes to achieve total customer satisfaction and improve business results by eliminating wasted and non-value added activities.

The role of the Director of Total Quality Management is one of a pro-active catalyst working in partnership with the Senior Management Team.

Principal Duties and Responsibilities

1. Planning and support to the Senior Management Team in the implementation of the Total Quality Management Strategy throughout the company.

2. To act as quality specialist to the Senior Management Team by pro-actively facilitating the integration of quality into the planning, marketing, finance, engineering, operations, and all other business processes.

Figure 12-10. Position Description Example

3. To support the Management Team in applying quality and cycle time tools to drive work improvements in achieving annual objectives and longer-term goals.

4. To support management in defining and implementing effective means for measuring and managing customer satisfaction, quality, and cycle time improvement.

5. To be personally responsible to support senior management in upgrading their knowledge and skills in Total Quality Management (TQM).

Knowledge, Skills, and Abilities Required

1. A bachelor's degree in a non-liberal arts field.

2. Practical experience relating to quality, the marine industry, program management, and supervision.

3. Formal training in a recognized Quality Management System.

Disclaimer Clause

This position description is not intended, and should not be construed, to be an all inclusive list of responsibilities, skills, efforts, or working conditions associated with the job of the incumbent. It is intended to be an accurate reflection of the principal job elements essential for making a fair decision regarding the pay structure of the job.

Working Conditions

Work will normally be performed in an air-conditioned office environment with a comfortable setting. May encounter stressful situations prevalent in a senior management position. Will travel frequently and will entertain clients and business associates as deemed appropriate.

Reporting Relationships

Reports directly to the Chairman and Chief Executive Officer.

Revision History

Revision Number	Revision Summary	Effective Date
0	Initial Issue	2 April 1993
1	Revised position description manual	1 April 1996

Figure 12-10. Position Description Example—*Continued*

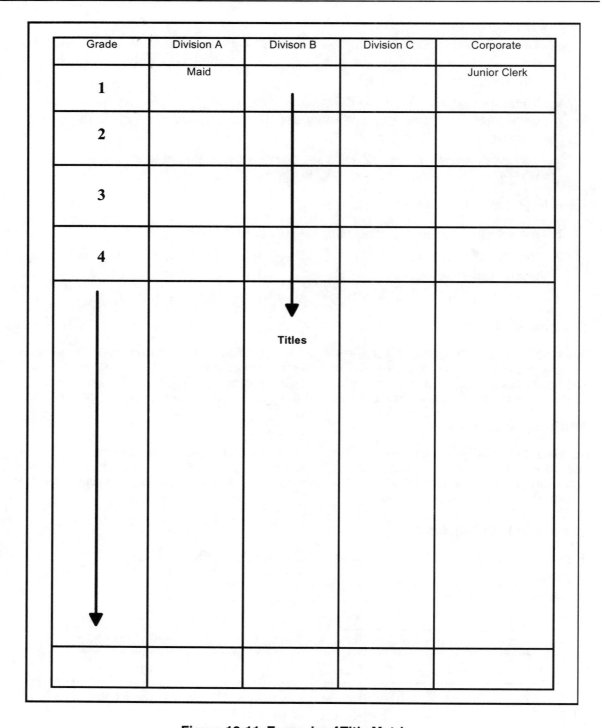

Grade	Division A	Divison B	Division C	Corporate
1	Maid			Junior Clerk
2				
3				
4				
		Titles		

Figure 12-11. Example of Title Matrix

Organization Charts Manual

The Organization Charts Manual is normally a company confidential reference document rather than a controlled document. The need for an organization charts manual is highly dependent upon the size and structure of the company, as are its contents.

Traditional organizational charts and matrix cross-functional charts should be considered for inclusion. The Organization Charts Manual should be updated at least annually or when any significant changes occur.

Not all companies are of sufficient size to need an Organization Charts Manual. Even though this may be the case, organization charts in some configuration are still necessary and must be kept reasonably up-to-date.

Organization charts should be dated and signed with a distribution listing maintained to ensure any updates are sent to the same people/locations who received the original issue.

Local organization charts associated with departments and/or small offices are not usually included in the organization charts manual. Instead, they are maintained on a local basis. These local organization charts might also include the associated delegation of authority by each person's name on the chart.

> Position
> Persons name (A, B,...)
> > A = Signature authority
> > B = Designates "in-charge" when manager not in office

DELEGATION OF AUTHORITY MANUAL

The Delegation of Authority Manual is also dependent upon the company size and structure. It is usually considered to be a controlled document with a defined format and controlled distribution. Companies that do not have an actual manual still need some documented means to cover the delegation of authority within the company.

An Introduction and a Table of Contents should be considered in the formatting of the manual.

Introduction Section

The Introduction should be relatively short—no more than one or two pages—and should include the following:

> **Objective/Scope:** A single paragraph describing the objective and scope of the Delegation of Authority Manual.

> **Related Guidance:** Brief sentence-length statements describing any related documents to the manual.

Applied Example:

> *This Policy Statement represents only one of several media that define the management environment.*

- Position descriptions set forth a general summary, principal duties and responsibilities, and other characteristics of each management position.

- Policies, organized by subject, define principles or "rules for action" governing the manner in which recurring types of situations in the conduct of business affairs are expected to be handled.

- Procedures and Work Instructions include the following components:

Contents Section

The Table of Contents should consider the following:

I. **Introduction:** To be structured as stated above.

II. **Organizational Overview**: Is usually one to three pages in length and describes, in summary form, the key features of the company's organization.

III. **The Concept of Delegation**: Reviews principles underlying the delegation of responsibility and authority and the corresponding accountability for performance and illustrates their application. This review should only be one to three pages in length.

IV. **Specific Delegations of Authority**: Delineates, by type of business transaction or decision, the level of authority delegated to the operating functions, as well as to executives and staff. The format may be in the form of matrices or written.

CONCLUSION

The following are the steps to be taken in identifying and documenting the Primary Work Processes of an organization.

List the top level functions within the organization

- Name and number these top level functions
- Brainstorm and list all work processes for each
- Determine which of these are primary processes
- Determine the work categories associated with each process
- Format listing into processes and categories

Determine the listing of work process procedures

- Group the procedures into the categories
- Name and number the procedures
- Determine the listing of associated work instructions for each procedure
- Group the work instructions by procedure
- Number the work instructions

Once the procedures and work instructions have been determined as described above, the associated training and knowledge of those performing the processes need to be established.

The training of those who are in the direct process related to the delivery of the product or service to the customer is essential in order to reduce the possibility of problems affecting the quality of that product or service.

Training is a process-controlling factor that is the responsibility of management. The placing of someone in a process without the proper training invites quality problems. Each procedure or work instruction needs to state what the training and knowledge requirements are and each person performing those processes must be trained, and perhaps certified, in the respective process. Doing so will greatly improve consistency of the output and reduce nonconformances.

Quality System Procedures dealing with training need to be prepared. A company-wide training approach or plan needs to be in operation—one that considers feedback and is continually being improved. Individual training needs assessments are generally the beginning of a plan, followed by the plan, budget for implementing the plan, and, of utmost importance, the implementation and tracking of the training.

Closely coupled with the training and knowledge requirements are the position descriptions of the personnel associated with each process.

Not all companies are large enough to need specific manuals for position descriptions, organization, and delegation of authority. However, each company needs to have position descriptions and organization charts that show the relationship between functions and some form of authority delegation. It is not necessary to place each of these items in a dedicated manual. In summary, these documents need to be available in some useable form if independent from a Position Description and Delegation of Authority Manual. In addition, these documents need to be maintained and up-to-date, which implies that they are issued in a controlled manner to ensure that the latest versions are being used.

Chapter 13

Assignment and Preparation
Procedures, Work Instructions, and Check Sheets

WORK PROCESS PROCEDURES

The Quality System Manual has been written; the Quality System Procedures have been completed or are close to completion; and the procedures and associated work instructions have been listed, grouped into categories and processes, and numbered. Now it is time to begin the task of preparing the individual procedures, work instructions, and associated check sheets for the Primary Work Processes.

The key to accomplishing this task in the most expeditious and cost-effective manner is to prepare a thought-out plan before launching the task. The steps of the planning process for this element of implementation should include the following:

1. Designate a team, department, or individual within the organization to handle the logistics associated with assignment and tracking of this effort. This assigned entity should also be the designee for collecting and reviewing the completed documents for form, fit, and function.

2. Prepare a matrix of the procedures and work instructions to be done by extending the matrices developed in Chapter 10 for determining the listings. See Figure 12-10 and Figure 12-11.

3. Prepare a simple code to designate the status of each procedure and work instruction.

4. Prepare a sample of a typical procedure and a typical work instruction, which includes a checklist and a Training and Knowledge Worksheet. This sample should actually be one of the needed procedures and work instructions.

5. Determine who is best qualified to write each procedure and each work instruction within the entire organization. If possible, only one task should be assigned to an individual. Place the names of the assignees on the matrix to be used for tracking the development process.

6. Prepare a software template on disk—one for the preparation of a procedure and one for the preparation of a work instruction. In this way, the developer only needs to complete the text and it can easily be edited and configured into the final form.

7. Prepare a packet for each developer that includes:

- Task assignment description (which procedure or work instruction to develop)

- Quality System Procedure (development of a Quality System Procedure or Work instruction document)

- Sample Quality System Procedure or Work Instruction to be used as a guide

- Copy of the disk with the format pre-entered

- Where to call for help

8. Forward the packet to the developer. Be sure the person's supervisor is in agreement.

9. Monitor and track progress on the Tracking Matrix Chart.

The average time to develop a Quality System Procedure or Work Instruction is about two hours. If it takes longer, then too much detail is being generated.

The tendency is to make the Quality System Procedures or Work Instructions more complex than necessary. They should be kept simple and use flowcharts where practical. The objective is to simply write down what you do, not what you would like to do. Keep it simple and make it more complex later if necessary. This approach is much easier than simplifying later.

Provide a "sanity" check for each completed document—an expert within the company in the respective technical field should be able to do this. Also, provide a format check to ensure the adherence to the Quality System Procedure requirements and to ensure documentation completeness. The assigned entity of Item 1 above can ensure this is accomplished.

CHECK SHEETS

In conjunction with the development of Quality System Procedures or Work Instructions, one needs to consider the additional need for a procedure titled "Check Sheets" that provides guidance in the development, need, and use of check sheets as applied to work processes. Such a procedure would addresses specific requirements when check sheets are used.

Check Sheets—General

The purpose of Quality System Procedures is to state the overall requirements of the process, but not how to do the process or carry it out. In addition, one Procedure may cover several work processes. Therefore, Procedures are not a viable alternative to the use of Check Sheets in carrying out work.

Work Instructions, on the other hand, describe how the work is done in sufficient detail to allow one to follow the instructions and accomplish the work. As a result, the process instruction is usually too detailed for the experienced practitioner to need each time the process is carried out. In normal circumstances, the Work Instruction is used for training and certification of the practitioner to the process, and for referral should the need arise during the performance of the associated work. Work Instructions are not usually used as Check Sheets, but could be used as Check Sheets.

The purpose of Check Sheets is to ensure that certain steps are carried out in a process. The completed Check Sheets are evidence that these steps were carried out and as such are considered quality records.

Check Sheets are simpler than Work Instructions. Check Sheets are used as a reminder or memory-jogger to the practitioner to ensure that he/she does not forget or bypass any steps that are important to the integrity of the associated process. Check Sheets also ensure that the practitioner knows where he/she is when interruptions affect the work effort.

Check Sheets are an assurance tool forming part of a work process control which ensures all work processes are performed; they provide evidence that all listed steps of a work process have been performed and support consistent service delivery regardless of where or by whom the work process is performed.

Check Sheets also serve as the document of record for verification that one is doing that which is written down in the associated work instruction or procedure. Finally, Check Sheets help to ensure that multiple practitioners are consistent in how they do their work, giving the client a consistent product.

Check Sheets should and must be simpler than Work Instructions. They should include only those items necessary to ensure that all pertinent steps affecting the integrity of the process output are covered, and they must take virtually no additional time to use as a tracking tool/document.

Criteria for the Use of Check Sheets

The use of a Check Sheet must be an evaluated decision, one that is challenged as to its value relative to the quality of the process output. The only question that must be asked relative to Check Sheets is, "How does one assure oneself and others that they have covered all of the key steps of the process, and what is the visible evidence of such?" If one can adequately answer this question and show it with a simplified Check Sheet or none at all, then one meets the requirements.

The process owner/manager determines whether a Check Sheet is needed based on informed judgments as to relative risks associated with doing (or not doing) the process consistently. The degree of confidence required by the manager to ensure a certain quality of work is also a factor in the decision. Questions that might be asked to assist in this determination include:

- Is a check sheet needed to ensure that the process is being carried out the same way or consistently in all locations?

- Is a check sheet needed to ensure that all critical items are checked prior to dispatch to the client?
- Will the process or service quality suffer if a Check Sheet is not used?

PREPARATION AND ASSIGNMENT

The preparation, assignment, and tracking progress until completion is the next step in the Quality System Implementation Process. The assigned person should be technically qualified to prepare the document and provided with guidance examples and requirements to minimize variation between those preparing documents. The need for Check Sheets should also be considered. Accountability and schedules should be established with monthly progress reports provided to management.

One should also keep in mind that all of the documents do not need to be completed before implementation, as they can be implemented in groups. However, the entire set of documents whose need is anticipated should be planned and scheduled.

CONCLUSION

Planning the Process Procedure, Work Instructions and Check Sheet preparation as outlined in this chapter is one of the keys to success. In so doing, one can use the matrices developed in Chapter 10. Don't make the procedure or work instruction more complex than necessary.

The answer to the question, "How does one know when a procedure, work instruction, or check sheet is needed?" is important to remember. Generally, the answer to the additional question, "Will the absence of a procedure, work instruction, or check sheet cause a quality problem for the output of the associated process?" will provide the insight needed to make an appropriate determination. If the answer to this question is no, then a check sheet is not needed. However, be sure that all factors have been considered before making that judgement.

Chapter 14

Controlled Document Issuance

The ISO 9001:2000 Standard describes the Documentation Control requirements in the following manner:

> *Documents required by the quality management system shall be controlled. A documented procedure shall be established to define the controls needed:*
>
> - *to approve documents for adequacy prior to issue,*
> - *to review and update as necessary and re-approve documents,*
> - *to ensure that changes and the current revision status of documents are identified,*
> - *to ensure relevant versions of applicable documents are available at points of use,*
> - *to ensure that documents remain legible and readily identifiable,*
> - *to ensure that documents of external origin are identified and their distribution controlled, and*
> - *to prevent unintended use of obsolete documents, and to apply suitable identification to them if they are retained for any purpose.*

The term generally accepted for documents meeting the above requirement is "controlled document," which carries the definition of: any document issued to a particular department or individual that is uniquely identified as a controlled document and is traceable for recall.

It is easy to get carried away in the classification of documents as *controlled*, even though it is not necessary for them to be so classified. In general, only those documents for which failure to use the latest revision will directly affect the end product or service need be classified as controlled documents.

Controlled documents normally include Work Process Procedures, Work Instructions, Quality System Manuals, Quality System Procedures, Technical Software lists, and any other documents that might be utilized in the production of product or service, including forms. In addition, management might decide to include other documents as controlled documents to track and ensure that the latest revisions are being utilized. Such documents might include Personnel Position Descriptions, Delegation of Authority Manual, Safety Manual, etc.

Being a controlled document implies that the document needs to be dated, numbered, signed, and the revision indicated (by date or number). There must also be a listing of who has received each specific document and a master listing of controlled documents showing the latest revision levels. A number of companies also require a signed acknowledgment of receipt of a controlled document and verified destruction of the outdated document. This is not necessary if distributed electronically.

Controlled documents may be electronic and distributed electronically. This is perfectly acceptable so long as those individuals who need the documents to perform their work tasks have access to them, and avail themselves of that access prior to performing work controlled by the documents.

Quality Records are a special type of controlled document and are required to provide evidence of conformity to requirements and of the effectiveness of the quality management system. Records are also required to remain legible, readily identifiable, and retrievable. A documented procedure is required to define the controls needed for the identification, storage, protection, retrieval, retention time, and disposition of records.

A typical controlled document distribution list for hard copies might look like that shown in Figure 14-1 and Figure 14-2. A typical master listing of controlled documents might look like that shown in Figure 14-3. If the document control is electronic, then such a listing can be an electronic version of the listing. If all employees have access, then no listing is necessary, since that which is on the electronic system is the updated document. It is more cost effective and more easily controlled to have an electronic document management system in place.

In acknowledgment of a controlled document one may use a bar coding and scanning approach, a signed and returned acknowledgment form, or any other suitable method, such as e-mail. An example of each approach is shown in Figure 14-4 and Figure 14-5. If controlled documents are accessible through an electronic system which is maintained and updated, then an acknowledgment system is not necessary. However, the users of such a system must access it each time before work is performed to ensure that they are using the latest documents to perform work.

CONCLUSION

There is no right or wrong way to issue controlled documents. An all-electronic system, with immediate access to the latest version of the documents by all parties, is the most efficient and cost-effective manner for the control of documents. If the document control system is manual or hard copy, then a record needs to be maintained of the people who have the documents so that management can be assured that these same people receive the latest revisions to the issued documents. This chapter offers examples of some methods for such tracking and confirmation of receipt of documents. The simplest method that meets the requirements is best.

CONTROLLED DOCUMENT MATRIX 1 JULY 2001		Control Copy Number	Master List (Vol. 0)	Quality System Manual (Vol. 1)	Quality System Procedures & PIs (Vol. 2)	Worldwide Procedures & PIs (Vol. 3)	IS General Procedures & PIs (Vol. 3s)	IS Engineering Procedures & PIs (Vol. 4s)	IS Inspection/Consulting Procedures & PIs (Vol. 5s)	MS All Procedures & PIs (Vol. 4m)	Delegation of Authority Manual	Position Descriptions
Manager of Actg.	Singapore	001	X	X	X	X	X				X	X
Operations Manager	New York, NY	026	X	X	X	X	X	X	X	X	X	X
Engineering Manger	Houston, TX	037									X	
		688	X	X	X	X	X		X		X	X
		038	X	X	X	X	X		X	X	X	X
		795	X	X	X	X	X	X	X	X	X	X
		939	X	X	X	X	X	X	X		X	X
		004	X	X	X	X	X				X	X
Name of Office or Department or Function		010	X	X	X	X	X	X	X	X	X	X
		443	X	X	X	X	X	X	X		X	X
		994	X	X	X	X	X		X		X	X
		072	X	X	X	X	X		X		X	X
		558	X	X	X	X	X	X	X	X	X	X
		973	X	X	X	X	X			X	X	X
		016	X	X	X	X	X					
	Location	427	X	X	X	X	X		X	X	X	X
		637	X	X	X	X	X				X	X
		401	X	X	X	X	X		X	X	X	X
		071	X	X	X	X	X		X	X	X	X
		979	X	X	X	X	X		X	X	X	X
		066	X	X	X	X	X				X	X
		428	X	X	X	X	X				X	X
		007	X	X	X	X	X				X	X
		079	X	X	X	X	X				X	X
		514	X	X	X	X	X				X	X
		683	X	X	X	X	X	X	X	X		
		656	X	X	X	X	X	X	X		X	X

Figure 14-1. A Typical Controlled Document Distribution Matrix for Offices/Departments/ Functions

PERSONNEL CONTROLLED DOCUMENT DISTRIBUTION MATRIX — 1 JULY 2001

Name of Person and Functional Title	Location	Control Copy Number	Master List (Vol. 0)	Quality System Manual (Vol. 1)	Quality System Procedures & PIs (Vol. 2)	Worldwide Procedures & PIs (Vol. 3)	IS General Procedures & PIs (Vol. 3s)	IS Engineering Procedures & PIs (Vol. 4s)	IS Inspection/Consulting Procedures & PIs (Vol. 5s)	MS All Procedures & PIs (Vol. 4m)	Delegation of Authority Manual	Position Descriptions
	Houston	001	X	X	X	X	X				X	X
	Singapore	026	X	X	X	X	X	X	X	X	X	X
	DuBai	037									X	
		688	X	X	X	X	X			X		X	X
		038	X	X	X	X	X			X	X	X	X
		795	X	X	X	X	X	X		X	X	X	X
		939	X	X	X	X	X	X		X		X	X
		004	X	X	X	X	X					X	X
		010	X	X	X	X	X	X		X	X	X	X
		443	X	X	X	X	X	X		X		X	X
		994	X	X	X	X	X			X		X	X
		072	X	X	X	X	X			X		X	X
		558	X	X	X	X	X	X		X	X	X	X
		973	X	X	X	X	X				X	X	X
		016	X	X	X	X	X					X	X
	Location	427	X	X	X	X	X			X	X	X	X
		637	X	X	X	X	X					X	X
		401	X	X	X	X	X			X	X	X	X
		071	X	X	X	X	X			X	X	X	X
		979	X	X	X	X	X			X	X	X	X
		066	X	X	X	X	X					X	X
		428	X	X	X	X	X					X	X
		007	X	X	X	X	X					X	X
		079	X	X	X	X	X					X	X
		514	X	X	X	X	X					X	X
		683	X	X	X	X	X	X		X	X		
		656	X	X	X	X	X	X		X		X	X

Figure 14-2. A Typical Controlled Document Distribution Matrix for Individuals

MASTER LIST OF CONTROLLED DOCUMENTS	Revision Number 1	Date Effective 1 April 2001	Section Number 5
Engineering Procedures	Prepared By C. Biczynski	Approved By R. Murphy	Page 1 of 1

Title Effective	Number	Rev.

Structural Modeling, FEA .... EIZ-101-01-P01 .... 1 .... 1 April 2001

◆   Structural Analysis
    - Finite Element Modeling .... EIZ-101-01-P01-W001 .... 1 .... 1 April 2001

Fatigue Analysis .... EIZ-101-01-P02 .... 1 .... 1 April 2001

◆   Pressure Vessel Fatigue Analysis .... EIZ-101-01-P02-W001 .... 1 .... 1 April 2001

Applied Forces .... EIZ-101-01-P03 .... 1 .... 1 April 2001

◆   Wind Load Conditions .... EIZ-101-01-P03-W001 .... 1 .... 1 April 2001
◆   Nozzle External Load Conditions .... EIZ-101-01-P03-W002 .... 1 .... 1 April 2001
◆   Wind Load Conditions .... EIZ-101-01-P03-W003 .... 1 .... 1 April 2001

Procedure title or name

Work Instruction

Figure 14-3. Typical Master Listing of Controlled Documents

Company Name

Controlled Document Transmittal Record

Attached are controlled copies of approved documents. Please include these in your records and discard superseded copies. Please return one signed copy of this transmittal record to the undersigned within six weeks of receipt.

Date: _____   Initial Transmittal: _____   Revision Transmittal: _____

ISSUED TO:

Address:

Control Copy:

Document Name	Document Number	Section Number	Revision Number	Revision Date

I have received and filed these documents, and will thoroughly familiarize myself with their content before doing the work they govern:

_____
Document Recipient's Signature

_____
Date of Acknowledgment

Issuer of Document:

Name: _____
Title: _____
Address: _____
_____
_____

Document Control, QSZ-999-99-P02   Attachment A - Revision 1   Page 1 of 1

Figure 14-4. Signed and Returned Acknowledgment—Applied Example

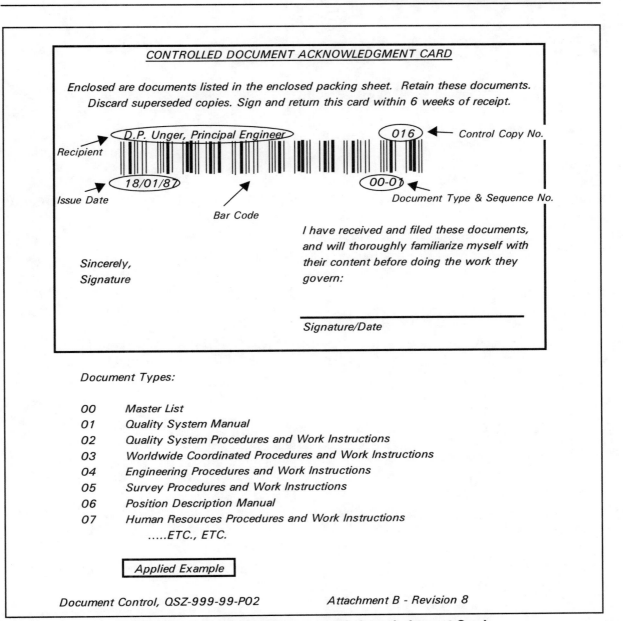

CONTROLLED DOCUMENT ACKNOWLEDGMENT CARD

Enclosed are documents listed in the enclosed packing sheet. Retain these documents. Discard superseded copies. Sign and return this card within 6 weeks of receipt.

Recipient → D.P. Unger, Principal Engineer — 016 ← Control Copy No.

Issue Date → 18/01/87 — 00-01 ← Document Type & Sequence No.

Bar Code

Sincerely,
Signature

I have received and filed these documents, and will thoroughly familiarize myself with their content before doing the work they govern:

_____

Signature/Date

Document Types:

00	*Master List*
01	*Quality System Manual*
02	*Quality System Procedures and Work Instructions*
03	*Worldwide Coordinated Procedures and Work Instructions*
04	*Engineering Procedures and Work Instructions*
05	*Survey Procedures and Work Instructions*
06	*Position Description Manual*
07	*Human Resources Procedures and Work Instructions*
	.....ETC., ETC.

Applied Example

Document Control, QSZ-999-99-P02   *Attachment B - Revision 8*

Figure 14-5. Controlled Document Acknowledgment Card

Chapter 15

Quality System Implementation Instructions

Controlled Documents have been distributed to the various offices, departments, and individuals. Now comes the task of ensuring that those who receive these documents know what to do with them so that quality becomes "just the way we do our work." This effort can be accomplished in a number of ways, but one of them is *to make it happen with a planned effort.* In order to be successful, the implementation of the system should be planned and executed with feedback, like any other step of the process.

The first task, then, is to determine the implementation plan for each office/country/ region/department/etc. For single location companies, this plan may be for departments.

- Select the key person or task team charged with implementation.
- Determine the implementation method (modules or scattered).

     The *scattered approach* is to have no pre-planned groupings of documents.

     The *modular approach* is to group related documents together.

     A typical module might include:

          QSM Section

          Associated Quality System Procedure

          Supporting Procedure(s)/Documents

- Implement even if other parts of the organization are not yet ready.
- Educate all participants of requirements and processes.
- Follow-up to ensure compliance and to work out any discovered problems.
- Begin with full effort.

IMPLEMENTATION HANDBOOK

One method of Quality Management System Implementation for organizations is to prepare an ISO 9001:2000 Implementation Instruction Handbook for use by all employees, issued in an uncontrolled manner to each office/department. This Implementation Instruction Handbook would have about a three-month life span, used mostly for training and as a guidance document.

The layout of such a handbook may be modular in nature for larger organizations, combining all of the Quality System procedures and work instructions into groups dependent on their respective content and providing explanations for each group. For smaller organizations, a single section Handbook would suffice. Such a Handbook is certainly optional. The important thing is to plan the implementation and provide the best documentation method for that implementation.

A typical Quality Management System Implementation Handbook is best configured as outlined for QSM Option 3, Process Orientation, of Chapter 9. This is the case even if Option 2, ISO 9001:2000 Standard Orientation is chosen for the QSM. In actuality, both Option 2 and Option 3 contain exactly the same material, only grouped differently. An Implementation Handbook might include the following sections, with each section containing References, Immediate Actions, and Implementation Instructions. Not all implementation modules will contain Immediate Actions. Each module should be customized for the specific status of the company. Smaller, single sight companies may not need this handbook but should read and consider the approach in their implementation planning.

Implementation Modules

Module 1—Quality Management System Implementation Plan *(Applies to all employees)*

This module would be a concise plan of implementation which describes the deployment methodology and provides some awareness information, and which can be used in the provision of training. It would include a description of the Quality Management System, including its overall purpose. This module should be kept short.

Module 2—Quality Management System *(Applies to all employees)*

References

This module would reference the Quality System Manual Section(s) that contain the Quality Management System Scope, General Explanation of the Quality Management System, Quality Policy, Quality Policy Implementation, and Quality Objectives. The purpose of this module is to acquaint the employee with the requirements of the Quality Management System and its purpose. This module addresses Clauses 1.0, 4.1, and 5.3 of the ISO 9001:2000 Standard.

Implementation Instructions

The actions taken in implementing this module would include but not be limited to the following:

1. Supervisors and above read entire Quality System Manual, with a special focus on the sections that include the items listed in the above Reference.

2. Managers and above may want to memorize the Mission, Vision, and Quality Policy or be sure that they understand them and can find the printed copy easily.

3. Assess the Quality Policy and Mission Statement needs for each part of the organization or location and complete the order form (attached). Prepare a simple order form to be completed by those receiving the handbook.

4. Recommendation is to have a minimum of one set of implementation instructions in each geographical office location (not each employee office). For larger offices, such as regional, more copies or larger size copies may be desirable.

5. Display the Quality Policy when received. This can be coupled with the display of the organization's Mission Statement and Vision Statement.

6. All employees familiarize themselves with the Quality Policy, Mission Statement, and Vision Statement.

7. Managers and above should be sure that they understand the General Comments section of the QSM. Each should know what it means to them and the work processes for which they are responsible.

8. Supervisors and above should also be sure that they understand how the Quality Policy is implemented throughout the organization (see Quality System Manual). One method would be for each to write it out for group review with their team.

9. Make the Quality Objectives and the specific function's (Department or Office) Operations Objectives available for the all of the function's (Department or Office) employees.

10. Supervisors and above understand the Quality and specific function's Operating Objectives and their part in accomplishing those objectives. One method would be for each to write their part out for review with their respective team.

    • What does each Objective mean to them and their job?

    • How do they measure success of these objectives?

Note that the Operations Objectives are not stated in the Quality System Manual or the Quality System Procedures, but are those that are determined by each Operating Unit in accordance with the requirement for quality objectives for those needed to meet requirements for product or service.

Module 3—Planning *(Applies to those responsible for the QMS Planning)*

This module explains the purpose of planning as it relates to the Quality Management System in respect to process management and addresses Clause 5.4.2 of the ISO 9001:2000 Standard. This Module is applicable for those responsible for QMS Planning and not necessary for the general employee. The general employee must know, however, who the Quality Management Representative is.

Module 4—Management Responsibility *(Applies to top management)*

References

This module applies to management personnel, especially top management, and would include Management Commitment, Customer Focus, and Internal Communication, and addresses Clauses 5.1, 5.2 and 5.5.3 of the ISO 9001:2000 Standard.

Implementation Instructions

Management must read and know their responsibilities relative to the demonstration of their commitment to the quality management system, which are stated in the QSM. These actions include:

11. Visible evidence of Top Management's

    - Communicating to all employees the importance of meeting customer as well as statutory regulatory requirements,

    - Establishing the quality policy and ensuring that this policy is understood by all employees,

    - Ensuring that the quality objectives are established and reviewed for continuing suitability and adequacy when necessary,

    - Conducting management reviews, and

    - Ensuring the availability of resources.

12. Top management ensures that customer requirements are determined and met with the aim of enhancing customer satisfaction.

13. Top management ensures that appropriate communication processes are established within the organization and that communication takes place regarding the effectiveness of the QMS.

Module 5—Organizational Responsibility *(Applies mostly to supervisors and above, but also to employees in part)*

References

This module covers the responsibilities and authorities of personnel for implementing and maintaining the Quality Management System and is directed at those personnel. However, the general employee must know certain parts of this module. This module addresses Clauses 5.5.1 and 5.5.2 of the ISO 9001:2000 Standard.

Implementation Instructions

Top management defines and communicates the responsibilities and authorities of all employees within the organization. The documents that describe and define organizational relationships within the company, as well as the responsibilities and authorities for activity affecting quality must be available and familiar to all employees, but especially to supervisors and above. Organizational charts, position descriptions, functional process relationship charts, and delegation of authority document may support this module.

14. All managers and above read the section of the QSM that denotes organizational responsibility for the QSM for understanding.

    - Know the Responsibilities and Authorities for the organization or be able to show documentation that shows the responsibilities and authorities

    - Know who the Management Representative is.

    - Be familiar with the Quality Management System Structure and the key players.

15. All employees must know who the Management Representative is and be familiar with the organizational structure, responsibilities, and documents wherein these are defined.

Module 6—Management Review *(Applies top management and the management team of the organization)*

References

This module addresses Clause 5.6 of the ISO 9001:2000 Standard and covers the Management Review of the Quality Management System. There may be a Quality Management System procedure titled, "Management Review", associated with this module as well. If so, it should be included for training purposes.

Implementation Instructions

This module applies to all CISC members (if such has been established) or the team of senior managers plus top management who will be reviewing the Quality Management System. The method established for the Management Review, either through a Management Review Board or through a continuous management review as part of the CISC or regular management team meetings is communicated to those involved. Management reviews will then be held on a regular basis and shall include:

16. Understanding of the review inputs as stated in the QSM and Management Review Procedure, if applicable.

17. Understanding of the required outputs and actions relating to the review itself.

18. This training is perhaps best conducted during the first management review meeting, which should be held early in the development and implementation of the Quality Management System.

Module 7—Documentation Requirements *(Applies to the entire organization)*

References

This module addresses Clauses 4.2.1, 4.2.2, 4.2.3, and 4.2.4 of the ISO 9001:2000 Standard and focuses on imparting understanding of the structure of the Quality Management System documentation, as well as the requirements for, and contol of, these documents to all employees. Documents that support this module would include the Quality System Manual, Procedures for Document Control (a required procedure), Quality Records (a required procedure), and any other related procedures that the organization may have generated.

Implementation Instructions

Each office/department must establish the means with which they will comply with the requirements of the procedures. This module covers documentation requirements, the quality manual, the control of documents, the control of records, and the Quality Management System documentation structure. Consideration might be given to a File Management Guide such that the basic file types within each office or department would be the same and carry the same file reference number.

19. Determine who is responsible for "setting up" the document control requirements within each office or department.

20. Provide the referenced documents to each responsible individual or group for review and study and provide training for those individuals to ensure their understanding.

21. Implement the process as stated in the referenced documents (procedures) and present the requirements to all employees within the office/department. Ensure that they understand the Quality Management System structure as presented in the Quality System Manual.

22. Follow-up to ensure compliance and understanding.

Module 8—Resource Management *(Applies to supervisors and up, those who manage the organization's resources)*

References

There is no required procedure relative to resource management. However, one must answer the question, "Does the absence of a procedure for this requirement negatively affect the output or the consistency of the output of the related processes?" If the answer is "yes?" then one should consider a policy or procedure that controls resource management. This module addresses Clause 6 of the ISO 9001:2000 Standard and includes the Provision of Resources, Human Resources, Competence, Awareness and Training, Infrastructure (buildings, process equipment and supporting services), and the Work Environment. The appropriate QSM Section and any related procedures or policies should be provided to Supervisors and above.

Implementation Instructions

Everyone involved with resource management must understand and comply with the referenced documents for their respective part of this process. If employees are expected to complete work processes without proper training, skills, or physical resources, the work environment can negatively affect the quality of the associated processes' outputs. For this reason, Resource Management is a Controlling Factor of the process as it controls certain aspects of quality of the process.

23. Determine those individuals within each office/department responsible for resource management as defined in the referenced documents.

24. Provide each with the referenced material to read and study.

25. Implement the process as stated in the referenced documents. This may involve meeting with each employee, evaluating the employee training needs, establishing a training plan, certifying each employee for the process in which they are participating, and documenting employee competency for the respective work processes.

26. Follow-up to ensure compliance and understanding.

Module 9—Product Realization Planning *(Applies to those individuals or functions responsible for the planning of product realization within the organization)*

References

This module addresses Clause 7.1 of the ISO 9001:2000 Standard. The Planning of Product Realization and the associated responsibilities are included. Product realization planning is for the Production and Service Provision of the organization. There is no required procedure for this planning, but one must be able to demonstrate that it is done for each part of the operation that delivers product or service to customers. The appropriate section of the Quality System Manual must be provided to each person responsible for the planning of product realization.

Implementation Instructions

Each person responsible for the planning of product realization must be familiar with the requirements and ensure that they comply with them. This includes but is not limited to the following:

27. Quality objectives and requirements for the product or service,

28. The need to establish processes and documents, and to provide resources specific to the product or service,

29. The required verification, validation, monitoring, inspection, and test activities specific to the product or service, and the criteria for customer acceptance.

30. The records evidencing that the production and service delivery process meets the requirements.

The format of the output of this planning process must be determined and may be a part of the various operations procedures that control each specific process. The major implementation training ensures that the requirements for planning are understood. Then follow-up to ensure completion. This is done as part of the Internal Audit program yet to come.

Module 10—Customer Related Processes *(Applies to those responsible for the determination, review, and communication of product or service requirements for customer related products and services)*

References

This module addresses Clause 7.1 of the ISO 9001:2000 Standard and includes the determination of the requirements related to the product or service, the review of those requirements, and customer communication—including communications related to product/service information, inquiries, contracts, amendments to contracts, contract changes, and customer feedback (including complaints). The documentation provided to those involved in these requirements includes the appropriate sections of the QSM and any associated procedures that control customer communications. This might include review procedures for service requests, initiation of projects, contract review, customer feedback, contract changes and/or amendments, proposal generation, etc.

Implementation Instructions

31. List the applicable procedures associated with this module and other related documents as applicable.

32. Determine those individuals/departments involved in Customer Related Processes and provide each with the referenced material to read and study.

33. Everyone who is involved with this specific work process must understand and comply with the referenced documents and then implement the process as stated in those documents.

34. Appropriate records must be maintained as stated in the requirements.

35. Follow-up to ensure compliance and understanding.

Module 11—Design and Development *(Applies to those organizations that design and develop product and services)*

Reference

This module covers the Design and Development Planning, Inputs to the process, Outputs from the process, Review, Verification, Validation, and Change Control. It applies to those departments and individuals involved with and/or responsible for the design and development of products and services. This module addresses Clause 7.2 of the ISO 9001:2000 Standard. There is usually an associated operations procedure for this function, but the ISO Standard does not specifically require it.

36. Determine those individuals/departments involved in Design and Development.

37. Provide each with the referenced material to read and study.

38. Implement the process as stated in the referenced documents.

39. Follow-up to ensure compliance and understanding.

Module 12—Purchasing *(Applies to those departments and individuals responsible for verifying that purchased product conforms to the specified purchasing agreements)*

References

This module addresses Clause 7.4 of the ISO 9001:2000 Standard and includes the purchasing process, purchasing information, and verification of purchased product. Although not required, there is usually an operating procedure associated with this requirement, to ensure process consistency and conformance.

Implementation Instructions

40. List all applicable procedures associated with purchasing and supplier control, including those associated with subcontracted labor, as applicable.

41. Everyone involved in the purchasing and supplier control as well as those involved in the engagement of labor-supplying subcontractors must understand and comply with the referenced documents.

42. Determine who is responsible for purchasing and supplier control within each respective office/department.

43. Provide the referenced documents to each of those responsible for review and study.

44. Implement the process as stated in the reference documents.

45. Follow-up to ensure compliance and understanding.

Module 13—Production and Service *(Applies to production and service delivery processes and all employees involved in those processes)*

References

This module addresses Clause 7.5 of the ISO 9001:2000 Standard. It includes the control of production and service, the validation of processes for production and service provision, identification and traceability of product throughout the process, the handling of customer property used in the process, and the preservation of product associated with the processes. Documentation associated with this requirement includes the appropriate section of the QSM and those procedures, work instructions, and check sheets that control the production and work provision process.

Implementation Instructions

This module applies to all employees involved in Work Processes.

46. Make the Work Process Procedures and Work Instructions available to each employee involved in the work process.

47. Employees engaged in the work process must read the work process documents and comply with their requirements.

48. After the supervisor for the work process certifies the employee, implement the Work Process Procedures in accordance with the requirements. (Note: This should be an academic step of the process, as the written work instructions should reflect how we do our work. If this is the case, the personnel who have been doing the work process are certainly qualified and only need to read the documentation for that process).

49. Utilize the Check Sheets in accordance with the instructions of the associated Work Instruction.

50. Follow-up to ensure compliance and understanding.

51. **Note:** Supervisors carry a responsibility in this module.

Module 14—Control of Monitoring and Measuring Devices *(Applies to those individuals and functions responsible for the establishment of monitoring and measurement and the monitoring and measuring devices needed to provide evidence of conformity of product to determined requirements)*

References

This module addresses Clause 7.6 of the ISO 9001:2000 Standard and states the requirements associated with the control of monitoring and measuring devices. Although the ISO Standard does not require a procedure for this clause, organizations usually have one in order to ensure consistence and compliance. These procedures and the appropriate section of the QSM must be made available to those responsible for the actions.

Implementation Instructions

This module is generally applicable to manufacturing organizations that have a specific department to handle this requirement, but it may be applicable to others as well.

52. Provide the associated QSM requirements and the procedure controlling the process (as applicable) to those involve in ensuring the requirements are met.

53. Verify their understanding and compliance with the requirements.

Module 15—Measurement, Analysis and Improvement *(Applies to those responsible for the planning, implementation, and follow-up analysis of measurement, analysis, and improvement and usually includes awareness of all employees)*

Reference

This module addresses Clause 8.1 of the ISO 9001:2000 Standard and includes the requirements and responsibility for the planning and implementation of monitoring, measurement, analysis, and improvement processes needed to demonstrate conformity of the product and/or service to the QMS requirements. Although not specifically required, there may be an associated procedure for this requirement to ensure that everyone addresses the issue in the same manner.

Implementation Instructions

54. Make all relevant documentation available to those ensuring the requirements associated with this module. See that they understand the requirements and their part in ensuring compliance.

55. Ensure that monitoring and measuring is considered in the planning of the various activities of the organization, including (but not limited to) production and service delivery.

56. Provide the necessary training to all employees in improvement of work processes and the monitoring and measuring of those processes. This may require an in-house course on continual improvement and instruction in the use of the various continual improvement tools.

Module 16—Monitoring and Measurement *(Applies to those departments/individuals responsible for customer satisfaction, internal audits, the monitoring and measurement of processes and product, as well as all employees)*

Reference

This module addresses Clause 8.2 of the ISO 9001:2000 Standard, which requires a procedure and records for Internal Audits. The organization may have an additional procedure covering customer satisfaction with associated quality records and also for the monitoring and measuring of processes and product. The latter may be included in specific procedures/work instructions covering the product or service provided by the organization.

Implementation Instructions

There are 3 parts to this module that may apply to different individuals or departments of the organization. They are treated separately in respect to implementation.

Customer Satisfaction

57. Ensure that all individuals and functions within the organization are familiar with the customer satisfaction requirements and their respective responsibilities for such. This includes the necessary documentation and records.

58. Provide the necessary training to ensure that customers are treated equally and include the methods by which customer satisfaction is determined.

59. Provide a means to handle customer complaints (may include a procedure) and the necessary training in the process to do so effectively.

60. Ensure that all feedback from customers is evaluated as to potential process changes resulting from corrective and preventive actions associated with that feedback. Document such feedback and changes and monitor for effectiveness.

61. Remember that customer satisfaction is the perceived satisfaction of the customer.

Internal Audits

Although internal audits are the responsibility of top management, it involves everyone in the organization. The internal auditors are already selected, audit checklists developed, and auditors trained prior to this module implementation.

62. Provide awareness training to all employees as to the purpose, requirements, process, and the schedule of the internal audits. This can be part of the overall awareness training provided to all employees during the training phase of implementation.

63. Provide the internal audit checklist to each department for their familiarization.

Monitoring and measurement of processes and products

64. During the employee awareness training, provide the necessary information to the employees such that they are familiar with the purpose of monitoring and measurement.

65. Provide employees in specific work processes with the necessary training to effectively monitor and measure the processes and product in which they are involved. The associated operational procedures and work instructions should contain the monitoring and measurement points.

66. Ensure through the internal audit that monitoring and measurement is taking place in accordance with the stated requirements and that it is understood.

Module 17—Control of Nonconforming Product *(Applies to all employees involved in the control of nonconforming product)*

References

This module addresses Clause 8.3 of the ISO 9001:2000 Standard, establishing the requirements for controlling nonconforming product. The appropriate QSM Section and the required Quality System Procedure, Control of Nonconforming Product *(Procedure Number)* should be provided to those involved in the process.

Implementation Instructions

This module is generally only applicable to manufacturing organizations.

67. Determine the work categories involved; acquaint each person within those categories with the requirements associated with their work and the control of nonconforming product.

68. Set up a system to ensure compliance within each office/department performing work involving these requirements.

69. Follow-up to ensure compliance and understanding.

Module 18—Analysis of Data *(Applies to all individuals/departments responsible for gathering data, its subsequent analysis, and resulting follow-up actions)*

Reference

This module addresses Clause 8.4 of the ISO 9001:2000 Standard and includes the determination of what data to collect, the collection of that data, and the analysis of that data to evaluate where continual improvement of the effectiveness of the QMS can be made. The relevant section of the QSM should be provided.

Implementation Instructions

This is a new requirement of the ISO Standard and may require training of personnel in the methodology and techniques of Continual Improvement Tools and methodology. This needs to be determined and provided as necessary by management.

Module 19—Improvement *(Applies to all employees as led by top management)*

Reference

This module addresses Clause 8.5 of the ISO 9001:2000 Standard and includes Continual Improvement, Corrective Action, and Preventive Action as it applies to the Quality Management System and the Operating Procedures. A Quality System Procedure is required for both Corrective and Preventive Action. Provide them as well as the appropriate QSM Section during the training of employees in these requirements.

Implementation Instructions

70. Supervisors and up review and understand the referenced documents.

71. Set up the requirements of the Corrective and Preventive Action Procedures within each office/department.

72. Train all employees in the use of the Corrective and Preventive Action System. Use the referenced procedures as part of the training.

73. Make Corrective and Preventive Action forms available to all employees.

74. Implement the process with monitoring as to effect by top management.

75. Follow-up to ensure understanding and compliance.

Continual Improvement is affected by the actions of the Management Review Team as well as management in general addressing the root cause of problems and effecting their resolution.

CONCLUSION

This chapter deals with the Quality System and Operating System Implementation instructions. Actual implementation should be based on the status of the company's journey towards an ISO 9000 System. What is offered in this chapter is one method to implement the system, a method geared more for a company that has multiple offices in many locations and utilizes a single Quality System (recommended method). However, the content is applicable to implementation in general and should be reviewed.

One should not make the implementation instructions more complex than necessary for the specific application. In many cases, the implementation modules discussed above would not be necessary. Remember, however, to plan the implementation—this is the real key to success. This plan should be coupled with a follow-up to ensure understanding and compliance with the requirements of the plan.

Chapter 16

Internal Audits

Internal audits are a key in determining whether or not the Quality Management System is properly designed, implemented, and effective in meeting the stated objective of the Quality Management System.

Although the overall internal audit is Top Management's responsibility, it is usually assigned to the Management Quality Representative. This representative is specifically responsible for:

- Maintaining overall internal audit scheduling
- Ensuring the qualifications of selected internal auditors
- Ensuring that the internal audits take place as scheduled
- Reviewing all internal audit reports for content and finding accuracy
- Assuring that corrective and preventive action has taken place relative to the audit findings
- Analyzing the findings for trends and appropriate actions taken

The Management Quality Representative is required to report the results of internal audits and the overall effectiveness of the quality and operating systems to the Continuous Improvement Steering Committee—or to senior management should there not be such a committee—for Management Review.

Audits are of fundamental importance to a Quality Management System. Because audits uncover system deficiencies, they are a very powerful tool in developing and improving a Quality Management System that will help ensure a zero defect mentality and that processes are done right the first time. An effective internal audit program provides assurance that the documented quality and operating systems have been implemented and are maintained. Such a program also will verify that corrective actions have been taken, preventive actions are implemented to resolve further nonconformances, and that their effectiveness has been verified.

Internal audits are concerned with the organization's operating procedures, products, services, the requirements of the ISO Standard, and customers. All offices/departments and activities that affect product or service quality should be included in the audit program, including Finance, Human Resources, Information Management, Manufacturing, Engineering, Business Development, etc.

The following are objectives of internal audits:

- Determine the conformity of the quality and operating system to specified and planned requirements
- Determine the effectiveness of the quality and operating system in meeting the quality objectives
- Provide a basis for inputs directed at continual improvement of the work processes
- Meet certification requirements

AUDITOR TRAINING AND QUALIFICATIONS

Auditor training and qualifications are an important consideration in ensuring the effectiveness of the audit program. Formal auditor training is essential, although it need not be an IQA- or RAB-approved lead auditor course. However, I have found that having such training is a plus. Auditor training programs are readily available in a classroom environment, public or private. A successful training program must include participant workshops designed to simulate an audit.

Each internal auditor must be very familiar with the organization's Quality Management System and the ISO 9001:2000 Standard. Finally, internal auditors should have experience, which can be a part of the internal auditor training and certification process. This usually involves, after training, the new internal auditor accompanying an experienced auditor as an observer and then acting as the lead auditor while being observed by an experienced auditor. Periodic follow-up auditor monitoring is recommended.

It has been said that good auditors are born and not made. While it is maintained that training can improve an auditor's skills, it is also true that certain basic personal attributes are important when selecting internal auditor candidates. The successful auditors are open-minded and mature. They must be able to exercise sound judgment in employing analytical skills. They should have a "hound-dog" mentality to tenaciously follow trails. Above all, they must be fair in their judgments and sensitive to the feelings and egos of those being audited.

PLANNING AND CONDUCTING AN AUDIT

Planning and conducting the audit is the next essential element for the success of the internal audit program. A schedule of area activities to be audited must be established to ensure all elements of the quality and operating systems are audited annually, as a minimum. The frequency that an area or activity is audited is dependent upon several factors, such as the following:

- the number of nonconformances found during the previous audit,
- severity of the nonconformances,
- the cost of possible nonconformances,
- the criticality of the function,
- the age of the process,

- experience of personnel performing the task,
- any special requirements of the customer,
- past history of problems, and
- any adverse trends.

The Management Quality Representative is generally responsibility for defining the scope and sample size of each audit. Often a generic internal audit checklist is prepared from which the audit categories can be selected. In addition, notification of the office, department, or function to be audited needs to be given no later than four weeks prior to the planned audit date. The selected lead auditor for the audit normally provides this notification.

Unlike most external or third party audits, there is generally no requirement for a formal opening meeting, but some formalities should be observed. Before beginning the audit, the auditor should meet with the respective manager(s) to confirm awareness of the audit being performed and to set a time for a brief closing meeting involving the managers, supervisors and the employees (dependent on the size of the organization) of the audited functions. The manager or designee should accompany the auditor as an escort for the duration of the audit.

INTERNAL AUDIT PLAN

An Internal Audit Plan is another essential part of making an internal audit successful. Such a plan should include the following:

- An audit schedule
- Applicable reference documents
- Responsibilities associated with the audit defined
- Provision for audit notification and verification 4 weeks prior to the audit
- A defined audit format
- Clear audit objectives and scope
- Flexibility to improvise
- Identified audit contact points
- Provision of confidentiality
- A planned report format and distribution

AUDIT CHECKLIST

The use of an Audit Checklist is recommended. The checklist is normally used as a guide rather than literally reading and checking each item on such a list. The auditor needs to be flexible during the audit.

The checklist should identify the following:

- What you want to look at
- What you want to look for
- Whom you want to speak to
- What you want to ask

Numerical scoring is to be avoided to reduce subjectivity. Questions that can be answered "yes" or "no" or by a brief explanation are best.

When designing the content of a checklist, keep in mind that the completed audit will have accomplished the following:

- Determined the extent of conformance to existing policies, procedures, and work instructions
- Determined whether existing policies, procedures, and instructions comply with requirements
- Assured availability, understanding and use of policies, procedures, and work instructions
- Determined need for new documentation or changes to existing documentation

Audit Report

The Audit Report should be comprehensive yet simple in its presentation. It should contain the following elements and may also include the completed audit checklist as an attachment. The reason for leaving a complete report with the audited office/department is to enhance communications and to initiate corrective actions in a timely manner. Therefore, the audit report should also contain the completed Corrective Action Requests for each finding and an Action Plan format that makes it easy for the auditee to respond. Software packages are available that make the audit report generation both simple and cost effective. ABSG Consulting Inc offers one of the better packages I have seen.

Cover Page

The cover page (Figure 16-1) contains the audit report number, name of the company, name of the office/function(s) being audited, those interviewed during the audit, the audit team, audit dates, and signatures.

Instructions Page

The second page of the document is an instruction page, an example of which is shown in Figure 16-2. This page should be customized for each specific company and checklist, as might be applicable.

Conclusion Page

The third page of the document contains the Opening/Closing Meeting Attendance Register, the Auditor's Conclusion, the Auditor's Recommendation, the Report Distribution Matrix, and the Report Distribution Date as shown in Figure 16-3.

Attachments to the Audit Report

The following list of attachments should be a part of the Audit Report.

1. Internal Audit Category Listing (Figure 16-4)
2. Summary of Audit Findings (Figure 16-5)
3. Action Plan (Figure 16-6)
4. Corrective Action Request for each of the Findings (Figure 16-7)
5. Auditee's copy of the completed audit checklist (Optional) (Figure 16-8)

THE ADMINISTRATION OF INTERNAL AUDITS

This is another of the key elements in a successful internal audit program.

The manager/supervisor of the office/department being audited must be notified prior to an audit using established channels of communication. This is known as *audit notification*. The information provided should include the scope of the audit, auditor names, schedule, any support needs (rooms, phone, etc.), and other needed logistical information (flights, hotel, etc.).

If the audit team is composed of more than one auditor, a *pre-audit meeting* should be held with the auditors to review the purpose of the audit, scope, resources to be applied, who has authorized the audit criteria/standards, and to answer any questions that might arise. The internal audit checklist to be used should be discussed and revised as necessary for the specific audit. This meeting could be held on the day of the audit.

The *lead auditor* must remain in control of the audit and the audit team. The lead auditor is responsible for the integrity of the audit. Support auditors can audit independently or as teams.

One reason to team two auditors might be that one may have a stronger technical knowledge of the function being audited and the other possess stronger auditor process skills, but weak specific knowledge.

The *audit escorts* should allow persons being interviewed to answer all questions independently. Their function is to act as a guide and to ensure cooperation. It should be noted that an escort is not necessary for smaller offices, but may be a wise idea to ensure a third party presence and to clarify any misunderstandings that may occur.

The *collection of data* during the audit is also very important. The auditor should document the audit results as factually as possible. Objective evidence should be collected and only the facts recorded on the audit checklist.

Auditor Meetings

Two types of auditor caucus meetings may be held as deemed necessary by the audit team: audit team meetings and daily briefings.

The duration of audit team meetings should be as brief as possible so that the auditee representatives are not kept waiting to continue the audit and so that valuable audit time is not wasted. It is a good idea to schedule audit team meetings as a part of the audit plan. This type of meeting is a private one for the audit team members only (the auditee representatives are not included). Audit team meetings are conducted to:

- Keep the audit team informed of developments
- Make revisions to the audit schedule
- Review and discuss evidence presented
- Examine observations and reach consensus on findings
- Inform team members of any change of assignments
- Have the team members examine confusing or complex issues or documents
- Determine the acceptability of compliance
- Examine specific documentation or evidence of compliance for pitfalls
- Develop the Audit Report as the audit progresses (begin drafting the report on the first day of the audit)

Two short meetings should be held with the auditee representatives daily. These are usually conducted in the morning and near the end of the audit day. In each of these meetings, the lead auditor takes the opportunity to advise the auditee of:

- Planned daily activities
- Any schedule changes
- Summary of observations and nonconformances (findings)
- Areas of concern

Such meetings keep the auditee informed of how the audit is progressing and gives the auditee the opportunity to produce any evidence of compliance or conformance in inconclusive areas of concern.

The Finding Statement

The Finding Statement is the primary result of the internal audit. The statement should cite the specific Quality System or operating system requirement and the specific nonconformance or observation. Objective evidence should be included wherever possible (i.e. copies of records, instructions, etc., or references to such). It must be noted that sensitive data must not be copied. Although not recommended by this author, if the system contains categories of nonconformances, categorize the findings as either major or minor. A major nonconformance is a finding that is systemic and puts product or service quality at risk. A minor nonconformance poses no immediate threat to product or service quality. An observation is a finding that, if not corrected, could lead to a nonconformance. For internal audits, it is recommended that only nonconformances (without major or minor classification) and observations be utilized. The associated definitions in such a case would be:

Nonconformance = Nonfulfillment of a specified requirement

Observation = A detected weakness that, if not corrected, may result in a degradation of product or service quality

At the conclusion of the internal audit a *closing meeting* should be held. The lead auditor should control and conduct the meeting. Thanks should be expressed for cooperation, the purpose of the audit summarized, and the findings summarized with each one reviewed. Copies of the audit summary should be provided. Recommendations and conclusions on the acceptability of the system can also be given at this time. An attendance roster is needed for the formal report later.

The Audit Report can either be the combined audit checklist as noted above or a separate report. In either case, the audit report should be completed as soon as possible after the conclusion of the audit (preferably before leaving the site). The report should be factual and include:

- Name of audited organization
- Date and location of audit
- Purpose of audit
- Scope of audit
- Auditor(s) names
- Summary of the findings
- Checklist element by element assessment showing nonconformances and observations
- Conclusion and recommendations
- Exhibits (attendance rosters, nonconformance reports, and any pertinent documentation)

Equally important as the items included in the formal audit report are those items that should be excluded:

- Any confidential or proprietary information
- Any subjective opinions
- Unsolicited recommendations. In most cases, it is wise to omit solicited recommendations as well.
- Nit-pick items
- Emotional argumentative statements
- Items neither discussed nor mentioned during the closing meeting

The overall internal auditor's function is to determine whether a quality system is in place, and then evaluate its effectiveness. A single paragraph is sufficient for the statement of this analysis.

The Audit Report should be as simple, clear, and concise as possible. Based on the nature of the audit and the auditor's authority, it may be necessary to order the auditee to stop work on an order, project, or contract. The Audit Report must state exactly what work must be stopped.

CORRECTIVE AND PREVENTIVE ACTION

Corrective and preventive action is the responsibility of the auditee and not the auditor. The auditee must develop a Corrective and Preventive Action Response Plan that addresses the root cause of the finding and an associated action plan. Provisions must be made for follow-up to assess the effectiveness of any action taken as well as if the action was actually completed. Formal closure should not be done until verification is complete and a follow-up internal audit report is issued.

The internal audit results should be used as part of management reviews of the quality and operating systems and their implementation. Future audits should use the results of past audits and serve as a basis to evaluate the effectiveness of corrective and preventive action.

CONCLUSION

Early in the Quality System Implementation, auditors can assist those being audited by teaching them the requirements of the system. Auditors can also help identify changes needed for compliance with selected ISO 9000 Series Standard.

A well-designed and implemented internal quality audit program is vital in the successful implementation and continuance of the Quality System. Without an effective internal quality audit process, the Quality System will die in a relatively short period of time. One key to the success of such a program is to have a well-developed internal audit checklist (and report or combination checklist and report) and well-trained internal auditors. Coupled with these two items is a good analysis of the audit results with follow-up of findings to resolution.

The ISO Standard, ISO 10011-1, ISO 10011-2, and ISO 10011-3 should be used for guidance relative to internal audits.

Audit Report No.: *(Add the Report Number here and on every page)*

(Add the Organization's Logo here)

Quality Management System Internal Audit

Audit Report

Functions Audited	Personnel Interviewed
(List the Functions audited here)	*(List the personnel interviewed here)*

Audit Team/Signature: **Lead Auditor**   *(Name/Signature of Lead)*

                                         Auditor   *(List Signatures of auditors)*

Date(s) of Audit: *(Provide the dates of the audit)*

Figure 16-1 Cover Page

Audit Report No.:   *(Add the Audit Report Number here)*

Introduction This Internal Audit Report/ Checklist is based on the requirements of the *(Name of Organization)'s Quality Management System. The checklist is configured in such a manner so as to allow customization by the audit team for the office or function(s) being audited.* Suggested improvements should be forwarded to the Management Representative.

Report/Checklist Configuration

This Internal Audit Report/Checklist is configured in a manner that will allow the completed document to meet the requirements of the concluding audit report and the checklist for which the audit report is based. Copies can be made and distributed, while the original remains with the audited Department or Function.

Internal Audit Function

The Function for which the specific Report and Checklist is configured is for the *(Name of Office/Department)*.

Audit Scope

The scope of the Internal Audit is the evaluation of the operation for compliance with the documented policies and procedures as contained in the Quality System Manual, Quality System Procedures, Operating Procedures and Work Instructions.

AUDIT APPROACH

The purpose of the audit is to collect objective evidence, through interview with personnel and review of pertinent records to assess the level of compliance to the documented requirements. The approach is to be positive and constructive with open dialogue. All previous audit findings will be reviewed for close-out and noted accordingly as a new finding or as closed out in the conclusion of this report. Audit Items will be selected in advance for each specific audit cycle. Not every item listed in this document will be audited each time.

Audit Finding Follow-up Action Plan

The audited function is reminded that a Follow-up Action Plan is required and is to be submitted within 4 weeks of receipt of the Audit Report. *(Note: If this is not a requirement of the Quality Management System, then leaves this paragraph out. However, one is encouraged to make it a requirement.)*

Note: Each audited item listed on the audit check sheet must have a comment or note clarifying the sample size or audited details, even if there are no associated finding.

Figure 16-2 Instructions Page

Audit Report No.:   *(Add the Audit Report Number here)*

Opening/Closing Meeting Attendance Register

No Meeting Held   ☐

Name	Opening	Closing
(Name of Attendees at each Meeting)	☐	☐
	☐	☐
	☐	☐
	☐	☐
	☐	☐
	☐	☐

Auditor Conclusion

(Auditor to add his overall conclusion comments related to the audit here)

(Make a statement that the last Internal Audit findings have been verified and closed. Include the audit report number as reference.)

Auditor Recommendations

(Add the auditor's recommendations here, such as the need for a follow-up audit, etc.)

Distribution   **Date of Distribution**

(List the distribution of the Audit Report and date of distribution)

Figure 16-3 Conclusion Page

Internal Audit Categories

List of Selected Categories, which are included in this audit

Audit Report No.: *(Add the Audit Report Number here)*

CATEGORY	TITLE
101	Quality Management System
102	Quality Policy
103	Quality Objectives
104	Planning
105	Management Responsibility
106	Organizational Responsibility
107	Documentation Requirements (Quality Manual, Document Control, Control of Records, Documentation Structure)
108	Resource Management
109	Product Realization
110	Customer Related Processes
111	Design and Development
112	Purchasing
113	Production and Service Provision
114	Control of Monitoring and Measuring Devices
115	Measurement, Analysis and Improvement
116	Customer Satisfaction
117	Internal Audits
118	Monitoring and Measurement of Processes
119	Monitoring and Measurement of Product
120	Control of Nonconforming Product
121	Analysis of Data
122	Continual Improvement
123	Corrective Action
124	Preventive Action

Figure 16-4 Internal Audit Category Listing

Summary of Findings   **Audit Report No.:**   *(Add the Audit Report Number here)*

CATEGORY   *(List the Category Number associated with the Finding here – 101, etc.)*

OBS/NC Findings (Associated with this category)

FINDING 1: Nonconformance (NC)

Write the Nonconformance Statement here and site the reference (QSM Section, Procedure, etc.)

FINDING 2: Observation (OBS)

Write the Observation Statement here and site the reference.

Figure 16-5 Summary of Audit Findings

Action Plan for **Audit Report No.:**   *(Add the Audit Report Number here)*

FINDING 1: Nonconformance (NC)

Write the Nonconformance Statement here and site the reference (QSM Section, Procedure, etc.)

Proposed Action:

Status of Action:

FINDING 2: Observation (OBS)

Write the Observation Statement here and site the reference.

Proposed Action:

Status of Action:

Figure 16-6 Action Plan

Corrective and Preventive Action Request (CAR)
Improving the way we do our work

To (Quality Coordinator):	CAR Number:

Reason for Initiation:

(OI) ☐   Opportunity for Improvement of a Procedure or Work Instruction

(NC) ☐   Nonconformance Audit Number (if applicable):

(EM) ☐   Environmental Management System Improvement Opportunity

(CF) ☐   Client Feedback

Description:	**Source of CAR** (Check one)
(Provide a complete description of the finding or opportunity for improvement *or client feedback here)*	Day-to-Day Operation ☐
	Client Feedback ☐
	Internal Audit ☐
	External Audit ☐
	Management Review ☐
	Environmental Issue ☐
	Other ☐

CAR Initiator's Recommendation:

(State here the CAR initiator's recommendation on how to address the finding, as applicable)

CAR Forwarding: **To:**   **Date:**

(If the issue cannot be resolved locally, forward the CAR for Management Review and resolution assignment)

Investigation Summary:

(Include here a description of the investigation results associated with this CAR)

Figure 16-7 Corrective Action Request (Part 1)

Corrective and Preventive Action Request (CAR)

Improving the way we do our work

Action(s) taken to resolve the CAR: Target date for completion of action:

(List and describe here all of the actions taken to resolve this CAR and to prevent it from occurring again)

Action by: **Date:**

Affects other processes: Yes ☐   No ☐

Measurement of completion and requirements for follow-up

(required for nonconformances, client feedback and environmental related CARs)

What measurements will be used to determine that the CAR resolution has been implemented?

Who is responsible for follow-up action to ensure effectiveness?

How is follow-up action verification of effectiveness to be accomplished?

Corrective and Preventive Action Request Close-Out (After implementation has been completed)

Closed – Out by: **Comments**

Date:

Closed-Out CAR Distribution   **Date**

(List the Distribution recipients here

Figure 16-7 Corrective Action Request (Part 2)

Audit Report No: *(Add the Audit Report No. here)*

Category 103   **Training and Development**

Finding 1 Type   **Finding Detailed/Notes/Comments**

> *(List the finding details here associated with this category)*

Finding 2 Type   **Finding Detailed/Notes/Comments**

> *(List the finding details here associated with this category)*

103-1   Has a Training Needs Assessment been done for the office/department?

(Add Quality System Document reference here)

103-2   Has an Office/Department Training Plan been completed which includes all employees in the office/department?

(Add Quality System Document reference here)

103-3   Is there evidence of completed training course feedback forms having been submitted to HR?

(Add Quality System Document reference here

103-4   Is the training plan maintained? (Is it kept up-to-date?)

(Add Quality System Document reference here

Figure 16-8 Audit Checklist (Sample)

Chapter 17

Corrective and Preventive Action System

The Corrective and Preventive Action System is a system for identifying, analyzing, and implementing improvements and corrective action in a company's products, services, and work processes.

ESTABLISHING AN EFFECTIVE SYSTEM

An effective Corrective and Preventive Action System (often called a CAS) is a key element of the quality process and is based on every employee becoming a problem identifier and, more importantly, a problem solver. An effective Corrective and Preventive Action System provides a mechanism for every employee to identify and communicate process improvement opportunities to management and for these opportunities to be evaluated with positive changes implemented. The CAS also provides the means for addressing and tracking nonconformances and observations.

The responsibility for the overall direction of the CAS lies with the Quality Management System Steering Committee(s) or, if there isn't one, with the Management Review Team, or simply with top management. Any real success resulting from the CAS must come from the commitment and dedicated effort of all employees as participants in the CAS. The required CAS must be an integral part of the Quality Management Process.

Continual Improvement

The purpose of Continual Improvement, which includes the Corrective and Preventive Action System, is to provide a structured and disciplined approach for identifying, analyzing, and implementing improvement opportunities related to work processes that support the company's mission and Quality Policy. Improvement opportunities include:

- Investigating root causes of nonconformances and the application of corrective and preventive actions
- Reducing the cycle time of work processes
- Making work processes more efficient
- Increasing customer satisfaction
- Improving the work environment
- Strengthening teamwork and communication at all levels of the organization
- Eliminating the cost associated with errors

ORGANIZATION AND RESPONSIBILITIES

The Corrective and Preventive Action System does not replace the normal management functions of decision making and resource allocation. The teams described in this section solve problems and make recommendations, but it remains with the respective supervisors, managers, and senior managers to take final action.

Quality Management System Steering Committee

The CISCs (reference Chapter 4 for further information) have the responsibility for the overall direction of the CAS. In the absence of a CISC, the Management Team or management would have this responsibility. The CISCs are comprised of management personnel. Their functions related to the Corrective and Preventive Action System include:

- Establishing guidelines and priorities for operation of the CAS
- Assuring that all employees are trained and the CAS is operating efficiently at all levels within the organization
- Addressing major quality and cycle time issues
- Forming Corrective Action Teams on critical quality matters
- Reviewing recommendations and taking action on recommendations
- Resolving Corrective and Preventive Action Requests (CARs)

Continual Improvement Teams

Continual Improvement Teams (reference Chapter 4) manage parts of the Total Quality Management process on behalf of the Quality Management System Steering Committee. In respect to the CAS, these teams would be responsible for the above listed functions for their respective areas.

Management and Supervisor Responsibilities

Managers and supervisors play a key role in the Corrective and Preventive Action System. Their responsibilities include:

- Educating and training employees on the benefits and use of the CAS
- Encouraging employees to originate Corrective and Preventive Action Requests (CARs), provide solutions to problems, and become involved in Corrective Action Teams
- Responding quickly to all submitted CARs
- Tracking the review and resolution status of departmental CARs and providing timely feedback to originators on the actions taken
- Creating employee awareness and recognizing employee achievement
- Implementing approved recommendations in a timely and efficient manner

Employee Responsibilities

For the Quality Process to work, employees at every level of the organization must be trained to use the quality tools and techniques by the Corrective and Preventive Action System. They must also participate in the CAS by originating CARs, by offering solutions to issues raised by CARs, by becoming members of Corrective Action Teams and Continual Improvement Teams, and by making a commitment to the principles of "continuous performance improvement" and "doing every task right the first time."

Management Systems and Quality

Some companies have separated the Quality Management System from management systems and found out that it does not work. Employees will tend to separate the two as well and think of quality as an additional burden, as additional work. Although it is paramount to remember that the Quality Management System does not manage the company, one must also remember that the Quality Management System is just one of the many management systems and processes of a successful company (reference Chapter 18). In fact, one major objective of management should be to have quality become "just the way we do our work." When this occurs, the word "quality" will disappear and become a natural part of our management systems and processes.

The management systems and processes of the company (reference Chapter 18) incorporate the Quality Management System. Management should identify and solve problems independent of the Corrective and Preventive Action System. One should not assign all of the management responsibilities for addressing management issues to quality. Doing so will cause problems and will be detrimental to proper system integration. The Quality Management System must not be the only way for management to identify inputs for business process improvements.

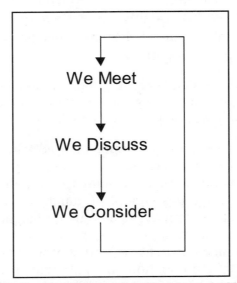

Figure 17-1. Method of Addressing Problems in Many Companies

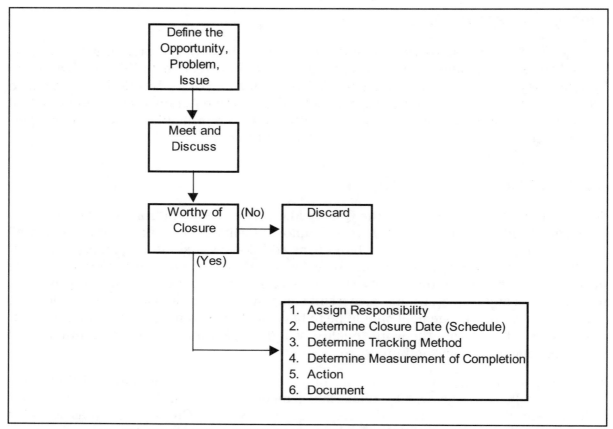

Figure 17-2. Correct Method of Bringing Issues to Closure

The stages of problem identification and solutions, including problem identification, analysis solution determination, decision to implement, implementation, and follow-up, are all management system responsibilities, not Quality System responsibilities. If this is the case, then where does the Quality Management System—specifically, the Corrective and Preventive Action System—fit into the equation?

The Quality Management System needs to be supplemented by a consistent, company-wide methodology for addressing problems. One method is presented in Chapters 18 and 19 as part of the continual improvement training provided to employees.

The Quality Management System must be supplemented with tools and techniques for problem identification, root cause determination, tracking, measurement, and follow-up for use by management, individuals, or management appointed problem-solving teams. The use of these tools and techniques should be taught as part of the overall training program. The tools must teach all employees a common language associated with all aspects of problem identification and problem solving. Actual utilization of the method presented in Chapters 18 and 19, an equivalent method of problem identification and problem solving, the tools, techniques, and common language remain management system decisions—to be used or not used. One important additional quality-related approach is to establish an environment that allows for effective problem identification and problem solving.

What is the real problem in most companies? The questions are "Is the management system utilizing these tools and techniques to address and solve problems?" and "Is the management system fostering an environment conducive to problem identification and problem solving?" An observation of several companies has been that they do not use the identification and solving of problems within the established management system that has historically been set in place. One might say that they have identified problems as they surfaced, discussed them, considered them, and then repeated the process over and over again without performing the remaining steps leading to successful solution and close out. Instead, problems continue to surface without being solved, causing the organization to become problem-saturated, which often causes organizational immobility.

If the established management system is not a problem-solving system and if an ISO 9001:2000-based Corrective and Preventive Action System is introduced, the tendency is for management to use it in lieu of what they are lacking. This causes confusion and misuse of the Quality Management System.

Therefore, the statement made earlier that all problem identification, analysis, solution determination, decision to implement, implementation, and follow-up are management system responsibilities verifies that these are not Quality Management System responsibilities.

USES OF THE CORRECTIVE AND PREVENTIVE ACTION SYSTEM

The Quality System, via the Quality System Manual and Quality System Procedures, normalizes the "documentation of what we do" for the purpose of consistency and control. In other words, it ensures that we write down what we do in our work processes in a consistent manner and that there is a formalized process for changing and controlling this documentation.

The Corrective and Preventive Action System is the mechanism for change and improvement of the work processes and their associated procedures and instructions. These opportunities for improvement come from employees involved in the work processes. The CAS is an all-employee, "bottom up" approach and requirement. This approach is one of the parameters of the CAS that is outside the less formal, management system problem-identification and problem-solving responsibilities.

The Corrective and Preventive Action System is used to document nonconformances in order to track corrective action, investigation, preventive action, and follow-up to ensure effectiveness. The actual documentation of a nonconformance uses the CAR form itself; no other form is necessary (reference Figure 16-7).

The Corrective and Preventive Action System is also used to document the findings of external audits. A CAR is completed for each finding (nonconformance or observation). Again, this is for the purpose of tracking to closure, as stated above for nonconformances, as well as to provide formalized documentation, analysis, and follow-up.

The Corrective and Preventive Action System is also used to document negative customer feedback (complaints), when those complaints may affect work processes. The CAR form is used to accomplish this and is tracked to closure as is done for nonconformances.

The Corrective and Preventive Action System is also used to track CARs generated as a result of trend analysis. Should a trend be detected relative to customer feedback, analysis of internal or external audit findings, or any other trending gained from the application of statistical methods, it is documented and tracked through the use of the CAS.

The Corrective and Preventive Action System can be applied to Quality, Environmental, Health, and Safety Management Systems.

Corrective and Preventive Action Requests (CARs)

A properly designed and implemented Corrective and Preventive Action System allows any employee to originate a CAR and assures that the CAR will be considered by management with timely feedback to the originator. CARs are used to:

- Identify problem areas associated with work processes (procedures and work instructions) that need corrective action
- Identify opportunities that will improve work processes and services
- Address identified nonconformances
- Address environmental issues associated with the work processes
- Identify customer feedback and follow-up action
- Provide trending data inputs

A typical CAR form might look like Figure 16-7, but can be customized to fit the respective company. For multiple office companies, it is recommended that only one Corrective and Preventive Action System be implemented using the same CAR form. It is beneficial to have the CAR form printed on a certain color paper, such as yellow, so that the originals can easily be differentiated from copies. It is also very cost effective to have the Corrective and Preventive Action System totally electronic, such as a Web Based System.

- The CAR form should contain the following information:
- The name of the person receiving the CAR
- The name of the person who originated the CAR
- The date initiated
- The office/department of the initiator
- The CAR number (assigned by the Quality Coordinator or MQR in accordance with the quality system requirements)
- The reason for initiation (as a result of an opportunity for improvement, nonconformance, customer feedback, environmental system finding or trend analysis)
- A description of the problem
- The CAR recommendations of the initiator or auditee if the initiator is an internal auditor
- Investigation results for nonconformances and client feedback-related CARs
- Actions taken to resolve the CAR and signature of who has taken the action

- The target closure date
- Whether or not the CAR affects other processes
- The measure of completion and requirement for follow-up stated on the CAR form
- The close-out of the CAR, with the signature and date of the authorized person closing it out
- The distribution of the closed-out CAR and date of distribution

Corrective and Preventive Action System—Definitions

The Corrective and Preventive Action System is the heart of successful continuance and improvement of any Quality Management System. For this reason, it is worthy of a great deal of detail.

To ensure that there is no miscommunication relative to the CAS, the following definitions are offered for consideration:

The Corrective and Preventive Action System (CAS) —the system for identifying, analyzing, and implementing improvements and corrective action in a company's products, services, and work processes.

A Corrective and Preventive Action Request (CAR)—a documented request to improve a procedure, a work instruction, or to initiate an internal investigation of the cause of a nonconformance for applying corrective or preventive action.

Product—the output of any process. It consists mainly of goods, software, or services.

Nonconformance—non-fulfillment of a specified requirement.

Opportunity for Improvement—an input to the Corrective and Preventive Action System that is not initiated by a nonconformance, but is nevertheless an opportunity for improving a procedure or a work instruction.

Corrective Action—an action to eliminate the causes of an existing nonconformance, nonconforming service, or other undesirable situation. Consists of the correction of the problem, investigation of the root cause, and implementation of steps to prevent the problem from occurring again. It is said that a Corrective Action implies "Don't make the same mistakes."

Preventive Action—action to eliminate the causes of a potential nonconformance, nonconforming service, or other undesirable situation. It is said the Preventive Action implies "Don't make the first mistake."

Assign—for the purposes of the CAS, the term "assign" means to transfer responsibility, with mutual consent, for action to an individual or group (i.e., team or committee).

Corrective and Preventive Action System—Initiation

Any employee or subcontractor should be able to initiate a CAR using the equivalent of the form shown in Figure 16-7. The CAR is issued to document and track corrective and preventive action as a result of:

- Customer feedback

- Internal or external audit findings

- Analysis of trends associated with the following:

  Customer data

  Customer feedback

  Nonconformances

  Process monitoring

- Identify improvement opportunities that involve changes to procedures or work instructions that are beyond the originator's area of responsibility associated with quality, environmental, health, or safety issues.

- Nonconformances

The CAR initiator must be required to provide recommendations and obtain as many facts as possible before initiating the CAR. If the CAR initiator is an internal auditor, the originator recommendations are to be completed by the auditee.

In general, a CAR is not needed to change a procedure or work instruction within one's own area of responsibility. These are documented and tracked according to the Quality System Procedure, Development of Procedures and Work Instructions, using the respective tracking sheet.

Corrective and Preventive Action System—General Description

The intent should be for corrective and preventive actions to occur at the lowest possible organizational level. In addition, overall awareness by the respective Continuous Improvement Steering Committee is also necessary to ensure correct and documented resolutions. Such actions are intended to address situations that require correction and identify preventive action to diminish the opportunity for nonconforming services.

The simplified flow chart, Figure 17-3, shows an applied example of the path of a CAR through the Corrective and Preventive Action System of ABS Consulting.

The design of the CAS should consider paths for CARs that require immediate action, the effects on other work processes, and an appeal process for solutions in which the originator does not agree.

The completed CAR forms are considered quality records and must be retained for presentation to the external and internal auditors.

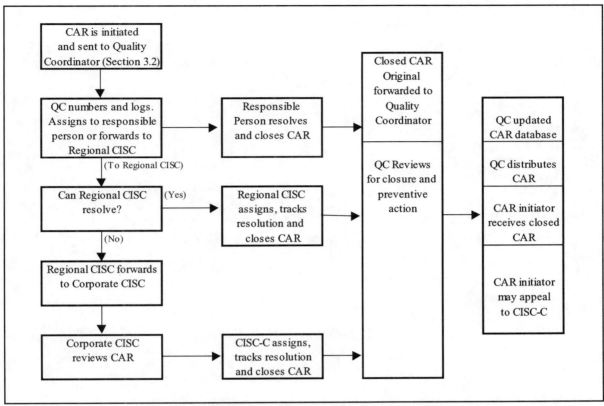

Figure 17-3. Simplified Flow Diagram—Applied Example

CONCLUSION

This chapter has presented considerations for a Corrective and Preventive Action System. The CAS is essential, besides being required, for the success of the Quality Management System and its continuation. A working CAS can provide management with insights and opportunities for continual improvement of the work processes. It is a very formal, documented system and must not replace or be used in lieu of an informal system of problem solving and continual improvement. This informal system should be dominant and only involve the more formal CAS when a change to a procedure or work instruction is necessary.

The CAS is not an employee suggestion system and should never be used as such.

Each completed CAR form should be a stand-alone document with all necessary attachments to make it so.

Software programs are commercially available for Corrective and Preventive Action Systems, but they must be selected with care since many of them do not meet the needs of the system. Unfortunately, this is usually not found out until after both money and resources are wasted. It may be best to design one's own system by utilizing available off-the-shelf software.

It is important to keep the CAR form as simple and easy to complete as possible, especially from the initiator's point of view. This may help to increase the number generated and forestall any excuses for not generating them.

Chapter 18

Beyond ISO 9000 Certification

Once the ISO 9001:2000 Quality Management System has been installed, implemented, and in operation, a company has several options:

- To stop with ISO 9001 Certification and just maintain that system
- To continually improve the work processes
- To improve all of the company's management systems and processes

The ISO 9001 Quality Management System is part of process management, which itself is only one of the management systems and processes necessary to become a Malcolm Baldrige (or equivalent) Award-winning company. The ISO 9001:2000 Quality Management System may be thought of as representing Phase 1 in a company's Journey to Excellence. One can decide how far along this journey the respective company wishes to travel.

JOURNEY TO EXCELLENCE

The Journey to Excellence approach recommended in response to *Beyond ISO 9000 Certification* is one which aligns the activities of all employees and all management systems and processes within the organization with the *common focus of customer satisfaction through continual improvement of all activities, goods, and services*. Within this context, "customer" means "a person or group, internal or external to the organization, to whom a service is provided."

The Journey to Excellence can be accomplished in *four concurrent phases*, as shown in Figure 18-1.

Phase 1—Process Management

Phase 1 is the implementation of process management, which includes the installation of a Quality Management System based on the International Organization for Standardization (ISO) 9001 Standard. Phase 1 involves the following ten-step plan of action:

1. Senior management education and commitment
2. Quality awareness for all employees
3. Quality foundations—ISO 9001
4. Establishment of operating procedures/work instructions
5. Education and training of all employees
6. Establishment of a communication system

7. Installation of a corrective and preventive action system

8. Setting of goals

9. Establishment of measurements company wide

10. Continual improvement and simplification of all company work processes

Phase 1 of the Journey to Excellence needs to be solidly installed and forms the foundation for the remainder of the Journey. The receipt of ISO Certification to ISO 9001 evidences phase 1 completion.

Phase 2—Improve the Processes

Phase 2 provides all employees with the tools and techniques to continuously improve the foundation processes established in Phase 1. If a company decides not to take the complete Journey to Excellence, they should at least proceed through Phase 2. Key aspects of this phase of the journey are elimination of non-value added process steps, mapping of processes, barrier identification and removal, team problem solving and process improvement, planning and metrics.

Part 1 of Phase 2—Continual Improvement Training

Phase 1 of Phase 2 can be accomplished through an investment of 16 hours of intensive Tools for Continual Improvement (TFCI) classroom training for every employee of the company. The end result of such training is the knowledge by the employee of how to use the tools and techniques applied to process improvement, and a systematic approach or way of thinking in so doing. Any of the tools and techniques can be used by the employee, at any time and in any order the tools are needed.

The TFCI training provides the employee with the tools and skills for process improvement. The tools that are provided by such training should include:

- Work Process Chart
- Histograms
- Pareto Charts
- PERT Chart
- Help-Hindrance Diagram
- Run Chart
- Cause-Effect Diagram
- Matrix Chart
- Gantt Chart
- Cost Benefits Chart

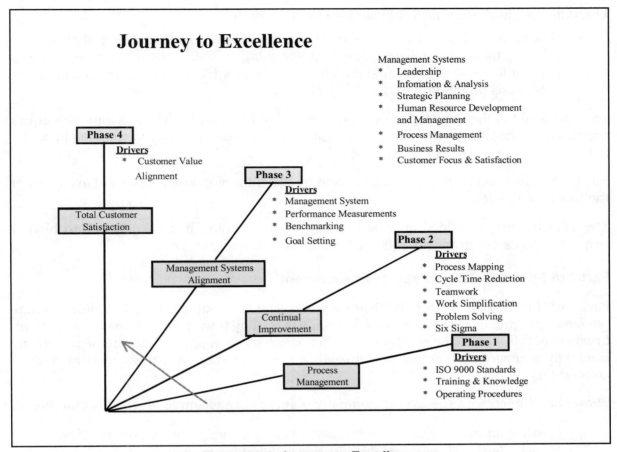

Figure 18-1. Journey to Excellence

The techniques provided by TFCI training should include:

- How to prepare and analyze the cost and benefit of proposed improvements
- How to write a problem or opportunity for improvement statement
- How to define a process and scope the area for analysis
- How to measure the outputs of a process
- How to brainstorm causes and solutions
- How to prioritize solutions
- How to map work processes
- How to evaluate work processes relative to value added, necessary non-value added, and non-value added steps
- How to plan, implement, and measure the proposed improvement
- How to present the proposed improvement to management
- How to reduce/eliminate non-value adding steps from the work processes
- How to look at work processes innovatively
- How to work in teams

The skills taught during the TFCI training should include:

- How to actually apply all of the tools and techniques to a real project that is selected by the participant prior to the training. In other words, the training for the employee should include the solution of a problem or the improvement of a process as an integral part of the training.

The end result is the knowledge by the employee of how to use the tools and techniques applied to process improvement, and a systematic approach or way of thinking in so doing.

Any of the tools and techniques can be used by the employee, at any time and in any order the tools are needed.

The TFCI training should simply be training for the employee to take back into his/her respective work environment and use for continuous improvement.

Part 2 of Phase 2—The Workplace Environment

Part 2 of the Phase 2 effort establishes a workplace environment that will allow the employee to provide innovative solutions and ideas leading towards continual improvement. Creation of this workplace environment often involves changing the culture of a company from tight management control to control through leadership, processes, metrics, and accountability.

Phase 2 is aligned with the overall company objective, an example of which would be:

> *Creating an environment for our employees that encourages innovative thinking, personal initiative, problem identification and problem solving, prevention, commitment to continuous improvement, and encouraging decisionmaking at the lowest practical levels.*

Part 2 of Phase 2 of the Journey to Excellence Plan changes the traditional, functional, hierarchical organizational structure to a matrix structure involving teams (cross-functional and departmental) and employee empowerment. Every employee becomes a "problem identifier" and "problem solver" and operates with a strong feeling of "I can make a positive difference." The change also involves a change in mindset, to one where management is responsive to the needs of the work processes, and where employees are responsible for their work. To achieve this mindset, it is necessary to establish a proper working environment that will both promote and allow for improvement opportunities to be identified and acted upon by employees in an innovative and empowered manner.

Phase 3—Management Systems Alignment

Phase 3 is the establishment of management systems and processes where needed and improvement of the organizational effectiveness of systems already established. Phase 3 maps the current management systems and processes and compares them to benchmarks from national and business standards, as well as to other world class companies.

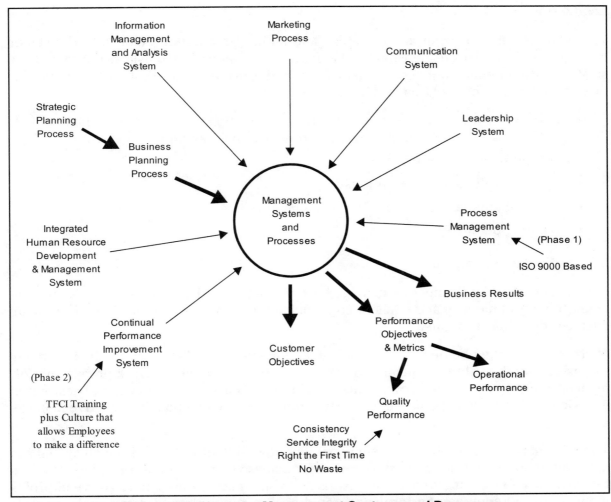

Figure 18-2. Phase 3—Management Systems and Processes

Some of the Management System categories include (but are not limited to):

- Leadership
- Information and Analysis
- Strategic and Business Planning
- Human Resource Development and Management
- Process Management
- Business Results
- Customer Focus and Satisfaction

In considering the imperatives of each respective company's business, one must identify certain key strategic elements to incorporate so that the company can compete effectively in the chosen markets. These elements, discussed below, involve the alignment of management systems with the business objectives of the Journey to Excellence.

Leadership

The responsibility for leadership strategy and its implementation belongs to the senior management team. This responsibility includes how the leadership translates the company's strategy into an effective overall organization and a management system that is performance-based. Elements of this system include:

- Developing and maintaining an effective leadership system focused on individual development, high performance, and organizational learning
- Setting strategic direction
- Creating value and expectations
- Building company capabilities
- Building teamwork

Information and Analysis

Information of all kinds must be managed for competitive advantage. In today's environment, the use of modern and efficient communications systems to support effective management decisions is a must.

Measurements must be developed, tracked, and managed to show continually improving trends in overall quality, financial performance, core competencies, work process performance, employee satisfaction, cycle time reduction, and customer satisfaction. These seven generic measurements should be regularly reported to the company's executive management.

The Information and Analysis System considers how well information from all systems is aggregated and analyzed to support reviews, business decisions, and planning. The system includes how competitive comparisons and benchmarking are used to drive improvement of overall company performance, rapid access and update of data capability, user needs considerations, reliability, and selection and management of information. The Information and Analysis System is the "brain center" for the alignment of the company information system with its strategic directions.

Strategic and Business Planning

A fact-based strategic and business planning and market planning process should be used to identify, select, and address those markets where the company has or can achieve competitive advantage.

The Strategic Planning System focuses on how strategy and plans are translated into key business drivers and includes such elements as:

- Operational performance requirements
- Customer performance requirements
- Long range view of key influences, challenges, and requirements that might affect the company's future opportunity and direction

The Business Planning System focuses on the plan's deployment throughout the organization, integration into the review/measurement system, and overall effectiveness. The Business Planning System takes the key business drivers and translates them into:

- Action plans
- Spelling out the key performance requirements
- The alignment of work units
- How productivity, cycle time, and waste reduction are addressed
- The principal resources committed
- How alignment and consistency are achieved

Human Resource Development and Management

The Integrated Human Resource Development and Management System ties the HR practices into the company's strategic directions. Included are the employee education, training, and development processes, the setting up of high performance work systems, employee well-being and satisfaction, HR planning and evaluation, and employee incentive alignment.

The development of the entire workforce and the needs of a high performance workplace are addressed. The approach to enhance employee well being, satisfaction, and growth potential are addressed. Employee recognition, compensation, discretion, decision-making, well-being, and satisfaction are some of the other elements to be addressed, as well as teamwork, job design, and work environment.

Process Management

A time-based management approach for understanding, managing, and continuously improving all key work processes and support to customers is recommended. The ISO 9000-based Quality System comprises the Quality Assurance System, which needs to be used throughout the company.

The Process Management System is the focal point for all key work processes and includes support services.

Business Results

Measurements must be developed, tracked, and managed to show continually improving trends in the overall quality of the service delivery processes and in the support processes. Each category of service should be compared to the performances of industry leaders, with targets set to achieve world class performance and excellence.

Business Results include performance objectives and measures of quality performance, operational performance, competitive performance, and customer and market performance.

The Business Results provide a results focus for all processes and process improvement activities as well as "real time" information (measures or progress) for evaluation and improvement. Included are company operational and financial results, product and service quality results, and service performance results.

Measures also include comparative information and current level and trends for each.

Customer Focus and Satisfaction

The Customer Focus and Satisfaction System is a closed-loop measurement and management system for identifying, understanding, and fully satisfying customer requirements at competitive costs to the company and its customers. This system is the focal point for a detailed understanding of the voices of customers and the marketplace, with inputs from results and trends.

Some elements to include are customer relationship management (ease of customer access to information, complaint management, how customer follow-up is accomplished); customer market and knowledge (processes for determining requirements and expectations, processes for addressing future customer requirements and expectations); customer satisfaction results (customer dissatisfaction measurements, customer satisfaction measurements); customer satisfaction comparison (comparisons of gains and losses of customer accounts and customer satisfaction relative to competitors, trends in gaining or losing market share).

Communication System

The Communication System relates to how communicated information is "made real" throughout the company and reinforced through the organization, management system, and work processes. This communicated information includes company values, company expectations, company directions, review of work process assessments, company performance, and work unit performance.

The communications system must constantly reinforce "truth testing" and "walk the walk."

Phase 4—Total Customer Satisfaction

Phase 4 is the alignment of the entire organization (people and processes) with the evolving needs of the company's targeted market. Phase 4 involves getting closer to the market (customers and competitor's customers) than the competitors do, being market driven, understanding customer needs and expectations, getting closer to customers, and being customer driven.

CONCLUSION

The foregoing Journey to Excellence is presented as one of the paths a company can take beyond ISO 9000 Certification. Any path, however, including the one presented, must have the full commitment of senior management from the very beginning, as they must be the champions for such a Journey to be successful. Planning the Journey prior to launch is essential, as is being willing to modify that plan en route.

Company-wide training in problem identification and problem solving is also a key factor in the success of the Journey, independent of the path chosen. All employees are involved in the effort.

It is easier to stop the Journey after ISO 9001 Certification (Phase 1 of the Journey to Excellence presented)—many companies do so—than move forward. However, one need only ask those who have gone forward to see the positive results that are possible.

In reality, many companies are already on the Journey to Excellence, needing only to assess where they are and what gaps need to be filled in order to get to where they want to go.

As shown in the highlighted path of Figure 18-2, one very important consideration is the Strategic Planning Process through the Business Planning Process to the outputs of Customer Objectives, Performance Objectives and Metrics, Operational Performance, and Quality Performance. All employees should be tied into this path, with everything that they do supporting this path in some manner.

Notice that the Process Management System (Phase 1) in Figure 18-2 (the ISO 9000 Quality System) is only one small part of the overall Management Systems and Processes and that it is not at the center. Many people have the perception that the Quality System resides at the center, and although it may seem so at times, it is important to keep it in its place. The Continual Improvement System (Phase 2) is likewise only one part of the overall Management System and Process.

It is recommended that one obtain a copy of the Malcolm Baldrige National Quality Award Criteria for Performance Excellence (available from the United States Department of Commerce). This document is an excellent model for Phase 3 of the Journey to Excellence and for Management Systems and Processes.

Chapter 19

Continual Improvement

As described in Chapter 18, continual improvement is Phase 2 of the Journey to Excellence and is absolutely vital for a company if that company does not want to become stagnant and fall behind its competitors. Continual Improvement is also a requirement of the ISO 9001:2000 Standard. It is likely that a company left alone will improve. However, what distinguishes companies from one another is the rate of this improvement.

Will Rogers once said:

> *You may be on the right track, but if you ain't moving fast enough you will get run over anyway.*

The same is true relative to continual improvement. You may be on the right track of improvement, but one needs to move along that track at a pace that is faster than the competition. To do this, every employee needs to be a part of the continual improvement process.

One method of accomplishing continual improvement is to set up the foundation for that improvement to take place. In other words, establish the procedures and work instructions that describe what and how the respective company does the work. Of course, the ISO 9001:2000 Quality Management System does this beautifully. Then, one needs to train all employees in the tools for continual improvement. This will supply them the time necessary to apply those tools to their work processes, either individually or as part of a team.

TOOLS FOR CONTINUAL IMPROVEMENT

There are many methods and sources of tools for continual improvement and, in general, no one is preferable over another. What is imperative is the establishment of the method and selection of the tools that best fit each particular company, and then the teaching of those tools to all employees. The primary reason for this is so that all employees talk the same language and use the same methodology in addressing improvement opportunities.

The tools described in the method presented here compare favorably to any tool presented for continual process improvement. The key is to apply and use the tools in order to improve a project or process problem or to resolve the problem in a classroom environment. In this manner, the participant walks away with applied learning rather than just theoretical learning. After learning how to apply all of the tools to a real process, the participant can then selectively use the tools as needed. It is important that the organization provide the opportunity for employees to address issues and problems or any learning will be lost.

This method is through a 12-step process that involves applying the tools to actual work processes an employee brings to the class. In this approach, employees are placed into teams of two to four individuals. These teams then select a work process to work on during the formalized training sessions. Guidelines must be furnished to ensure that the project chosen is a viable one—a project for which all of the tools being taught can be applied.

The students then receive four sessions of four hours each in learning and applying the tools for continuous improvement. These four sessions are shown in Figure 19-1. The actual tools and techniques taught are listed in Chapter 19.

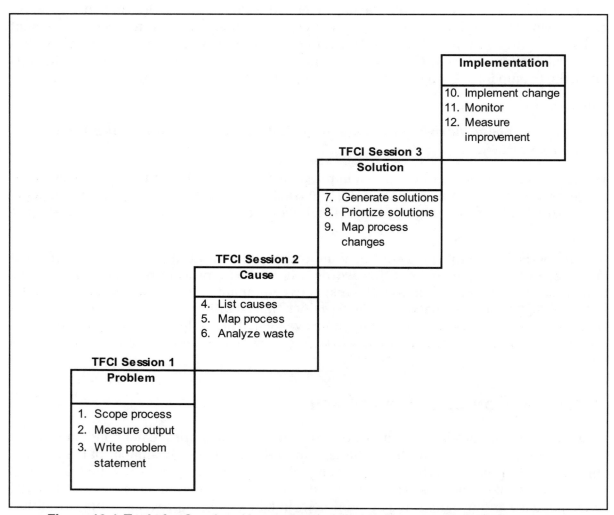

Figure 19-1. Tools for Continual Improvement (TFCI)—Process Improvement Model

Some of the basic project improvement tools taught during these sessions include:

Session 1: Work Process Chart

Run Chart

Histogram

Session 2: Cause-Effect Diagram—Causes

Process Map of existing process

Pareto Chart of causes

Session 3: Cause-Effect Diagram—Solutions

Process Map of revised process, incorporating solutions

Matrix chart prioritizing solutions

Session 4: PERT Chart

Project Cost-Benefit Chart

Gantt Chart

Figure 19-5 shows the tools that are included in each session.

One of the key tools that should be included in any continual improvement program is that of process mapping.

Process Mapping

If one defines quality as "the way we do our work," then mapping is the term used for diagramming "how we do our work."

There are three types of mapping: mapping associated with processes, mapping associated with the office conducting the process, and mapping associated with information transfer. Process mapping is very precise and simply documents, in a diagram format, the written words that describe how one does his or her work. Office mapping utilizes the same tools as process mapping but is approached differently. Information transfer mapping maps the information flow between each process and the suppliers and customers of that process.

Process Mapping may be done in several levels, beginning at Level 1, which is simply the name of the overall process. Examples would include corrective and preventive action, contract review, document control, logging, filing, getting dressed, etc. Level 2 includes the steps that make up the Level 1 process, presented in the sequence in which they occur. Level 3 selects any one of the Level 2 steps and breaks it up into the individual steps from which it is made, presented in the sequence in which they occur. Level 4 and further levels do the same as the Level 3 approach. In general, one does not map below Level 5.

The Purpose of Process Mapping is to present, in a visible format, all of the process steps for the process being mapped. The end result of doing so allows one to easily see the redundant and non-value-added steps, giving a clearer picture of opportunities and ways to improve the process. Process mapping is also a way of documenting the process in a user-friendly format. Analysis of such mapping includes the number of process steps, the cycle time of each step, and of the overall process and the duplication of process steps. Duplication of work within each step is easily seen through the Level 3 mapping of the chosen Level 2-process step (reference Figure 19-2).

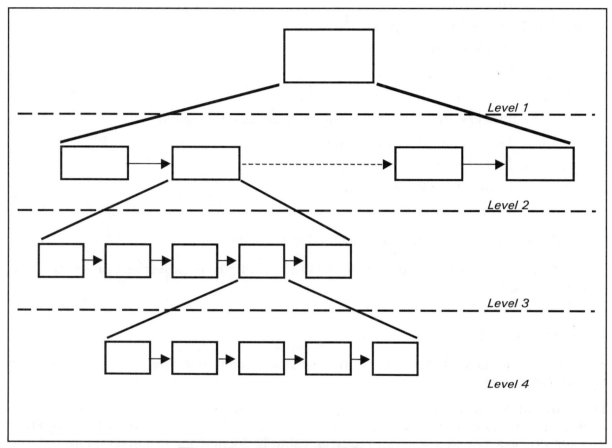

Figure 19-2. Process and Office Mapping

The Purpose of Office Mapping is to identify opportunities for improvement within the office through the analysis of the existing work and the generation of suggestions for possible improvement. This is accomplished through the preparation of process maps incorporating the identified improvements. The office process map will be no different in format than the process map.

The Purpose of Information Flow Mapping is to identify all of the information that flows from each process within a department/office to other departments, from suppliers and customers. It does not address information within the process itself, just the process communications with the "outside world."

The Approach to Process and Office Mapping is to have the personnel who perform the process work as a team to build the map. This is accomplished by using "Post-It" notes to construct the map, as shown in Figure 19-3. Following the mapping effort, the team identifies the opportunities associated with the process, identifies any better methods to accomplish the process, and then proceeds to make a new process map that incorporates these improvements. These identified improvements may include the elimination of process steps, the reduction of cycle time, the elimination of logging, photocopying, and duplicating files. Always in a mapping effort, a Cost-Benefit Analysis must be done of the proposed changes in order to justify making the changes. The cost analysis must include the cost of implementation (training, documentation, equipment, etc.).

After the process map is completed, it is generally converted into a *flow diagram*. So doing allows for a better presentation for future use in training, analysis, documentation within procedures, and/or work instruction, etc. Figure 19-3 shows a portion of a process map using "Post-it" notes. Figure 19-4 shows that process in the format of a flow diagram.

It is not necessary to show the map in the style as shown in Figure 19-3. One can show only those steps in the specific level being mapped. In addition, all process steps should be shown, including the wait steps and move steps associated with the item flowing through the process. These steps are not shown in the referenced figure. Typically, incoming letters wait in the in-box until picked up, as would the incoming faxes.

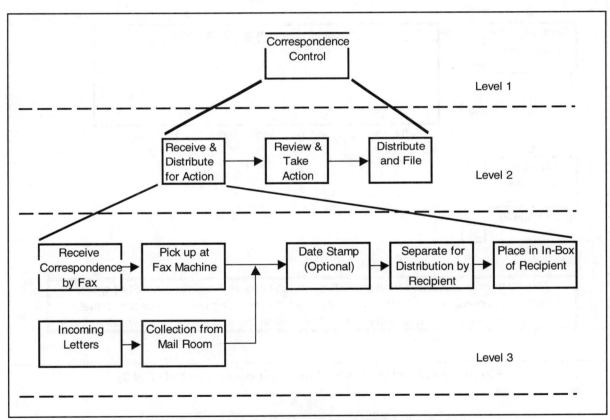

Figure 19-3. Process Map—Correspondence Control

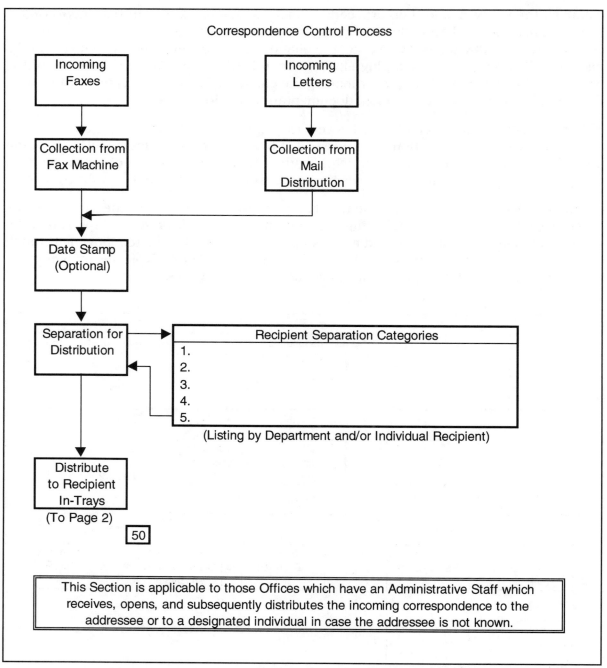

Figure 19-4. Flow Diagram—Correspondence Control (1 of 3)

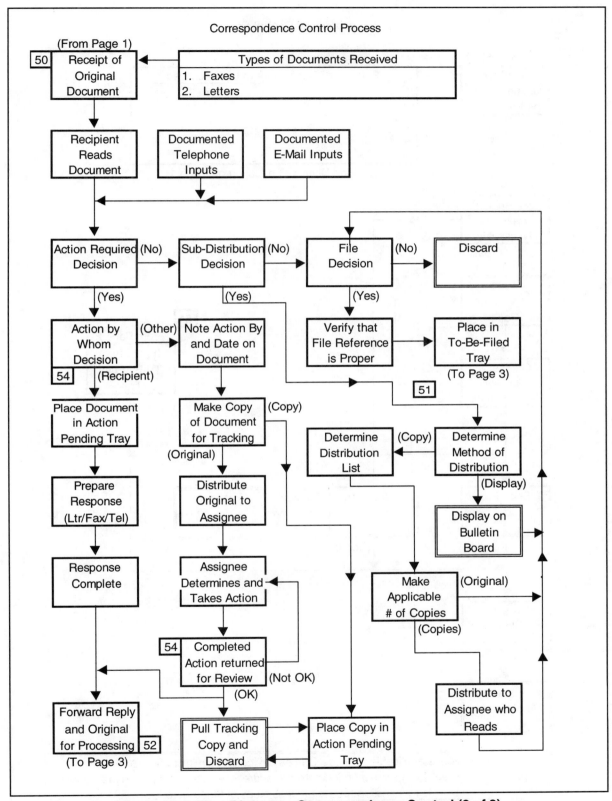

Figure 19-4. Flow Diagram—Correspondence Control (2 of 3)

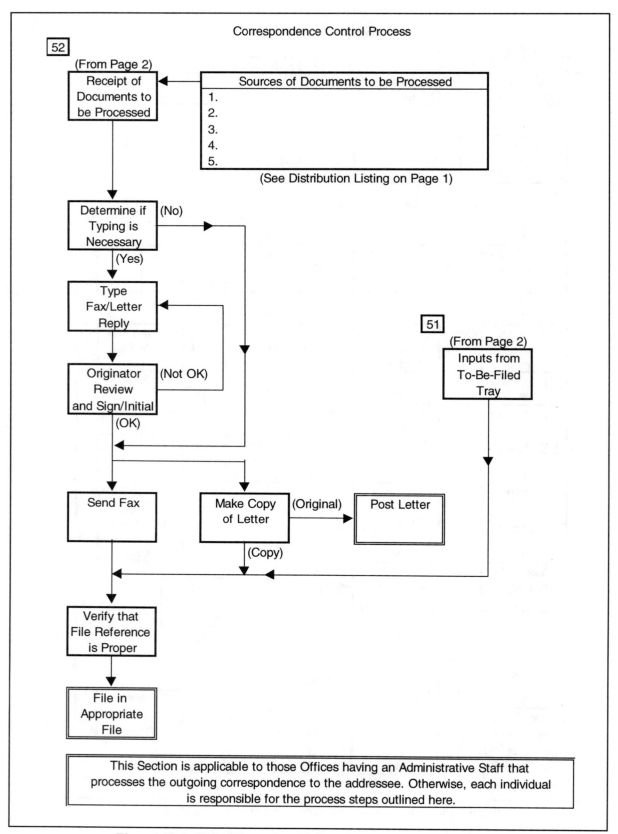

Figure 19-4. Flow Diagram—Correspondence Control (3 of 3)

Office Mapping

The Office Mapping, though different from Process Mapping, is accomplished utilizing the same tools and techniques as Process Mapping, and involves a majority of the staff members in the mapped office. The integral parts of the Office Mapping process include:

1. The identification of all of the processes occurring within each function of the office. Remember that a process is "a series of actions that produce a result," or "the work we do to convert process inputs to process outputs." From this listing will come those processes to be analyzed using the Office Mapping techniques.

2. The estimation of the types and percent of time spent in doing the work done within each function of the office. The breakdown is for each category of employee, such as Administrative Assistant, Engineer, Office Supervisor, etc.

3. The listing of all logs and databases maintained by each function within the office.

4. The listing of all file types kept and maintained within the office.

The work processes initially chosen for mapping are determined by their relative contribution to work performed—the larger the contribution, the greater the opportunity for mapping. In addition, the contribution of the process towards non-value added work within the office itself is considered in the process selection.

The Deployment of Office Mapping is then accomplished by spending time with the personnel associated with the chosen processes to be mapped, allowing them to map the chosen process as it currently is performed, including all process steps and who accomplishes them. If logs or databases are kept, then each data field is listed. If copies are made, then the process path for each copy must be shown until it is either filed, destroyed, or ends its journey through the process.

The viewpoint in the mapping effort must be from that of the item going though the process (that which is happening to the item) and not from the viewpoint of who is performing the process. In other words, if a fax is waiting in an in box, that is a process step from the viewpoint of the fax, even though no work is being performed at that time on the fax.

After the mapping of the current process steps for the process chosen, the participants hold a brainstorming session to list the current problems, issues, and barriers being experienced with the process. In addition, the participants list "challenge" goals for the new or revised process map, which is to be generated. These "challenge" goals might include such items as:

- Eliminate the making of photocopies.
- Eliminate duplicate files.
- Eliminate all logging or, as a minimum, reduce data fields associated with logging.
- Eliminate duplicate process steps.
- Eliminate duplicate processes.

The chosen process is then re-mapped utilizing the existing process map, the identified problems, issues and barriers, and the listed goals, beginning with a fresh piece of paper rather than modifying the existing process map.

After mapping, each identified problem, issue, and barrier is "bounced" against the new process to see if it was eliminated or reduced. This may cause further adjustments to the re-mapped process map. In a similar manner, the listed goals are "bounced" against the re-mapped process.

A "sanity check" should be performed on the re-mapped process to determine if the changes make sense from a number of different viewpoints. In addition, as stated earlier, a Cost-Benefit Analysis must be done for the re-mapped process, comparing the revised versus the current processes. This Cost-Benefit Analysis must be based on the respective process maps and must be coupled with a plan of implementation.

During the design of the re-mapped process, measurement points should be selected that will best determine the "health" of the process, so that the process can be accurately monitored, with the idea of continuous improvement in mind. Remember, if it is not measured, it is not managed—and you cannot have quality without measurements. All processes can be measured.

Finally, one may want to convert the process map into a flow diagram format to better display and use in the future.

A resulting comprehensive report should be prepared containing an overall summary and the documentation associated with the mapping effort in the form of analysis and flow diagrams, if convenient.

Generally, management participates in the process, and approval of revisions is gained on the spot, with a corresponding plan for implementation prepared prior to the completion of the effort.

Each office staff member receives, through the application of the tools and techniques applied to a process in which they are personally involved, the training and motivation needed to map other processes in a team environment. The key for so doing, however, is to ensure the employees be allowed the time and given the encouragement to do so.

One of the end results is learning to question, asking questions like, "Why are we doing this?" "What are the requirements?" "Who is requiring this, and why?" "Is there a better, simpler way of doing it?" and, finally, "What is the nature of the communication between internal supplier and internal customer?"

Environment for Continual Improvement

A Quality System requires adherence to the procedures and work instructions that each department has established. The concept of Continuous Improvement involves challenging those procedures and everything that is done, as well as the manner in which it is done, to constantly evaluate if there are better, smarter, or more efficient ways to operate.

Over the past ten years, the majority of companies in the U.S., and many others globally, have been striving to improve the quality of their products and services. A few have found the key to real improvement. But many have only a certificate of compliance to show for their efforts. They have confused the introduction of a system with the need to develop a management philosophy.

Those companies that have experienced real benefits are the ones that have instilled a culture of continuous improvement throughout their organization. The challenge is to understand and to encourage such a culture.

One of the first steps is to establish a workplace environment that will not just allow, but which will stimulate employees to suggest innovative ideas that could improve the way in which we operate.

According to Frank Iarossi, Chairman of the American Bureau of Shipping,

> *Our challenge is to create a workplace environment that encourages employee participation, teamwork, leadership, and innovation. All of this should be focused on fostering continuous improvement and appropriate decision-making at all levels of the organization. The challenge facing every ABS employee is to constantly ask themselves how they can do the jobs assigned to them more efficiently and more productively, and to then develop a broad consensus in support to the proposed change.*

This continuous improvement environment is an *informal* one. The formal procedures are contained in the Quality Management System. Continual improvement requires that everyone continue to question what we do and how we do it, challenging every aspect of our operations.

Frank Iarossi further states that

> *The major responsibility for fostering this new environment rests with managers at all levels who, in the new culture, must be prepared to not only encourage and support improvement suggestions from their subordinates, but to implement them.*

When this culture takes hold, one will be able to say, "We have found that as we have simplified the way that we work, we have become more innovative in the way that tasks are approached, and we have enhanced the quality of the entire work process."

Each employee holds the key to success. Every employee should know more about his or her individual work processes than anyone else. Everyone should have ideas for improving and simplifying these processes. The key to making these improvements happen is to encourage ideas to surface, to listen to the questions that are raised, and to respond to the challenges that are posed, without creating an environment of fear or of failure of rejection. Good ideas must be allowed to build momentum and achieve a broad consensus.

There is always the chance that, even though an idea may seem sensible to the person proposing it, it cannot be adopted for other reasons. Such a response should never be considered a failure, a reason to lose face, or, most importantly, a reason to feel that future suggestions will be rejected in the same way. It should never be considered a reason to stop participating in the process.

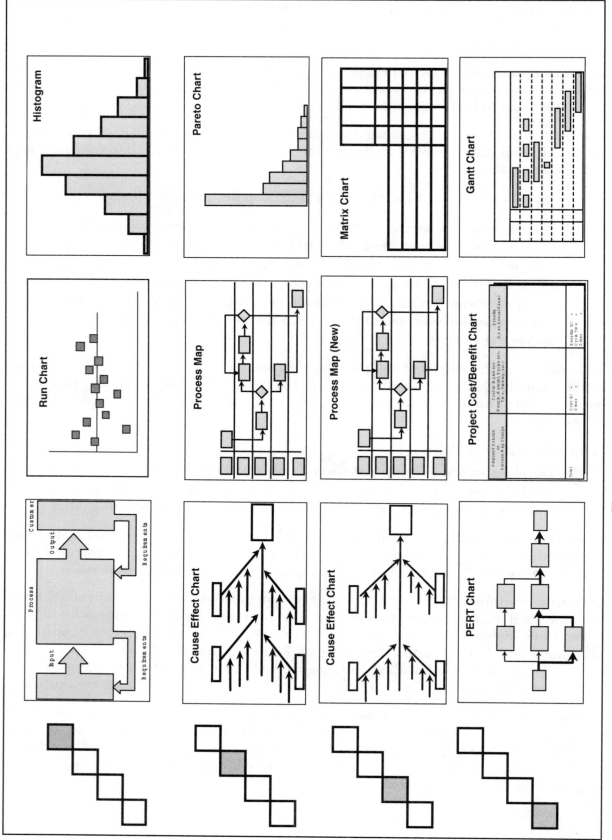

Figure 19-5. TFCI Project Tools

It can be difficult to make the time in a busy day to think through a work process and come up with a better method. But, by making time, and improving the way in which you do your job, you will be creating more time to think in the future. It is important that everyone resolves to take those risks, to make the time, and to have the courage to try to effect improvement.

If we do, then our jobs should be more enjoyable and less frustrating. By supporting and encouraging each other in a positive manner, blame will take a back seat. Instead, we will be able to learn from our mistakes and from others' points of view. We will be able to exert some control over our professional lives, and over the future success of the company for which we work.

HOW TO BE A PART OF CONTINUAL IMPROVEMENT

- Develop a work environment that encourages continual improvement.
- Identify those areas that are causing difficulty.
- Talk with each other and support each other in the search for better ways of doing things.
- Speak out when you have ideas or questions.
- Take the time to figure out why things aren't working as well as they should, rather than just complaining about the problems.
- Brainstorm the problem with your team.
- Identify and eliminate unnecessary "non-value" added steps from the way that work is done.
- Eliminate doing the same job twice (in part or in whole) because it was not done right the first time.
- Narrow alternatives down to the best solution.
- Develop consensus among those of your work mates who would be affected by a proposed change. Then the best, and most workable solution, is more likely to be developed and accepted.
- Carefully implement the agreed solution after informing all affected parties.
- Measure the impact of the new or revised way of doing things to determine if the change has really been for the better.
- Start the process all over again.

CONCLUSION

THERE IS NO FINISH LINE!

Chapter 20

Integrated Approach to Safety, Quality, and Environmental Management Systems
Including Management of Risk

This chapter provides the framework for developing an Integrated Management System using the International Standard ISO 9001:2000, Quality Management Systems—Requirements as presented in this book. This Standard has long been recognized in business and industry as an effective way of managing organizational work processes. ISO 9001:2000 addresses basic elements of Process Management, ISO 14001 addresses organizational concerns relating to environmental issues, and OHSAS 18001 provides international recognized requirements for safety. These three sets of elements combine to provide any organization a comprehensive approach to process management, generally referred to as SQE (Safety, Quality, and Environmental). This chapter will add an additional component to the SQE Process Management System in the area of Risk Management (R).

ISO 9001:2000 is an internationally recognized model for quality management systems. The standard is based on generally accepted practices and common sense, and it applies to the manufacturing industry, process industries, software developers, and service organizations. This standard presents the requirements for quality management systems, inclusive of work processes and encourages the adoption of the process approach for the management of the organization and its processes. The standard provides a means of readily identifying and managing opportunities for improvement. The ISO 9001:2000 Standard reinforces the overall management system of the organization but adds specific focus to the customer, leadership, involvement of people, process approach, system approach to management, continual improvement, factual approach to decision making, and mutually beneficial supplier relationships.

The ISO 14001 Standard addresses elements of management activities and processes that affect the external environment. ISO 14001 also reinforces the overall management system but adds specific focus to environmentally-related aspects associated with the management systems and processes. Also addressed are the organization's policy, mission, vision, corrective action, continual improvement, training, and measurement and management responsibilities. Approximately 80% of the ISO 14001 and ISO 9001 requirements are shared.

OHSAS 18001 addresses specific management practices related to increasing the chance that products and staff are safe. OHSAS 18000 addresses both the internal organizational operating systems at the organization level as well as those conditions affecting safety in the community and home. OHSAS 18000 establishes procedures for consistent safety practices that can be continuously monitored and improved. The OHSAS also shares many of the same basic requirements with the ISO 9001 and ISO 14001 Standard.

Risk Management provides for ongoing risk analysis that can be used to determine how potential hazards in operations affect safety and the environment, to produce risk profiles, to develop measures for managing identified risks, and to develop approaches for reducing and preventing safety and environment-related risks. Another aspect of Risk Management addresses the areas within management systems and processes where the organization should focus their resources, areas with the most organizational process-related risk.

The case for SQE plus R: Because the Safety, Quality, and Environmental Management Systems share a large percentage of overall management system requirements, it makes sense that they be integrated into a single management system. This comprehensive and integrated approach to management as presented here establishes consistency in practice and provides a solid baseline for continual process improvement. The result will be an "increase in public confidence, improved efficiency, cost savings, and most importantly, an increase in performance."

INTEGRATED APPROACH

An organization's journey to high performance begins with putting greater structure around what they do. This structure appears in processes with clear procedures (detailing what is required relative to the work) and work instructions (detailing how the work is done). It is also a first step in a Malcolm Baldrige National Quality Award effort.

Organizational leaders and subject matter experts often develop informal instructions, some of which are documented, but many only verbally communicated. This approach usually leaves quality in operations to be ensured by an individual and/or a small group. The addition of new requirements and demands for increased performance, coupled with unplanned crises occurring on a regular basis place a strain on these informal or semi-formal systems, and cause the quality of the processes to suffer. In today's culture, an organization that finds itself in this situation is operating in the Management Systems Stone Age, and will have increasing difficulty accomplishing its mission and objectives. Confusion over processes produces communications problems.

Rather than create an organized approach to system improvement, organizations frequently use a variety of techniques and tools that address, to a limited extent, specific operational problems as they arise. Actions take a narrow focus, generally based on a specific tool, technique, or program. In such cases, significant improvement generally does not occur. In addition, seminars and training courses are offered in an attempt to resolve the various issues that seem to arise faster than solutions can be found. More often than not, this effort still fails to satisfy the needs of the organization or individual, frustrating those served by the organization. It also wastes valuable time and resources, and negatively impacts customer satisfaction, performance results, and business results.

How can organizations step out of the box to design a more efficient management system and move forward in their journey to high performance? One method is to apply a three-step process designed to provide a clear picture of the journey.

The first step is to ascertain exactly where the organization wants to go, including a clear vision, mission, and goals. This means that every strategic and operational practice must contribute to the goals, such as "employees reaching high standards, a safe, stress-free environment, and an efficient, high performance operation." The planned activities to reach the goals must become a part of the day-to-day work of the organization.

The second step is to transition the organization to one where people know exactly where the organization is in respect to where the organization wants to go. This knowledge can be gained through performing a Gap Analysis or Gap Assessment between the "where we are" and "where we want to be." Such an assessment is organization-specific and is the document on which action plans are based.

The third step is to realize how to get from where you are to where you want to be. This involves planning. Remember, "If you fail to plan, you plan to fail." A plan is the road map used when taking a journey that helps you end up where you intend to go, and helps maintain focus on the goal. Planning includes strategic, business, and action plans, plus metrics to measure performance, and must include a corrective and preventive action process to ensure continual improvement.

The Journey - Baseline

The method to get from where your organization is to where you want it to be, is to establish a solid, documented baseline for work processes. This first step is simply to "write down what you do" in a formalized manner. The next step is to "do" what you write down followed by providing "visible evidence of what you have done." This documentation provides evidence of the process steps that are carried out. The final step is to measure and monitor the process (what you do versus what you have written down), ensuring that the process is being followed and continually improved. Reference Chapter 2.

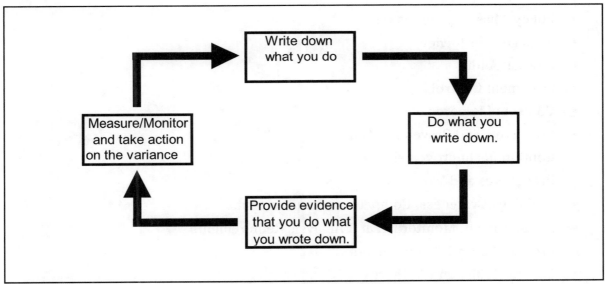

Figure 20-1. The First Step

Quality Management System

An efficient way to accomplish this phase of the journey is to establish a documented process management system as defined by the ISO 9001:2000 Standard (Quality Management System Requirements). The flow diagram at the beginning of the book shows the implementation steps for such a system.

Successful process management requires a solid understanding of work processes and is accomplished by fitting each work process into a **Work Process Model**, including all elements that might affect the quality of the process output. A picture of an ISO 9001-based model is described in Figure 11-5 of Chapter 11.

Adopting the ISO 9001 Standard as the baseline for process management provides a solid foundation for process definition, measurement, analysis, and continual improvement. Once the foundation is established, the focus is on improving the work processes by eliminating steps that do not add value to the process and ensuring those involved in the process are supported with training, equipment, a safe working environment, etc.

After this management system is operating, the organization may wish to seek ISO 9001 certification. Certification forces a discipline of doing what we say we do and of maintaining the management system and demonstrating continual improvement.

Environmental Management System

Because the ISO 14001 Standard (Environmental Management Systems—Specification with Guidance for Use) requirements include approximately 70+% of the ISO 9001:2000 Standard requirements and because the two standards are so closely configured, it is relatively easy for most organizations with ISO 9001 Certification to proceed to ISO 14001 Certification. Common elements to ISO 9001:2000 and ISO 14001, as well as Health and Safety (as discussed below) are:

- Policy, Mission, and Vision
- Management Review
- Internal Audits
- Document Control
- Control of Records
- Corrective and Preventive Action
- Continuous Improvement
- Procedures and Work Instructions
- Training, Awareness, Competence Requirements
- Measurement, Monitoring, and Analysis Requirements
- Process Control Requirements
- Responsibility and Authority

The primary benefit of the implementation of the ISO 14001 ISO Standard is the analysis of processes for improvement and the requirement for continual improvement of those processes.

Environmental management is not limited to how systems and processes affect the external environment. Environmental management includes the internal environment of the organization. Such considerations include any environmental aspects that negatively affect quality, such as conditions that disturb the working environment. In this respect, environmental management becomes a controlling factor with the potential of affecting the quality of the output of processes because it affects the people involved in the process. You cannot leave environmental considerations out of the overall management system and complete the journey to high performance successfully.

Safety Management System

In addition, the Safety Standards established by the organization also share the baseline ISO 9001:2000 Quality Management System requirements to the same degree as the Environmental Management System (listed above). Safety-related issues affect the internal operating environment, which affects the quality of the system. If the people performing the process and those involved in the process are trying to operate in an environment with a safety concern, it can easily have a negative impact on quality of the process. Therefore, an effective safety management system is essential for completing the journey to excellence. Safety considerations are those that are mandated as well as those that are determined by the organization and its stakeholders.

INTEGRATION OF SAFETY, QUALITY AND ENVIRONMENT (SQE) MANAGEMENT SYSTEMS

Because these systems share a relatively large number of the same or similar requirements, it is highly recommended to integrate them into one Management System. The end result of integrating these systems (Safety, Quality, and Environment) is a cost-effective Management System that establishes consistency, provides a baseline for improvement and training, and helps maintain focus. The case for an integrated system includes these benefits:

- The building of public confidence;
- Improved efficiency/economy;
- System consistency;
- Elimination of duplicate requirements and activities;
- Combined auditing/monitoring efforts;
- Minimization of documentation difficulties (defined, documented processes);
- Reduction in confusion about various programs among personnel;
- Encouraging a focus on the "best" way to manage operations rather than just complying with prescriptive requirements (investigations and improvements consider all issues and there is no sacrifice of one for the other);
- Single Work Instructions for each process which includes Health and Safety, Quality, and Environmental requirements (not several separate Work Instructions);
- Less resistance for the integration of new elements;

The Effect

All implemented, integrated management systems of quality, safety and environment will result in improved process efficiencies, realistic performance improvements, improved safety of personnel, improved response to the community, staff acceptance of responsibilities, and continual improvement.

An integrated management system allows the organization to operate in an efficient way and to become a high performance organization.

The **process for implementing** an integrated management system depends on the current state and structure of the organization.

The following are questions to consider in the preparation for an integrated management system:

- What are the benefits/drivers for integrating the Safety, Quality, and Environmental Management Systems?
- Is certification of the integrated system planned and useful?
- Is the internal know-how sufficient or will outside assistance be necessary?
- Are there the necessary support and resources available?
- Is there commitment to see it through to conclusion?

Risk Management

The integration of Safety, Quality, and Environmental Management Systems provides an excellent foundation for defining, controlling, and minimizing related risk through a risk assessment driven analysis. Such an analysis can be used to:

- Identify how hazards associated with operations/facilities potentially affect safety and the environment;
- Produce risk profiles for operations/facilities;
- Characterize the risk of the potential safety and environmental impacts focused on each of the organization's facilities;
- Assess the measures to effectively manage the identified risks;
- Develop recommendations for preventing and reducing safety related risks;
- Propose issues of potential national significance that district or national forums should address.

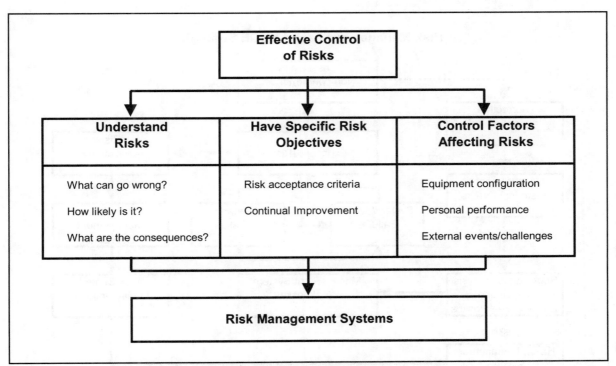

Figure 20-2. Risk Management

Risk Management is a very powerful means of preventive action and continual improvement. The integrated management system operates by applying corrective action to losses or non-conformances (procedures which violate the standard), evaluating the event, determining the root cause, pinpointing system weaknesses, and feeding this information into management system improvements. Applying Risk Management to this process takes the management system-identified weaknesses and applies risk assessment of the exposure. Coupled with management decisions relative to risk control and implementation, the results are applied back to the management systems for improvement to prevent recurrence. This process is shown in the figure on the following page.

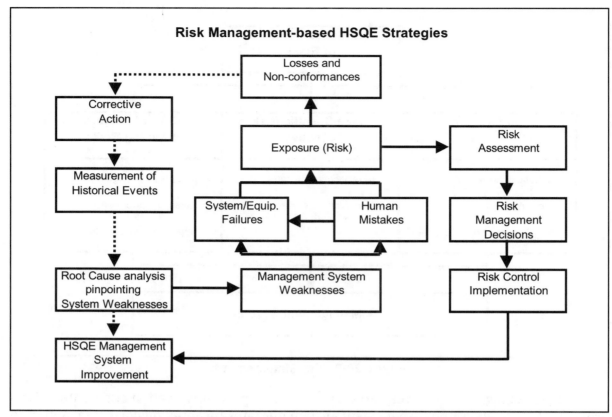

Figure 20-3. Risk Management Strategies for Improvement

CONCLUSION

The purpose of this chapter is to present an overall integrated management system approach coupled with the application of risk assessment, building off of an ISO 9001:2000 base. The integrated management system approach is not a complicated one and is mostly common sense coupled with the application of specific risk and management system tools. The demonstrated results for those organizations implementing this approach and those that have included risk analysis in that approach are impressive.

For organizations dedicated to being high performance, this approach provides the direction and tools necessary to attain the goal.

Chapter 21

Case Study:
American Bureau of Shipping (ABS)[1]

THE MISSION OF ABS

We, the employees of ABS, are to serve the public interest as well as the needs of our clients by promoting the security of life, property, and the natural environment primarily through the development and verification of standards for the design, construction, and operational maintenance of marine-related facilities.

THE MISSION OF ABS CONSULTING

The mission of ABS Group of Companies and its operating subsidiaries is to assist its clients to improve the safety of their operations, to enhance the quality of their services, and to minimize the environmental impact of their activities.

The ABS Group of Companies pursues this mission by offering integrated services related to awareness, evaluation, training, implementation, verification and certification.

In fulfilling our vision of this mission:

> *We seek to be the foremost marine classification society in the world.*
>
> *We seek to be the world's leader in the development of marine technology.*
>
> *We encourage similar aspirations on the part of our affiliated companies in keeping with their respective missions.*

BACKGROUND

ABS was founded in 1862 as a not-for-profit self-regulatory agency of the marine industry to promote the safety of life and property at sea. Since that time it has performed this function through a procedure known as ship classification, a procedure which determines the structural and mechanical fitness of ships and other marine structures for their intended service.

The classification work of ABS involves two fundamental aspects. One is development of ABS Rules—the process by which standards for the design, construction, and operational maintenance are established and updated. The other is the administration of ABS Rules—

---

[1] Includes the American Bureau of Shipping, its wholly owned subsidiary, ABS Group of Companies, and the operating subsidiary of the ABS Consulting.

the process of analyzing designs and surveying new building structures for conformance to the Rules, as well as surveying vessels in service to ensure maintenance in accordance with the Rules.

While the focus of ABS on ship classification has remained undiminished since its inception, the knowledge, experience, and resources of ABS have continuously progressed. ABS Group of Companies was established as a wholly-owned, taxable subsidiary dedicated to diversifying the activities of ABS by rendering, to industrial clients throughout the world, integrated services aimed at the management of risk, improving safety, enhancing quality, and promoting environmental protection.

ABS continues to forge an identification with two all-important words—Safety & Quality—with Safety defining what we do and Quality defining how we do it.

The ABS Journey—Overview

The ABS Journey to Excellence began in the spring of 1990, when ABS initiated a major strategic plan aimed at positioning ABS as a global enterprise providing a wide variety of maritime and industrial verification services. As explained by ABS Chairman, Frank J. Iarossi, "This strategic plan—called ABS 2000—is most importantly a renewal of our purpose, our principles, our values, and our dedication to providing a faithful balance of interests leading to the highest level of safety practical for the circumstances."

While the elements of ABS 2000 included a number of particular technical, administrative, and managerial objectives, a central objective running through all of the others is:

> *an emphasis on quality and quality management in all aspects of ABS activities in order to totally integrate quality in all functions and to become a model of quality management for other companies to follow.*

Consistent with this goal, ABS made a commitment in 1991 to establish and implement a Total Quality Management Process. This commitment soon turned into a journey which expanded beyond Total Quality Management. It is a process of continuous improvement which has no finish line and is called the "ABS Journey to Excellence."

The approach taken by ABS in its Journey to Excellence is one that aligns the activities of all employees and all management systems and processes within the organization with the *common focus on customer satisfaction through continuous improvement of all activities, goods, and services.* (Customer means a person or group, internal or external to the organization, to whom a service is provided.)

FOUNDATION OF THE ABS JOURNEY TO EXCELLENCE

In order to effect continuous improvement at an accelerated rate, ABS had to first establish a solid foundation on which to launch the journey. This involved writing down what we do (procedures and process instructions), doing what we wrote down, and having visible evidence that we have done it (check sheets)—the essentials of an ISO 9001-based Quality System. Additionally, ABS established an effective Corrective and Preventive Action System and an outstanding Internal Audit Program to ensure that we do what we wrote down.

From this foundation one need only close the loop by identifying opportunities for improving how we do our work and changing the written documents to reflect the changes. In addition, training plays a big part in this overall process. The focus in the following text will be specific to the ISO 9001 effort of ABS, which forms the foundation for the Journey to Excellence, the lessons learned, and the successes gained.

The Journey to Excellence by the ABS organization worldwide is being accomplished in four concurrent phases.

Phase 1 is the implementation of Process Management, which includes the installation of a Quality System based on the International Association of Classification Societies (IACS-QSCS) and the International Organization for Standardization (ISO) 9001-1994 standards. Phase 1 involved the following ten-step plan of action.

1. Senior management education and commitment
2. Quality awareness for all employees
3. Quality foundations—ISO 9001/IACS
4. Establishment of operating procedures/process instructions
5. Education and training of all employees
6. Establishment of a communication and recognition system
7. Installation of a corrective and preventive action system
8. Setting of goals
9. Establishment of metrics worldwide
10. Continued improvement and simplification of all ABS work processes

During 1992 this phase of the ABS Journey to Excellence, the Quality System was installed and was completed in December of 1994 as evidenced by the receipt of both the IACS-QSCS and the ISO 9001-1994 global certificates.

ABS's ISO 9001 Certification was unique in several respects:

- The first Classification Society to achieve certification to the ISO 9001 (1994) Standard
- Single, global certificate for 95 offices in over 60 countries on six continents
- Certification includes all ABS support functions—Information Management Systems, Human Resources, Finance and Administrative functions, as well as all Technical and Operational functions
- One hundred percent (100%) of the ABS offices worldwide are assessed every three years on a continuous basis

In addition:

- All ABS affiliates attained Single Certificate ISO 9001 (1994) certification for their worldwide operations in 1995.

Certification to this worldwide standard documents that ABS has in place the policies, practices, and procedures throughout the total company to provide ship classification, statutory, and related services in compliance with the ISO Model. It is also indicative of the worldwide consistency, integrity, and quality of the ABS services offered.

Certification of the ABS Global Quality System has been undertaken by SGS International Certification Services, Inc. (SGS-ICS), under accreditation to RvA and RAB. The initial assessment took place over a three-month period during September through October 1994, totaling 89 assessment days and 37 offices worldwide.

Where does one go from here relative to an ISO Certified Quality System itself and outside of its part in the overall journey? ABS, in conjunction with its registrar, has instituted a new approach to the ISO surveillance audits, one of looking at only 12 of the major offices each year and relying on a "visitless" audit of the remaining 83 offices. This cost-effective approach is based on the strength of the ABS internal audits, the effectiveness of the Corrective and Preventive Action System, and analysis of the five surveillance audits by the registrar. In other words, the focus is on the true certification and verification of the ABS Quality System and not a duplication of the Quality System functions by the Registrar. In addition, a "continuous surveillance" process has been implemented which forgoes the need for a renewal audit every three-year cycle.

The ISO 9000-based Quality System Implementation Process involved the following steps:

- Senior management commitment
- Establish the organization's quality structure
- Select the appropriate ISO standard
- Perform an internal, high level self-assessment
- Prepare a Quality System Implementation Plan
- Establish the organization's character:
    Values and Principals
    Code-of-Ethics
    Mission Statement
    Quality Policy
    Organization's Quality Goals and Objectives
- Prepare the Quality System Manual
- Prepare the Common Quality System Procedures
    Document Control
    Storage and Retention of Controlled Documents
    Corrective and Preventive Action
    Internal Quality Audits
    Operating Procedure Development
    Work Instructions Development
    Numbering and Indexing
    Management Reviews
    Nonconformance Reporting

> Purchasing and Supplier Control
> Contract Review
> Service Statusing
> Statistical Techniques
> Confidentiality
> Subcontracted Personnel
> Training and Development

- Define, list, and group the Primary Work Processes
- Determine the training and knowledge requirements for each work process
- Make writing assignments with a go-by and instructions for each procedure/work instruction
- Prepare a company-wide job title matrix
- Prepare a Position Description Manual
- Prepare an Organizational Chart Manual
- Prepare a Delegation of Authority Manual
- Provide training for all employees relative to the Quality System as defined
- Implement the Quality System
- Follow-up with frequent internal audits and management reviews

The lessons learned before, during, and after the implementation are numerous and varied, and many are company and culture specific.

Key success ingredients:

- Senior Level Management unanimous commitment, which is continuously demonstrated
- Detailed and thorough planning (if you fail to plan, you plan to fail)
- The establishment of a Senior Management Quality Steering Committee who meet regularly and review the plan progress and steps, making adjustments as necessary
- Good communications with employees as to the progress, what is to come, etc.
- Employee involvement from the very beginning, during, and after implementation
- Fast response in removing barriers discovered during the implementation process, including those related to specific personnel and specific processes
- Management must "walk the talk," as they will be tested by employees who will follow more of what management does rather than what management says to do.
- Keep everything very simple. The tendency is to exceed the requirements rather than meet them and there is a cost for so doing that is negative in the implementation phase. Simply write down what is done, do what is written down, provide visible evidence that you have done it, and then establish a means of continuous improvement that involves all employees, customers, and suppliers.
- Quickly eliminate programs that don't work or have out-lived their value.
- Keep the vision always in front of yourself and everyone else too.

Key Lessons Learned:

- Forced implementation generates a backlash reaction from employees.

- If there is a history of management programs that did not meet the advertisements, then employees may look on the effort as "just another program" that will go away if we just ignore it and/or if we go through the motions of compliance.

- Employees accept the quality system requirements as an add-on to what they are currently doing rather than integrating it into "just the way we do our work," thereby feeling it is just more non-value added work for them. Time is the cure for this.

- There will be some dissenters who will be an undercover counter-influence to the implementation effort.

- There will be some dissenters who will be very vocal.

- There will be those who cannot handle the controls associated with the Quality System.

- Do not start the process unless management is ready to support it because there is no turning back once the critical employee mass is reached.

- Base decisions on data but keep perception in the forefront because perception becomes one's reality.

- Metrics are important in that "what gets measured gets done" and "you can't manage what you don't measure."

ISO 14001, ENVIRONMENTAL MANAGEMENT SYSTEM CERTIFICATION

In 1999, ABS modified the ISO 9001 Quality Management System to "piggy-back" the Environmental Management System onto the ISO 9001 System. The level of effort was about 20% of the implementation of the Quality Management System, primarily because the two standards contain about 80% of the same requirements. As a result, the external audits for both systems are done at the same time and by the same auditor, saving both time and money.

CONCLUSION

The ABS Quality and Environmental Management System is fully implemented and has become "Just the way we do our work." Senior Management continues to be heavily involved through regular management reviews and through their "walking the talk," as a demonstration of their active involvement. The results remain impressive.

Appendix A

Quality Manual Configured to Option 3

{COMPANY NAME}

QUALITY MANAGEMENT

SYSTEM (QMS)

QUALITY MANUAL

Distribution Number: _____

Document Holder: _____

Option 3 – Process Orientation

{COMPANY NAME}			QUALITY SYSTEM MANUAL	
Title: **Table of Contents**	Prepared by: *{Name of Preparer}*	Approved by: *{Name of Approver}*	Page:	
	Effective date:	Revision number:	Section : **A**	

Section Number	Title	ISO 9001:2000 Reference	Revision Number	Revision Date
A	Table of Content and Cross-reference			
B	Quality Management System	1.0, 4.1, 5.3, and 5.4.1		
C	Planning	5.4.2		
D	Management Responsibility	5.1, 5.2, and 5.5.3		
E	Organizational Responsibilities	5.5.1 and 5.5.2		
F	Management Review	5.6 all		
G	Documentation Requirements	4.2 all		
H	Resource Management	6 all		
I	Product Realization	7.1		
J	Customer Related Processes	7.2 all		
K	Design and Development	7.3 all		
L	Purchasing	7.4 all		
M	Production and Service Provision	7.5 all		
N	Control of Monitoring and Measuring Devices	7.6		
O	Measurement, Analysis and Improvement	8.1		
P	Monitoring and Measurement	8.2 all		
Q	Control of Nonconforming Product	8.3		
R	Analysis of Data	8.4		
S	Improvement	8.5 all		
T	Glossary (Terms & Definitions)			
U	Record of Revision			

{COMPANY NAME & Logo}   QUALITY SYSTEM MANUAL

Title:	Prepared By/Date:	Approved By/Date:	Effective Date:	Page: 1 of 4
Quality Management System	Reviewed By/Date:	Approved By/Date:	Revision No.	Section No. B

Applicability: This section is applicable to all *{Company Name}* operations.

Standard Page Header

1.0 PURPOSE

The purpose of this section is to specify *{Company Name}*'s requirements for a Quality Management System (QMS) in order to demonstrate its ability to consistently provide *product* that meets *customer* and applicable regulatory requirements, and aims to enhance customer satisfaction.

2.0 REFERENCE DOCUMENTS

> Refer to the appropriate ISO 9001 paragraph, applicable other sections of the QSM and Quality System Procedures that support this QSM Section.

2.1 ISO 9001:2000 Clauses 1.0, 4.1 and 5.3

2.2 Quality Manual Section H, Resource Management

2.3 Quality Manual Section L, Purchasing

2.4 Quality Manual Section O, Management, Analysis and Improvement

2.5 Quality Manual Section P, Monitoring and Measurement

2.6 Quality Manual Section Q, Control of Nonconforming Product

2.7 Quality Manual Section R, Analysis of Data

2.8 Quality Manual Section S, Improvement

2.9 *{Applicable Supporting Quality System Procedures}*

3.0 DEFINITIONS

{For each section, italicize terms that may be necessary to understand the content of the QMS, especially those that are peculiar to the organization.}

3.1 See Section T, Glossary, for definitions of italicized terms.

4.0 QMS REQUIREMENTS

4.1 Scope

Top management of *{Company Name}* has specified the requirements for the *{Company Name}*'s QMS in order to demonstrate its:

- ability to consistently provide *product* that meets *customer* and applicable regulatory *requirements*, and

- aim to enhance customer satisfaction through the effective application of the QMS, including *process*es for *continual improvement* of the system and the assurance of conformity to customer and applicable regulatory *requirements*.

{COMPANY NAME & Logo} QUALITY SYSTEM MANUAL

Title:	Prepared By/Date:	Approved By/Date:	Effective Date:	Page:
				2 of 4
Quality Management System	Reviewed By/Date:	Approved By/Date:	Revision No.	Section No.
				B

4.2   Quality Management System - General (4.1)

<table>
<tr><td>
Add
Company
Name where
applicable.
</td><td>

{Company Name} has established, documented, and implemented a Quality Management System and continually improves its effectiveness in accordance with the requirements of the ISO 9001:2000 Standard.

{Company Name} maintains its Quality Management System by

</td></tr>
</table>

a)   identifying the processes needed for its QMS and their application throughout the organization,

b)   determining the sequence and interaction of these processes,

c)   determining the criteria and methods needed to ensure that both the operation and control of these processes are effective,

d)   ensuring the availability of resources, per Reference 2.2, and information necessary to support the operation and monitoring of these processes,

e)   monitoring, measuring, and analyzing these processes, per References 2.4 - 2.8 above, and

f)   implementing actions necessary to achieve planned results and continual improvement of these processes.

{Company Name} manages the QMS processes in accordance with the requirements of the ISO 9001:2000 Standard.

<table>
<tr><td>
If no
outsourcing is
done, use this
paragraph or
similar.
</td><td>

{Company Name} does not outsource any processes affecting product conformity with these requirements. Should any process be outsourced, *{Company Name}* will identify them and ensure control over such processes.

</td></tr>
</table>

OR

<table>
<tr><td>
If outsourcing
is done, use
this paragraph
text or similar.
List or
reference the
processes.
</td><td>

The below-listed processes affect *product* conformity with requirements; however, *{Company Name}* outsources these processes:

1)

2)

</td></tr>
</table>

{Company Name} ensures the control of these processes through the subcontractor control, per Reference 2.3.

{COMPANY NAME & Logo}			QUALITY SYSTEM MANUAL		
Title: Quality Management System	Prepared By/Date:	Approved By/Date:	Effective Date:	Page: 3 of 4	
	Reviewed By/Date:	Approved By/Date:	Revision No.	Section No. B	

4.3   Quality Policy (5.3)

This Quality System Manual is issued to describe the quality system employed by *{Company Name}*. Top Management of *{Company Name}* ensures that the Quality Policy

Make sure that the Quality Policy addresses items a), b), and c) in its text.

a)   is appropriate to the purpose of the organization,

b)   includes a commitment to comply with requirements and continually improve the effectiveness of the QMS,

c)   provides a framework for establishing and reviewing quality objectives,

Make sure that d) and e) are done and documented.

d)   is communicated and understood within the organization, and

e)   is reviewed for continuing suitability.

The following is the Quality Policy adopted by *{Company Name}*:

{State the organization's Quality Policy here exactly as it is. It is important that all distributed copies match the one contained here at all times.}

4.3.1   Quality Policy Implementation

The ways in which *{Company Name}*'s quality policy is implemented include:

Sample ways in which the quality policy is implemented are listed here. Customize them as necessary.

a)   being committed to continual improvement,

b)   making the quality policy available,

c)   providing a framework for establishing and reviewing objectives,

d)   reviews of the Quality Management System by top management,

e)   audits of the Quality Management System,

f)   defining and documenting the organization, responsibility, and interfaces of various functions,

g)   suiting our equipment and facilities to their intended purpose,

h)   our employees possessing sound skills in their own areas of responsibility and being offered the opportunity for the necessary training to ensure that they are capable to achieve quality in the work they perform.

Title:	Prepared By/Date:	Approved By/Date:	Effective Date:	Page: 4 of 4
Quality Management System	Reviewed By/Date:	Approved By/Date:	Revision No.	Section No. B

4.4 Quality Objectives (5.4.1)

It is the responsibility of *{Company Name}*'s top management to ensure that quality objectives, including those needed to meet work-related requirements and in support of the organizational objectives, are established at relevant functions and levels within the organization. These objectives are measurable and consistent with the quality policy.

The overall quality objectives are as follows:

{List the organization's quality objectives here. They must be obtainable and measurable. Sample objectives are shown below. Customize as needed.}

    a)   the provision of superior products and services to our customers,

    b)   continual improvement of our Quality Management System,

    c)   customer satisfaction as a paramount goal,

    d)   maintain the ISO 9001:2000 Certification,

    e)   create and maintain a work environment for our employees that encourages innovative thinking, leadership, decision making, and a commitment to continual improvement,

    f)   work with suppliers to ensure continuous adherence to *{Company Name}*'s requirements.

In addition, quality objectives, including those needed to meet requirements for *product* per Reference 2.3, have been established within the below-listed functions and levels of *{Company Name}*:

{List the functions here, if practical, or reference where they are listed or stated.}

5.0 RESPONSIBILITIES

It is top management's responsibility to ensure the quality policy is implemented and understood by all employees within the organization.

6.0 RECORDS

Records associated with the Quality Objectives are a part of the Management Review process.

{COMPANY NAME & Logo}			QUALITY SYSTEM MANUAL		
Title: Planning	Prepared By/Date:	Approved By/Date:	Effective Date:	Page: 1 of 1	
	Reviewed By/Date:	Approved By/Date:	Revision No.	Section No. C	
Applicability: This section is applicable to all *{Company Name}* operations.					

State the applicability of each QSM Section.

1.0   PURPOSE

This section establishes the planning of *{Company Name}*'s QMS and the quality objectives.

2.0   REFERENCE DOCUMENTS

2.1   ISO 9001:2000 Clause 5.4.2

2.2   Quality Manual Section B, QMS General Requirements

2.3   Quality Manual Section I, Product Realization

3.0   DEFINITIONS

3.1   See Section T, Glossary, for definitions of italicized terms.

4.0   QUALITY MANAGEMENT SYSTEM REQUIREMENTS

4.1   Quality Management System Planning (5.4.2)

{Company Name}'s top management ensures that:

a)   the planning of the QMS is carried out in order to meet the requirements given per Reference 2.2, as well as the quality objectives listed below, and

b)   the integrity of the QMS is maintained when changes to the QMS are planned and implemented.

4.2   Plan Development

{Add additional specific company information relative to Planning such as 4.2 Plan Development.}

5.0   RESPONSIBILITIES

QMS Planning is the responsibility of *{list the responsibility for QMS Planning.}*

6.0   RECORDS

Records associated with QMS Planning are maintained by *{state where Records associated with QMS Planning are maintained or equivalent.}*

{COMPANY NAME & Logo}			QUALITY SYSTEM MANUAL		
Title: Management Responsibility	Prepared By/Date:	Approved By/Date:	Effective Date:		Page: 1 of 2
	Reviewed By/Date:	Approved By/Date:	Revision No.		Section No. D
Applicability: This section is applicable to all *{Company Name}* operations.					

1.0 PURPOSE

This section establishes top management's responsibilities with regard to the continual improvement of *{Company Name}*'s Quality Management System and the enhancement of customer satisfaction.

2.0 REFERENCE DOCUMENTS

2.1 ISO 9001:2000 Clauses 5.1, 5.2 and 5.5.3

2.2 Quality Manual Section B, QMS General Requirements

2.3 Quality Manual Section C, Planning

2.4 Quality Manual Section E, Organizational Responsibilities

2.5 Quality Manual Section F, Management Review

2.6 Quality Manual Section H, Resource Management

2.7 Quality Manual Section J, Customer-Related Processes

2.8 *{List Quality System Supporting Procedures, as applicable.}*

3.0 DEFINITIONS

3.1 See Section T, Glossary, for definitions of italicized terms.

4.0 QMS REQUIREMENTS

4.1 Management Commitment (5.1)

Top management provides evidence of its commitment to the development and implementation of the QMS, and to continually improving the effectiveness of the QMS, by

a) communicating to all *{Company Name}* employees the importance of meeting customer as well as statutory and regulatory requirements,

b) establishing the quality policy, per Reference 2.2, and ensuring that this policy is understood by all *{Company Name}* employees,

c) ensuring that the quality objectives established, per Reference 2.3,

{COMPANY NAME & Logo}			QUALITY SYSTEM MANUAL		
Title:	Prepared By/Date:	Approved By/Date:	Effective Date:	Page: 2 of 2	
Management Responsibility	Reviewed By/Date:	Approved By/Date:	Revision No.	Section No. D	

    d)   conducting management reviews, per Reference 2.5, and

    e)   ensuring the availability of resources, per References 2.4 and 2.6.

{Add any additional evidence of management commitment that the organization may perform.}

4.2   Customer Focus (5.2)

Top management ensures that customer requirements are determined, per Reference 2.7. These requirements are met with the aim of enhancing the satisfaction of our customer.

4.3   Internal Communication (5.5.3)

Top management ensures that appropriate communication processes are established within the organization. These processes ensure that communication takes place regarding the effectiveness of the QMS.

5.0 RESPONSIBILITIES

It is the responsibility of top management to ensure customer focus and internal communication throughout the organization.

6.0 RECORDS

There are no quality records associated with this QSM Section.

Title:	Prepared By/Date:	Approved By/Date:	Effective Date:	Page: 1 of 2
Organizational Responsibility	Reviewed By/Date:	Approved By/Date:	Revision No.	Section No. E
Applicability: This section is applicable to all *{Company Name}* operations.				

1.0   PURPOSE

This section defines the responsibilities and authorities of *{Company Name}* Company personnel for implementing and maintaining the Quality Management System (QMS).

2.0   REFERENCE DOCUMENTS

2.1   ISO 9001:2000 Clauses 5.5.1 and 5.5.2

3.0   DEFINITIONS

3.1   See Section T, Glossary, for definitions of italicized terms.

4.0   QMS REQUIREMENTS

4.1   Responsibility and Authority (5.5.1)

{Modify the following paragraph to fit the organization, but address all issues contained therein:}

Top management within *{Company Name}* defines and communicates the responsibilities and authorities of all employees within the organization. Organizational relationships within the company are described in the organizational charts. Specific responsibilities and authorities for such activity affecting quality are defined in the respective job description.

4.2   Management Representative (5.5.2)

Top management has appointed the {Functional Title of person} who, irrespective of other responsibilities, has responsibility and authority that includes

a)   ensuring that processes needed for the QMS are established, implemented, and maintained,

b)   reporting on the performance of the QMS to the President, including any need for improvement, and

c)   ensuring the promotion and awareness of customer requirements throughout the *{Company Name}* organization.

{Provide descriptions of other QMS related job functions such as Quality Assurance Manager. Create a paragraph for each, 4.3, 4.4, etc. See example on following page.}

{COMPANY NAME & Logo}		QUALITY SYSTEM MANUAL			
Title:	Prepared By/Date:	Approved By/Date:	Effective Date:	Page: 2 of 2	
Organizational Responsibility	Reviewed By/Date:	Approved By/Date:	Revision No.	Section No. E	

Example

> **4.3   Quality Assurance Manager**
>
> The Quality Assurance Manager of each facility within the *{Name of organization}* will be the management representative for the ISO 9000 Quality Management System. The Management Representative is responsible for ensuring that the quality management system is established and maintained according to the ISO 9000 Standard, and has the following responsibilities:
>
> a)   coordinate Quality Assurance requirements with other departments;
>
> b)   ensure adequate training is given to Quality Department personnel;
>
> c)   establish quality policies and procedures to meet contractual requirements;
>
> d)   provide functional counseling and guidance on preparation of inspection and test plans;
>
> e)   ensure the appropriate quality representative participates in design review;
>
> f)   interpret quality requirements of contracts and notify affected areas of any changes;
>
> g)   report on the performance of the quality system to management for review.
>
> The Quality Assurance Manager is responsible for chairing the Quality Management System Review Meeting. *{Add any additional Quality-related organizational responsibilities here, as applicable.}*

5.0   RESPONSIBILITIES

Responsibilities are defined above. *{State the responsibilities here if not clearly stated in the text of paragraph 4.0.}*

6.0   RECORDS

{List the documents wherein the responsibilities mentioned in the text of Paragraph 4 are contained. Provided below are two examples.}

6.1   Organization Charts

6.2   Job Descriptions

{COMPANY NAME & Logo}		QUALITY SYSTEM MANUAL			
Title: Management Review	Prepared By/Date:	Approved By/Date:	Effective Date:	Page: 1 of 2	
	Reviewed By/Date:	Approved By/Date:	Revision No.	Section No. F	
Applicability: This section is applicable to all *{Company Name}* operations.					

1.0 PURPOSE

This section establishes the requirements for top management's review of the Quality Management System to ensure its continuing suitability, adequacy, and effectiveness.

2.0 REFERENCE DOCUMENTS

2.1 ISO 9001:2000 Clause 5.6

2.2 Quality Manual Section C, Planning

2.3 Quality Manual Section G, Documentation Requirements

2.4 Quality Manual Section P, Monitoring and Measurement

2.5 Quality Manual Section Q, Control of Nonconforming Product

2.6 Quality Manual Section G, Improvement

3.0 DEFINITIONS

3.1 See Section 20, Glossary, for definitions of italicized terms.

4.0 QMS REQUIREMENTS

4.1 Management Review – General (5.6.1)

Top management reviews *{Company Name}*'s QMS on an annual basis to ensure its continuing suitability, adequacy, and effectiveness. This review includes assessing opportunities for improvement and the need for changes to the quality management system, including the quality policy and quality objectives. Records from these reviews are maintained per Reference 2.3 (see paragraph 6.0 below)

4.2 Review Inputs (5.6.2)

Inputs to the management review include information on

a) Results of audits (Reference 2.4)

b) Customer feedback (Reference 2.4)

c) Process performance and product conformity to requirements (Reference 2.4 and Reference 2.5)

Title:	Prepared By/Date:	Approved By/Date:	Effective Date:	Page: 2 of 2
Management Review	Reviewed By/Date:	Approved By/Date:	Revision No.	Section No. F

    d)   Status of corrective and preventive actions (Reference 2.6)

    e)   Follow-up actions from previous management reviews (Reference 2.6)

    f)   Changes that could affect the QMS (Reference 2.2)

    g)   Recommendations for improvement (Reference 2.6)

4.3   Review Output (5.6.3)

The outputs from the review include all decisions and actions related to

    a)   Improvement of the effectiveness of the QMS and its processes

    b)   Improvement of product related to customer requirements, and

    c)   Resource needs

5.0   RESPONSIBILITIES

The *{Name of Function responsible for chairing the Management Review Meeting, such as Quality Assurance Manager}* is responsible for chairing the Quality System Management Review Meeting. Top management is responsible for reviewing the quality management system and ensuring its continuing suitability, adequacy, and effectiveness.

6.0   RECORDS

Records of management reviews are maintained by *{Name of Function responsible for maintaing the records and action items resulting from the review, such as Quality Assurance Manager}* in accordance with the requirements of Section G of this Manual.

{COMPANY NAME & Logo}			QUALITY SYSTEM MANUAL		
Title: Documentation Requirements	Prepared By/Date:	Approved By/Date:	Effective Date:	Page: 1 of 4	
	Reviewed By/Date:	Approved By/Date:	Revision No.	Section No. G	
Applicability: This section is applicable to all *{Company Name}* operations.					

1.0 PURPOSE

This section establishes the requirements for documentation of the Quality Management System (QMS). The system provides for the uniform preparation, revision, distribution, retrieval, and storage of documents and records.

2.0 REFERENCE DOCUMENTS

2.1 ISO 9001:2000 Paragraphs 4.2.1, 4.2.2, 4.2.3 and 4.2.4

2.2 Quality Manual Section B, Quality Management System

2.3 Quality Manual Section C, Planning

2.4 *{Quality System Procedure - Document and Data Control}*

2.5 *{Quality System Procedure - Control of Quality Records}*

3.0 DEFINITIONS

See Section T, Glossary, for definitions of italicized terms.

4.0 QMS REQUIREMENTS

4.1 Documentation Requirements - General (4.2.1)

The *{Company Name}* QMS documentation includes:

a) documented statements of a quality policy, per Reference 2.2, and quality objectives, per Reference 2.3,

b) this Quality Manual (see paragraph 4.2 below),

c) the documented procedures referenced within each Section of this Manual, where required by the ISO 9001:2000 Standard,

d) documents needed by the *{Company Name}* organization to ensure the effective planning, operation, and control of its processes, and

e) records required by the ISO 9001:2000 Standard (see paragraph 4.3 below).

{COMPANY NAME & Logo} QUALITY SYSTEM MANUAL

Title:	Prepared By/Date:	Approved By/Date:	Effective Date:	Page: 2 of 4
Documentation Requirements	Reviewed By/Date:	Approved By/Date:	Revision No.	Section No. G

4.2 Quality Manual (4.2.2)

The Quality System Manual provides an overall description of the scope of the Quality Management System, the general quality policies, quality objectives and documented procedures (referenced by this manual), and a description of the interaction between the processes of the Quality Management System (QMS). The Quality System Manual is subject to internal and external controlled distribution.

{Company Name} has established and maintains this Quality Manual that includes:

a) the scope of the QMS (see paragraph 4 within each Section of this Manual), as it applies to {product(s)/service(s)}. The justification(s) for exclusion(s) claimed under Clause 1.2 of the ISO 9001:2000 Standard is/are detailed below:

  1) *{List the ISO 9001:2000 related exclusions here and the associated justification for each. Also state this in the appropriate section of the Quality Manual. See the following example:}*

  2) *{Company Name}* does not hold any customer supplied property for exclusion of Element 7.l4.4, Customer Property.

b) inclusion or reference to the documented procedures established for the QMS, and a description of the interactions between processes of the QMS (see 4.5).

4.3 Control of Documents (4.2.3)

Documents required by the QMS are controlled as defined in Reference 2.4 above. Records are a special type of document and are controlled in accordance with Reference 2.5 above (see paragraph 4.4 below). Reference 2.5 defines the controls needed

a) for approval of documents for adequacy prior to issue,

b) for review and update as necessary and re-approval of documents,

c) for ensuring changes and the current revision status of documents are identified,

Title:	Prepared By/Date:	Approved By/Date:	Effective Date:	Page:
				3 of 4
Documentation Requirements	Reviewed By/Date:	Approved By/Date:	Revision No.	Section No. G

d)   for ensuring that relevant versions of applicable documents are available at points of use,

e)   for ensuring that documents remain legible and readily identifiable,

f)   for ensuring that documents of external origin are identified and their distribution is controlled, and

g)   for preventing the unintended use of obsolete documents, and to apply suitable identification to them if they are retained for any purpose.

A Master List has been established to identify the current revision of documents in order to control the issuance and revision status of the documents.

{If other than a Master List is used to track revisions, so state the method here and delete the preceding sentence.}

4.4   Control of Records (4.2.4)

Records have been established and are maintained to provide evidence of conformity to requirements and of the effective operation of the QMS. Records are maintained legible, readily identifiable, and retrievable. Reference 2.5 defines the controls needed for the identification, storage, protection, retrieval, retention time, and disposition of records.

4.5   Documentation Structure

The diagram below outlines the structure of *{Company Name}*'s QMS:

The Levels of documentation and instructions include:

Level 1 – Quality System Manual – A description of *{Company Name}*'s method of establishing, implementing, and maintaining a Quality Management System that meets the requirements of the ISO 9001:2000 Standard.

Level 2 – Quality System Procedures – Procedures which describe the overall activities corresponding to the major sections of this Quality System Manual.

Level 3 – *{List and describe each level of the Quality Management System as it is applied to your organization. The following structure shows the interrelationship between the parts of the QMS.}*

{COMPANY NAME & Logo}			QUALITY SYSTEM MANUAL		
Title: Documentation Requirements	Prepared By/Date:	Approved By/Date:	Effective Date:	Page: 4 of 4	
	Reviewed By/Date:	Approved By/Date:	Revision No.	Section No. G	

{Modify the following diagram or use some other method to accurately display the interrelationship between all parts of the Quality Management System.}

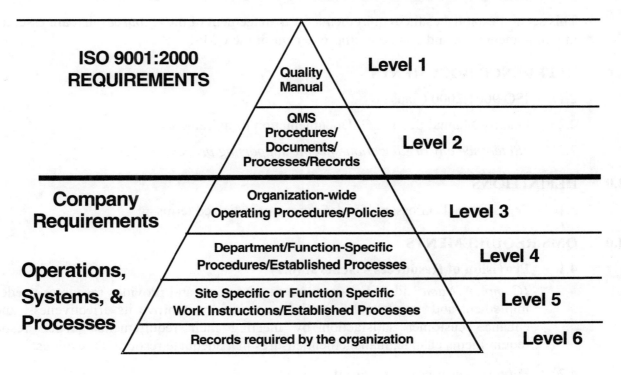

5.0 RESPONSIBILITIES

{State the responsibilities for the overall document control requirements for each requirement in this QSM Section. See the following example:}

The manager of each department is responsible for ensuring that issues of appropriate documents in their area are available for use, pertinent and periodically reviewed for removal of all obsolete issues.

6.0 RECORDS

{Identify and state the location of the associated records. See the following example:}

Record and retention requirements are contained in each respective procedure.

{COMPANY NAME & Logo}			QUALITY SYSTEM MANUAL		
Title: Resource Management	Prepared By/Date:	Approved By/Date:	Effective Date:	Page: 1 of 3	
	Reviewed By/Date:	Approved By/Date:	Revision No.	Section No. H	
Applicability: This section is applicable to all *{Company Name}* operations.					

1.0   PURPOSE

This section establishes the requirements for management of the *resources* that are essential to the implementation and continual improvement of the QMS.

2.0   REFERENCE DOCUMENTS

2.1   ISO 9001:2000 Clause 6

2.2   Quality Manual Section G, Documentation Requirements

2.3   *{Reference any organization-specific supporting procedures here.}*

3.0   DEFINITIONS

3.1   See Section T, Glossary, for definitions of italicized terms.

4.0   QMS REQUIREMENTS

4.1   Provision of Resources - General (6.1)

{Company Name} identifies resource requirements and provides resources needed to implement and maintain the QMS, to continually improve its effectiveness, and to enhance customer satisfaction by meeting their requirements. When resource requirements change, management ensures that adequate resources are allocated.

4.2   Human Resources – General (6.2.1)

All employees are verified to be competent in their specific job assignments on the basis of appropriate *education, training, skills,* and *experience.* All employees receive instruction in the QMS applicable to their specific work assignments. Personnel performing certain specialized activities identified and addressed in the QMS are formally qualified to perform those designated activities.

{COMPANY NAME & Logo}   QUALITY SYSTEM MANUAL

Title:	Prepared By/Date:	Approved By/Date:	Effective Date:	Page: 2 of 3
Resource Management	Reviewed By/Date:	Approved By/Date:	Revision No.	Section No. H

4.3 Competence, Awareness and Training (6.2.2)

In order to ensure continual improvement and customer satisfaction, *{Company Name}*:

a) determines the necessary competence for personnel performing work affecting product quality,

b) provides training or takes other actions in order to satisfy these needs,

c) evaluates the effectiveness of the actions taken,

d) ensures that its personnel are aware of the relevance and importance of their activities and how they contribute to the achievement of the quality objectives, and

e) maintains appropriate records of education, training, skills and experience, per Reference 2.2 (See paragraph 6.0 below).

> Modify as necessary to reflect how the organization accomplishes this function.

The *{Name of Department}* screens all applicants to ensure that all personnel are adequately qualified on the basis of appropriate skills assessment, education, training, and/or experience required.

As part of the orientation process, all new employees receive the following instruction as a minimum:

{List as appropriate}

4.4 Infrastructure (6.3)

> Customize paragraph but maintain the main content items.

{Company Name} determines, provides, and maintains the infrastructure needed to achieve conformity to *product* requirements. The infrastructure includes

a) buildings, workspace and associated utilities,

b) *process equipment* (hardware and software), and

c) *supporting services* (such as *transport* or communication)

4.5 Work Environment (6.4)

> Customize paragraph but maintain the main content items.

{Company Name} determines and manages the work environment needed to achieve conformity to product requirements.

{COMPANY NAME & Logo}   QUALITY SYSTEM MANUAL

Title:	Prepared By/Date:	Approved By/Date:	Effective Date:	Page: 3 of 3
Resource Management	Reviewed By/Date:	Approved By/Date:	Revision No.	Section No. H

5.0   RESPONSIBILITIES

{State the responsibilities for training requirements, identification, and implementation. Modify the following example as necessary.}

Top management is responsible for ensuring employee competence, awareness, and training, and to establish the infrastructure and work environment needed to achieve conformity to product requirements.

The *{Name of Department or Function}* is responsible for documenting the training of employees as requirements are identified. Job descriptions may be used as guidelines for training requirements.

6.0   RECORDS

{Identify training records that are maintained and state the locations of these records. Modify the following example as necessary.}

Data on education, training, skills and experience is recorded and maintained by the *{Name of Department or Function}* in accordance with Section G of this Manual.

{COMPANY NAME & Logo}		QUALITY SYSTEM MANUAL			
Title: Product Realization	Prepared By/Date:	Approved By/Date:	Effective Date:	Page: 1 of 2	
	Reviewed By/Date:	Approved By/Date:	Revision No.	Section No. I	
Applicability: This section is applicable to all *{Company Name}* operations.					

1.0 PURPOSE

This section establishes the requirements for planning and developing the processes needed for *product realization*. Planning of product realization is consistent with the requirements of all other sections of the Quality System Manual.

2.0 REFERENCE DOCUMENTS

2.1 ISO 9001:2000 Clause 7.1

2.2 Quality Manual Section B, QMS General Requirements

2.3 Quality Manual Section C, Planning

2.4 Quality Manual Section G, Documentation Requirements

2.5 Quality Manual Section H, Resource Management

2.6 Quality Manual Section J, Customer-Related Processes

2.7 Quality Manual Section K, Design and Development

2.8 Quality Manual Section M, Production and Service Provision

2.9 Quality Manual Section N, Control of Monitoring and Measuring Devices

2.9 Quality Manual Section P, Monitoring and Measurement

2.10 *{Reference any organization-specific supporting procedures here.}*

3.0 DEFINITIONS

3.1 See Section T, Glossary, for definitions of italicized terms.

4.0 QMS REQUIREMENTS

4.1 Planning of Product Realization (7.1)

{State what your Company does in words. This should match the scope of the ISO Certificate. See the following example:}

{Company Name} plans and develops the processes needed for product realization. Planning of product realization is consistent with the requirements of the other processes of the QMS defined in Reference 2.2.

{Include a simple flow chart that shows the overall process if desired to help clarify the Product Realization Process.}

{COMPANY NAME & Logo}				QUALITY SYSTEM MANUAL	
Title: Product Realization	Prepared By/Date:	Approved By/Date:	Effective Date:	Page: 2 of 2	
	Reviewed By/Date:	Approved By/Date:	Revision No.	Section No. I	

In planning product realization, *{Company Name}* determines the following:

<table>
<tr><td>

If any items are not appropriate, modify or delete.

</td><td>

a)   quality objectives and requirements for the product, per References 2.3 and 2.6;

b)   the need to establish processes, documents, and provide resources specific to the product, per References 2.2, 2.4, and 2.5;

c)   required verification, validation, monitoring, inspection, and test activities specific to the product and the criteria for product acceptance, per References 2.7, 2.8, 2.9, and 2.10;

</td></tr>
</table>

d)   records needed to provide evidence that the realization processes and resulting product meet the requirements, per Reference 2.5.

The output of this planning is in a form suitable for *{Company Name}*'s method of operations.

5.0   RESPONSIBILITIES

{State here what Functions have the responsibility for Product Realization.}

6.0   RECORDS

The *{responsible Department or Function}* is responsible for the records needed to provide evidence that the product realization process and resulting product meet requirements.

{COMPANY NAME & Logo}			QUALITY SYSTEM MANUAL		
Title: Customer-Related Processes	Prepared By/Date:	Approved By/Date:	Effective Date:	Page: 1 of 3	
	Reviewed By/Date:	Approved By/Date:	Revision No.	Section No. J	
Applicability: This section is applicable to all *{Company Name}* operations.					

1.0 PURPOSE

The purpose of this section is to determine, review, and communicate the product requirements for customer-related processes.

2.0 REFERENCE DOCUMENTS

2.1 ISO 9001:2000 Clause 7.1

2.2 Quality Manual Section G, Documentation Requirements

3.0 DEFINITIONS

3.1 See Section T, Glossary, for definitions of italicized terms.

4.0 QMS REQUIREMENTS

{Modify the following introductory paragraph to fit the organization:}

{Company Name} has established procedures detailing the methods for reviewing proposals and contracts to ensure that *{Company Name}* has the capability to meet all customer-specified requirements.

4.1 Determination of Requirements Related to the *Product* (7.2.1)

{Customize the following paragraph based on the product or service output of the organization:}

{Company Name} determines the requirements specified by the customer, including the requirements for delivery and post-delivery activities. Requirements not stated by the customer but necessary for specified use or intended use are reviewed and resolved prior to the delivery of the *{product or service}*. Any statutory or regulatory requirements are determined and acted upon by *{Company Name}*.

{Add any additional product-related requirements here. Modify the following example to fit the organization:}

Contracts are reviewed, as a minimum, for pricing, quantities, and ship-dates by the Sales Department before acceptance. Appropriate departments are consulted as necessary during the Contract Review.

Title:	Prepared By/Date:	Approved By/Date:	Effective Date:	Page: 2 of 3
Customer Related Processes	Reviewed By/Date:	Approved By/Date:	Revision No.	Section No. J

4.2　Review of Requirements Related to the *Product* (7.2.2)

{Modify the following description of what the organization does to match that which is done. Address all items listed below:}

{Company Name} reviews the requirements related to its product. This review is conducted prior to *{Company Name}*'s commitment to supply the product to the customer (e.g. submission of tenders, acceptance of contracts or orders, acceptance of changes to contracts or orders) and ensures that

a)　　product requirements are defined,

b)　　contract or order requirements differing from those previously expressed are resolved, and

c)　　the organization has the ability to meet the defined requirements.

Records of the results of the review and actions arising from the review are maintained per Reference 2.2 (see paragraph 6.0 below).

Where the customer provides no documented statement of requirement, the customer requirements are confirmed by *{Company Name}* before acceptance.

Where product requirements are changed, *{Company Name}* ensures that relevant documents are amended and that relevant personnel are made aware of the changed requirements. Any exceptions to the customer specifications shall be agreed upon with the customer prior to accepting an order or prior to finalizing a contract.

4.3　Customer Communication (7.2.3)

{Company Name} determines and implements effective arrangements for communicating with customers in relation to product information, inquiries, contracts, or order handling, including amendments, contract changes, and customer feedback, including customer complaints.

5.0　RESPONSIBILITIES

{State the responsibilities for customer related processes here. Modify the following as necessary to reflect actual responsibility.}

The responsibility for the determination of requirements related to the product is that of the *{Name of Function(s) or Department(s)}*.

The responsibility for the review of requirements related to the product is that of the *{Name of Function(s) or Department(s)}*.

{COMPANY NAME & Logo}			QUALITY SYSTEM MANUAL		
Title: **Customer Related Processes**	Prepared By/Date:	Approved By/Date:	Effective Date:	Page: 3 of 3	
	Reviewed By/Date:	Approved By/Date:	Revision No.	Section No. J	

The responsibility for Customer Communication is that of the *{Name of Department(s) or Function(s)}*.

| Example |

The Sales Department and the National Order Center share the responsibility for determination and review of the requirements related to the product as well as customer communications.

6.0 RECORDS

The results of Contract Reviews are documented and filed in the *{Name of Department(s) or Function(s)}*.

{COMPANY NAME & Logo}			QUALITY SYSTEM MANUAL		
Title: Design and Development	Prepared By/Date:	Approved By/Date:	Effective Date:	Page: 1 of 3	
	Reviewed By/Date:	Approved By/Date:	Revision No.	Section No. K	
Applicability: This section is applicable to all *{Company Name}* operations.					

1.0 PURPOSE

This section establishes the requirements for the design and development of *product* related to *{state that for which the Design and Development effort is applicable, such as the product or business}*.

2.0 REFERENCE DOCUMENTS

2.1 ISO 9001:2000 Clause 7.2

2.2 Quality Manual Section G, Documentation Requirements

2.3 Quality Manual Section J, Customer-Related Processes

3.0 DEFINITIONS

3.1 See Section T, Glossary, for definitions of italicized terms.

4.0 QMS REQUIREMENTS

4.1 Design and Development Planning (7.3.1)

{Company Name} plans and controls the design and development of product. During the design and development planning, *{Company Name}* determines

a) the design and development stages,

b) the review, verification, and validation that are appropriate to each design and development stage, and

c) the responsibilities and authorities for design and development.

{Company Name} manages the interfaces between different groups involved in design and development to ensure effective communication and clear assignment of responsibility.

Planning output is updated, as appropriate, as the design and development progresses.

{COMPANY NAME & Logo} QUALITY SYSTEM MANUAL

Title:	Prepared By/Date:	Approved By/Date:	Effective Date:	Page: 2 of 3
Design and Development	Reviewed By/Date:	Approved By/Date:	Revision No.	Section No. K

4.2 Design and Development Inputs (7.3.2)

Inputs relating to product requirements are determined and records maintained per References 2.2 and 2.3 (see paragraph 6.0 below). Inputs include

a)   functional and performance requirements,

b)   applicable statutory and regulatory requirements,

c)   where applicable, information derived from previous similar designs, and

d)   other requirements essential for design and development.

These inputs are reviewed for adequacy to ensure that requirements are complete, unambiguous, and not in conflict with each other.

4.3 Design and Development Outputs (7.3.3)

The outputs of design and development are provided in a form that enables verification against the design and development input and is approved prior to release. Design and development outputs

a)   meet the input requirements for design and development,

b)   provide appropriate information for purchasing, production, and for service provision,

c)   contain or reference product acceptance criteria, and

d)   specify the characteristics of the product that are essential for its safe and proper use.

4.4 Design and Development Review (7.3.4)

At suitable stages, systematic reviews of design and development are performed in accordance with planned arrangements, per paragraph 4.1 above,

a)   to evaluate the ability of the results of design and development to fulfill requirements, and

b)   to identify any problems and propose necessary actions.

Participants in such reviews include representatives of functions concerned with the design and development stage(s) being reviewed.

Records of the results of the reviews and any necessary actions are maintained per Reference 2.2 (see paragraph 6.0 below).

Title:	Prepared By/Date:	Approved By/Date:	Effective Date:	Page:
				3 of 3
Design and Development	Reviewed By/Date:	Approved By/Date:	Revision No.	Section No. K

4.5　Design and Development Verification (7.3.5)

Verification is performed in accordance with planned arrangements, per paragraph 4.1 above, to ensure that the design and development outputs have satisfied the design and development input requirements. Records of the results of the verification and any necessary actions are maintained per Reference 2.2 (see paragraph 6.0 below).

4.6　Design and Development Validation (7.3.6)

Design and development validation is performed in accordance with planned arrangements, per paragraph 4.1 above, to ensure that the resulting product is capable of meeting the requirements for the specified application or intended use, where known. Wherever practicable, validation is completed prior to the delivery or implementation of the product. Records of the results of validation and any necessary actions are maintained per Reference 2.2 (see paragraph 6.0 below).

4.7　Control of Design and Development Changes (7.3.7)

Design and development changes are identified and records are maintained. The changes are reviewed, verified, and validated, as appropriate, and approved before implementation. The review of design and development changes includes evaluation of the effect of the changes on constituent parts and product already delivered. Records of the results of the review of changes and any necessary actions are maintained per Reference 2.2 (see paragraph 6.0 below).

5.0　RESPONSIBILITIES

{State here the responsibility for the various Design and Development functions. The following example statement is given for reference.}

R&D has the responsibility for effective planning, design inputs, design outputs, review, verification, validation, and changes associated with the design and development for *{Company Name}* products.

6.0　RECORDS

{State here what records are maintained and who is responsible for such. See the following example.}

Records associated with product design are maintained in accordance with Section G of this manual and are the responsibility of the *{Name of Function}* Department.

{COMPANY NAME & Logo}			QUALITY SYSTEM MANUAL		
Title: Purchasing	Prepared By/Date:	Approved By/Date:	Effective Date:	Page: 1 of 2	
	Reviewed By/Date:	Approved By/Date:	Revision No.	Section No. L	
Applicability: This section is applicable to all *{Company Name}* operations.					

1.0 PURPOSE

This section establishes the requirements for verifying that *purchased product* conforms to the specified purchasing agreements.

2.0 REFERENCE DOCUMENTS

2.1 ISO 9001:2000 Clause 7.4

2.2 Quality Manual Section G, Documentation Requirements

3.0 DEFINITIONS

3.1 See Section 20, Glossary, for definitions of italicized terms.

4.0 QMS REQUIREMENTS

4.1 Purchasing Process (7.4.1)

{Company Name} ensures that purchased product conforms to specified purchase requirements. The type and extent of control applied to the supplier and the purchased product is dependent upon the effect of the purchased product on subsequent product realization or the final product. *{Company Name}* evaluates and selects suppliers based on their ability to supply product in accordance with *{Company Name}*'s requirements. Criteria for selection, evaluation, and re-evaluation are established. Records of the results of evaluations and any necessary actions arising from the evaluation are maintained per Reference 2.2.

4.2 Purchasing Information (7.4.2)

Purchasing information describes the product to be purchased including, where appropriate,

a) requirements for approval of product, procedures, processes, and equipment,

b) requirements for qualification of personnel, and

c) quality management system requirements.

{Company Name} ensures the adequacy of specified purchase requirements prior to their communication to the supplier.

{COMPANY NAME & Logo}			QUALITY SYSTEM MANUAL		
Title: Purchasing	Prepared By/Date:	Approved By/Date:	Effective Date:	Page: 2 of 2	
	Reviewed By/Date:	Approved By/Date:	Revision No.	Section No. L	

4.3 Verification of Purchased Product (7.4.3)

{Company Name} establishes and implements the inspection or other activities necessary for ensuring that purchased product meets specified purchase requirements. Where the organization or its customer intends to perform verification on the supplier's premises, *{Company Name}* states the intended verification arrangements and method of product release in the purchasing information.

5.0 RESPONSIBILITIES

{State the responsibilities for the Purchasing Process, Purchasing Information, and the Verification of Purchased Product here.}

6.0 RECORDS

Purchasing related records are maintained in accordance with Reference 2.2 above.

{COMPANY NAME & Logo}			QUALITY SYSTEM MANUAL		
Title:	Prepared By/Date:	Approved By/Date:	Effective Date:		Page: 1 of 5
Production and Service Provision	Reviewed By/Date:	Approved By/Date:	Revision No.		Section No. M
Applicability: This section is applicable to all *{Company Name}* operations.					

1.0 PURPOSE

This section establishes the requirements for *production and service provision* related to the *{state the scope of ISO certification here (describe the Company's business, specifically detailing the scope of the ISO certification)}*.

2.0 REFERENCE DOCUMENTS

2.1 ISO 9001:2000 Clause 7.5

2.2 Quality Manual Section G, Documentation Requirements

2.3 Quality Manual Section H, Resource Management

2.4 Quality Manual Section J, Customer-Related Processes

2.5 Quality Manual Section N, Control of Monitoring and Measuring Devices

2.6 Quality Manual Section P, Monitoring

{Add Operating Procedure References here that apply to this Section.}

3.0 DEFINITIONS

3.1 See Section T, Glossary, for definitions of italicized terms.

4.0 QMS REQUIREMENTS

4.1 Control of Production and Service Provision (7.5.1)

{Company Name} plans and carries out production and service provision under controlled conditions. Controlled conditions include, as applicable

a) the availability of information that describes the characteristics of the product, per Reference 2.4,

b) the availability of work instructions, as necessary, per Reference 2.2,

c) the use of suitable equipment, per Reference 2.3,

d) the availability and use of monitoring and measuring devices, per Reference 2.5,

e) the implementation of monitoring and measurement, per Reference 2.6, and

f) the implementation of release, delivery, and post-delivery activities, per References 2.4 and 2.6.

{COMPANY NAME & Logo}			QUALITY SYSTEM MANUAL		
Title: Production and Service Provision	Prepared By/Date:	Approved By/Date:	Effective Date:	Page: 2 of 5	
	Reviewed By/Date:	Approved By/Date:	Revision No.	Section No. M	

{Add descriptive paragraph here that describes how the procedures/work instructions are communicated to the required operations. If there are additional documents that control production, list them here as well. }

Example	Quality Assurance, Manufacturing Engineering, and/or Production communicate work instructions to required operations functions. In addition to work instructions, illustrations and samples may also be provided to show workmanship criteria.

4.2 Validation of Processes for Production and Service Provision (7.5.2)

{Company Name} validates any processes for production and service provision where the resulting output cannot be verified by subsequent monitoring or measurement. This includes any processes where deficiencies become apparent only after the product is in use or the service has been delivered. Validation demonstrates the ability of these processes to achieve planned results. *{Company Name}* establishes arrangements for these processes including, as applicable,

a)   defined criteria for review and approval of the processes,

b)   approval of equipment and qualification of personnel,

c)   use of specific methods and procedures,

d)   requirements for records, per Reference 2.2, and

e)   revalidation.

{Describe further how Validation occurs relative to the Production and Service Provision. See examples provided on next page.}

{COMPANY NAME & Logo}			QUALITY SYSTEM MANUAL		
Title: Production and Service Provision	Prepared By/Date:	Approved By/Date:	Effective Date:	Page: 3 of 5	
	Reviewed By/Date:	Approved By/Date:	Revision No.	Section No. M	

Examples

Processes are periodically reviewed by the Manufacturing Engineering Department through Maintenance Records, Statistical Charting, and First Part Inspections.

In-process functional tests are uniquely identified by the individual performing the tests. Test results are documented in accordance with control plans or inspection instructions.

Final inspection includes verification that appropriate in-process inspections and tests are performed. No product is to be sent to stock without an acceptance stamp affixed.

Final inspection is performed as described in control plans and/or inspection instructions to ensure that all customer-specified requirements are satisfied.

Inspection and test results are documented in the form of inspection and test reports. Final inspection and test results are also recorded.

Any product found to be nonconforming is handled as described in Section 16 of this manual.

4.3   Identification and Traceability (7.5.3)

Where appropriate, {Company Name} identifies the product by suitable means throughout product realization. This includes identification of product status with respect to monitoring and measurement requirements. Where traceability is a requirement, {Company Name} controls and records the unique identification of the product, per Reference 2.2 (See paragraph 6.0 below).

{Add additional descriptive paragraphs that describe the identification and traceability provided by the company of product as may be applicable. If this section is not applicable, such as in the case of a Service Company, so state.}

Title:	Prepared By/Date:	Approved By/Date:	Effective Date:	Page: 4 of 5
Production and Service Provision	Reviewed By/Date:	Approved By/Date:	Revision No.	Section No. M

4.4 Customer Property (7.5.4)

{Company Name} exercises care with customer property while it is under the organization's control or being used by the organization. Processes are in place to identify, verify, protect, and safeguard customer property provided for use or incorporation into the product. If any customer property is lost, damaged, or otherwise found to be unsuitable for use, this situation is reported to the customer and records maintained, per Reference 2.2 (see paragraph 6.0 below).

4.5 Preservation of Product (7.5.5)

{Company Name} preserves the conformity of product during internal processing and delivery to the intended destination. This preservation includes identification, handling, packaging, storage, and protection of all tangible aspects of our product. Preservation also applies to the constituent parts of the product.

{Add additional paragraphs here to describe or reference an associated procedure for the handling, storage, packaging, preservation, and delivery requirements of the company as may be appropriate.}

5.0 RESPONSIBILITIES

{State the responsibilities for paragraphs 4.1 through 4.5. Combine the responsibility statements of multiple paragraphs as applicable. Include:

Control of production and service provision,

Validation of processes for production and service provision,

Identification and traceability,

Customer property, and

Preservation of product.}

{COMPANY NAME & Logo}			QUALITY SYSTEM MANUAL		
Title: Production and Service Provision	Prepared By/Date:	Approved By/Date:	Effective Date:	Page: 5 of 5	
	Reviewed By/Date:	Approved By/Date:	Revision No.	Section No. M	

Plant Management is responsible for validation of processes for production and service provision, identification and traceability, and preservation of product.

Servicing of the products after installation is the responsibility of the Service Department.

Examples

The Quality Assurance Department is responsible for development of control plans with input from other departments as required.

The Shipping Department is responsible for delivery of products to the customer and for choosing a carrier to ensure that the product reaches the customer in good condition.

6.0   RECORDS

{State what the quality records are and where maintained for the Production and Service Provision or refer to an appropriate procedure that does so. See the following examples.}

The below-listed documents are maintained in accordance with Section G of this Manual:

The unique identification of the product for traceability purposes is *{state where}.*

The notification to the customer of any of their property that is lost, damaged, or otherwise found to be unsuitable for use is recorded *{state where}.*

{COMPANY NAME & Logo}			QUALITY SYSTEM MANUAL	
Title: Control of Monitoring and Measuring Devices	Prepared By/Date:	Approved By/Date:	Effective Date:	Page: 1 of 2
	Reviewed By/Date:	Approved By/Date:	Revision No.	Section No. N
Applicability: This section is applicable to all *{Company Name}* operations.				

1.0 PURPOSE

This section establishes requirements for monitoring and measurement to be undertaken by *{Company Name}*, and the monitoring and measuring devices needed to provide evidence of conformity of product to determined requirements.

2.0 REFERENCE DOCUMENTS

2.1 ISO 9001:2000 Clause 7.6

2.2 Quality Policy Manual Section G, Documentation Requirements

2.3 Quality Policy Manual Section J, Customer-Related Processes

{List additional, related Operating Procedure references here.}

3.0 DEFINITIONS

3.1 See Section T, Glossary, for definitions of italicized terms.

4.0 QMS REQUIREMENTS (7.6)

{Company Name} determines the monitoring and measurement to be undertaken and the monitoring and measuring devices needed to provide evidence of conformity of product to determined requirements, per Reference 2.3. *{Company Name}* establishes processes to ensure that monitoring and measurement can be carried out and are carried out in a manner that is consistent with the monitoring and measurement requirements.

Where necessary to ensure valid results, measuring equipment is

a) calibrated or verified at specified intervals, or prior to use, against measurement standards traceable to international or national measurement standards. Where no such standards exist, the basis used for calibration or verification is recorded;

b) adjusted or re-adjusted as necessary;

c) identified to enable the calibration status to be determined;

d) safeguarded from adjustments that would invalidate the measurement result;

e) protected from damage and deterioration during handling, maintenance, and storage.

Title:	Prepared By/Date:	Approved By/Date:	Effective Date:	Page: 2 of 2
Control of Monitoring and Measuring Devices	Reviewed By/Date:	Approved By/Date:	Revision No.	Section No. N

In addition, *{Company Name}* assesses and records the validity of the previous measuring results when the equipment is found not to conform to requirements, and takes appropriate action on the equipment and any product affected. Records of the results of calibration and verification are maintained in accordance with Reference 2.2 (see paragraph 6.0 below).

When used in the monitoring and measurement of specified requirements, the ability of computer software to satisfy the intended application is confirmed prior to initial use and reconfirmed as necessary.

5.0 RESPONSIBILITIES

{State the responsible function for the Control of Monitoring and Measuring Devices here. See the following two examples:}

The Quality Assurance Department is responsible for maintaining equipment calibration, per *{procedure reference number}*.

It is the responsibility of everyone using the measuring and test equipment to verify that the calibration status is current.

6.0 RECORDS

{State the related records associated with the Control of Monitoring and Measuring Devices here or reference where the records are so stated. See the following example:}

The results of calibration and verification are recorded on documents maintained in accordance with the requirements of *{procedure reference number}*.

{COMPANY NAME & Logo}			QUALITY SYSTEM MANUAL		
Title: Measurement, Analysis, and Improvement	Prepared By/Date:	Approved By/Date:	Effective Date:		Page: 1 of 2
	Reviewed By/Date:	Approved By/Date:	Revision No.		Section No. O
Applicability: This section is applicable to all *{Company Name}* operations.					

1.0   PURPOSE

This section establishes the *requirements* for the measurement, analysis, and improvement of the Quality Management System (QMS) processes.

2.0   REFERENCE DOCUMENTS

2.1   ISO 9001:2000 Clause 8.1

{Add additional references of associated procedures that deal with this Section.}

3.0   DEFINITIONS

3.1   See Section T, Glossary, for definitions of italicized terms.

4.0   QMS REQUIREMENTS (8.1)

{Company Name} plans and implements the monitoring, measurement, analysis and improvement processes needed to demonstrate conformity of the product and to ensure conformity of the QMS.

This includes the determination of applicable methods, including statistical techniques, and the extent of their use.

Modify these paragraphs as necessary to fit your specific company, but include the main content requirements.

{Company Name} uses *{list that which is used, such as Cost of Quality Reports, Scrap Reports, Nonconformance Reports, Final Inspection, In-Process Inspection, product audits, Statistical Analysis, Functional Product Analysis, Deviation Reports, Material Review Reports, and Monitoring of Production Equipment Maintenance}* to ensure product conformity to requirements.

{Company Name} ensures conformity to the QMS through internal and external audits, management reviews, and analysis of data from nonconformance reports and customer feedback.

{Company Name} uses Quality Assurance Reports, the results of internal and external audits, nonconformances, Corrective and Preventive Action reports, and customer feedback to continually improve the effectiveness of the QMS.

{Company Name} communicates the measurements and analysis for improvement to the affected responsible party(ies) for appropriate action.

{COMPANY NAME & Logo}			QUALITY SYSTEM MANUAL	
Title: Measurement, Analysis and Improvement	Prepared By/Date:	Approved By/Date:	Effective Date:	Page: 2 of 2
	Reviewed By/Date:	Approved By/Date:	Revision No.	Section No. O

5.0   RESPONSIBILITIES

<table>
<tr><td>

Customize
paragraph 5.0
as necessary.

</td><td>

The *{Name of Department or Function}* is responsible for monitoring, measuring, and analyzing the data to ensure product conformity to and continual improvement of the QMS.

The *{Name of Department or Function}* recommends action(s) based on the results of the monitoring, measuring, and analysis results dependent upon the criticality of the finding. The determination of applicable methods, including statistical techniques, and the extent of their use is the responsibility of the *{Name of Department or Function}*.

Management is responsible to follow through on recommended action(s).

</td></tr>
</table>

6.0   RECORDS

<table>
<tr><td>

Customize
paragraph 6.0
as necessary.

</td><td>

Records are determined and maintained by the *{Name of Department or Function}*.

</td></tr>
</table>

{COMPANY NAME & Logo}			QUALITY SYSTEM MANUAL	
Title: Monitoring and Measurement	Prepared By/Date:	Approved By/Date:	Effective Date:	Page: 1 of 3
	Reviewed By/Date:	Approved By/Date:	Revision No.	Section No. P
Applicability: This section is applicable to all *{Company Name}* operations.				

1.0 PURPOSE

This section establishes the requirements for monitoring and measuring the performance of the QMS.

2.0 REFERENCE DOCUMENTS

2.1 ISO 9001:2000 Clause 8.2

2.2 Quality Manual Section G, Documentation Requirements

2.3 Quality Manual Section I, Product Realization

2.4 Quality Manual Section S, Improvement

2.5 *{"Quality System Procedure - QMS Audits" (include the QMS Internal Audit Procedure reference here)}*

3.0 DEFINITIONS

3.1 See Section T, Glossary, for definitions of italicized terms.

4.0 QMS REQUIREMENTS

4.1 Customer Satisfaction (8.2.1)

As one of the measurements of the performance of the QMS, *{Company Name}* monitors information relating to customer perception as to whether or not the organization has met customer requirements. The methods for obtaining and using this information include *{list the methods here in the context of the paragraph. See the following examples:}*

customer surveys, customer feedback, field service inspection reports, and evaluation of warranty feedback.

Title:	Prepared By/Date:	Approved By/Date:	Effective Date:	Page: 2 of 3
Monitoring and Measurement	Reviewed By/Date:	Approved By/Date:	Revision No.	Section No. P

4.2   Internal Audit (8.2.2)

{Company Name} conducts internal audits at planned intervals to determine whether the QMS

a)   conforms to the planned arrangements, per Reference 2.3, to the requirements of the ISO 9001:2000 Standard, and to the QMS requirements established within this Manual and

b)   is effectively implemented and maintained.

An audit program is planned, taking into consideration the status and importance of the processes and areas to be audited, as well as the results of previous audits. The audit criteria, scope, frequency, and methods are defined, per Reference 2.5. Selection of auditors and the conduct of audits ensure objectivity and impartiality of the audit process. Auditors do not audit their own work.

The responsibilities and requirements for planning and conducting audits, and for reporting results and maintaining records, per Reference 2.2 (see paragraph 6.0 below), are defined in Reference 2.5.

The management responsible for the area being audited ensures that actions are taken without undue delay to eliminate detected nonconformities and their causes. Follow-up activities include the verification of the actions taken and the reporting of verification results, per Reference 2.4.

All elements of the QMS are audited a minimum of once per year.

Audits are conducted in accordance with Internal Audit Procedures, as per Reference 2.5.

The responsibilities and requirements for planning and conducting audits, and for reporting results and maintaining records, per Reference 2.2 (see paragraph 6.0 below), are defined in Reference 2.5.

The management responsible for the area being audited ensures that actions are taken without undue delay to eliminate detected nonconformities and their causes. Follow-up activities include the verification of the actions taken and the reporting of verification results, per Reference 2.4.

Title:	Prepared By/Date:	Approved By/Date:	Effective Date:	Page:
				3 of 3
Monitoring and Measurement	Reviewed By/Date:	Approved By/Date:	Revision No.	Section No. P

4.3 Monitoring and Measurement of Processes (8.2.3)

{Company Name} applies suitable methods for the monitoring and, where applicable, measurement of the QMS processes. These methods demonstrate the ability of the processes to achieve planned results. When planned results are not achieved, correction and corrective action is taken, as appropriate, to ensure conformity of the product.

4.4 Monitoring and Measurement of Product (8.2.4)

{Company Name} monitors and measures the characteristics of the product to verify that product requirements have been met. This is carried out at appropriate stages of the product realization process in accordance with the planned arrangements, per Reference 2.3.

Evidence of conformity with the acceptance criteria is maintained, per Reference 2.2 (see paragraph 6.0 below). These records indicate the person(s) authorizing release of product.

Product release and service delivery do not proceed until all the planned arrangements have been satisfactorily completed, per Reference 2.3, unless otherwise approved by a relevant authority, and where applicable by the customer.

5.0 RESPONSIBILITIES

The *{Name of Department or Function}* is responsible for all aspects of internal audits (see reference 2.5).

> Customize paragraph 5.0 as necessary.

The *{Name of Department or Function}*, in conjunction with {manufacturing}, is responsible for monitoring and measurement processes, and follow-up action(s).

Management is responsible for action(s) as a result of the internal audits.

The *{Name of Department or Function}* is responsible for all aspects of customer satisfaction.

6.0 RECORDS

The *{Name of Department/Function}* maintains all monitoring and measurement records.

> Customize paragraph 6.0 as necessary.

The *{Name of Department/Function}* maintains all customer satisfaction records in accordance with Section G of this Manual:

{COMPANY NAME & Logo}			QUALITY SYSTEM MANUAL		
Title: Control of Nonconforming Product	Prepared By/Date:	Approved By/Date:	Effective Date:		Page: 1 of 2
	Reviewed By/Date:	Approved By/Date:	Revision No.		Section No. Q
Applicability: This section is applicable to all *{Company Name}* operations.					

1.0   PURPOSE

This section establishes the requirements for controlling nonconforming *product*.

2.0   REFERENCE DOCUMENTS

2.1   ISO 9001:2000 Paragraph 8.3

2.2   Quality Policy Manual Section G, Documentation Requirements

2.3   Quality Policy Manual Section S, Improvement

2.4   *{Quality System Procedure – Control of Nonconforming Product}*

{Reference the above Control of Nonconforming Product procedure by number and name. See paragraph 5.0.}

3.0   DEFINITIONS

3.1   See Section T, Glossary, for definitions of italicized terms.

4.0   QMS REQUIREMENTS (8.3)

{Company Name} ensures that product which does not conform to product requirements is identified and controlled to prevent its unintended use or delivery. The controls and related responsibilities and authorities for dealing with nonconforming product are defined in Reference 2.4.

{Company Name} deals with nonconforming product in one or more of the following ways:

a)   by taking action to eliminate the detected nonconformity;

b)   by authorizing its use, release, or acceptance under concession by a relevant authority and, where applicable, by the customer;

c)   by taking action to preclude its original intended use or application.

Records of the nature of nonconformities and any subsequent actions taken, including concessions obtained, are maintained per Reference 2.2 (see paragraph 6.0 below). When nonconforming product is corrected, it is subject to re-verification to demonstrate conformity to the requirements. When nonconforming product is detected after delivery or use has started, *{Company Name}* takes action appropriate to the effects, or potential effects, of the nonconformity.

{COMPANY NAME & Logo}			QUALITY SYSTEM MANUAL		
Title:	Prepared By/Date:	Approved By/Date:	Effective Date:	Page: 2 of 2	
Control of Nonconforming Product	Reviewed By/Date:	Approved By/Date:	Revision No.	Section No. Q	

5.0   RESPONSIBILITIES

> Customize paragraph 5.0 as necessary.

The *{Name of Function}* is responsible for making disposition for nonconforming product in accordance with *{Procedure Name and Number}*.

The nature of nonconformities and any subsequent actions taken, including concessions obtained, are documented and maintained in accordance with the requirements of *{Reference document}*. See Reference 2.4.

6.0   RECORDS

> Customize paragraph 6.0 as necessary.

The nature of nonconformities and any subsequent actions taken, including concessions obtained, are documented on the below-listed forms and maintained in accordance with Reference 2.2.

{COMPANY NAME & Logo}			QUALITY SYSTEM MANUAL		
Title:	Prepared By/Date:	Approved By/Date:	Effective Date:	Page: 1 of 2	
Analysis of Data	Reviewed By/Date:	Approved By/Date:	Revision No.	Section No. R	
Applicability: This section is applicable to all *{Company Name}* operations.					

1.0 PURPOSE

This section establishes the requirements for the analysis of data regarding the QMS.

2.0 REFERENCE DOCUMENTS

2.1 ISO 9001:2000 Clause 8.4

2.2 Quality Policy Manual Section J, Customer Related Processes

2.3 Quality Policy Manual Section P, Monitoring and Measurement

3.0 DEFINITIONS

3.1 See Section T, Glossary, for definitions of italicized terms.

4.0 QMS REQUIREMENTS (8.4)

{Company Name} determines, collects, and analyzes appropriate data to demonstrate the suitability and effectiveness of the QMS and to evaluate where continual improvement of the effectiveness of the QMS can be made. This includes data generated as a result of monitoring and measurement and from other relevant sources.

Data generated as a result of monitoring and measurement or from other relevant sources aids the fulfillment of the analysis requirements through the trending of the data. The types of data include, but are not limited to *{adjust this list as necessary to fit your organization}*:

a) customer satisfaction metrics,

b) findings from internal and external quality system audits,

c) in-process inspection results,

d) supplier performance metrics,

e) statistical process analysis,

f) results from management reviews, and

g) customer feedback.

Title:	Prepared By/Date:	Approved By/Date:	Effective Date:	Page: 2 of 2
Analysis of Data	Reviewed By/Date:	Approved By/Date:	Revision No.	Section No. R

Based on the data, *{Company Name}* evaluates where continual improvement of the effectiveness of the QMS can be made.

In addition, the analysis of data provides information relating to:

a)   customer satisfaction, per Reference 2.3

b)   conformance to product requirements, per Reference 2.2

c)   characteristics and trends of processes and products, including opportunities for preventive action, and

d)   suppliers.

5.0   RESPONSIBILITIES

{Define the responsibility for data collection, analysis, and associated actions. Adjust the following example as necessary to fit your organization:}

Data collection, analysis, and associated action(s) are the responsibility of all functions within *{Company Name}*.

6.0   RECORDS

{Define the associated records relative to Data Collection, analysis, and associated actions. Adjust the following example as necessary to fit your organization:}

Records of data collection, analysis, and action are maintained by the respective department/function.

{COMPANY NAME & Logo}			QUALITY SYSTEM MANUAL		
Title: Improvement	Prepared By/Date:	Approved By/Date:	Effective Date:	Page: 1 of 3	
	Reviewed By/Date:	Approved By/Date:	Revision No.	Section No. S	
Applicability: This section is applicable to all *{Company Name}* operations.					

1.0 PURPOSE

This section establishes the requirements for ensuring *continual improvement* of the effectiveness of the quality management system.

2.0 REFERENCE DOCUMENTS

2.1 ISO 9001:2000 Paragraph 8.5

2.2 Quality Policy Manual Section G, Documentation Requirements

2.3 *{Quality System Procedure - Corrective Action}*

2.4 *{Quality System Procedure - Preventive Action}*

{Reference the above Corrective Action and Preventive Action Procedures by number and name. It is acceptable to combine these if there is a clear distinction between the two.}

3.0 DEFINITIONS

3.1 See Section T, Glossary, for definitions of italicized terms.

4.0 QMS REQUIREMENTS

4.1 Continual Improvement (8.5.1)

{Company Name} continually improves the effectiveness of its QMS through the use of the quality policy, quality objectives, audit results, analysis of data, corrective and preventive actions, and management review.

4.2 Corrective Action (8.5.2)

{Company Name} takes action to eliminate the cause of nonconformities in order to prevent recurrence. Corrective actions are appropriate to the effects of the nonconformities encountered.

> If combined with Preventive Action, state such here.

The Corrective and Preventive Action procedure is a combined Quality System Procedure, which makes a clear distinction between corrective action and preventive action and their inter-relationship. Reference 2.3 defines requirements for

{COMPANY NAME & Logo}			QUALITY SYSTEM MANUAL		
Title: Improvement	Prepared By/Date:	Approved By/Date:	Effective Date:		Page: 2 of 3
	Reviewed By/Date:	Approved By/Date:	Revision No.		Section No. S

a)   reviewing nonconformities (including customer complaints),

b)   determining the causes of non-conformities,

c)   evaluating the need for action to ensure that nonconformities do not recur,

d)   determining and implementing action needed,

e)   records of the results of action taken, per Reference 2.2 (see paragraph 6.0 below), and

f)   reviewing corrective action taken.

Corrective Action Requests may come from one or more of the following:

a)   Internal Quality System Audits

b)   External Audits

c)   Customer Feedback

d)   Preventive Opportunities

e)   Corrective Opportunities

f)   Supplier Audits

> Customize this listing to fit the organization.

{Company Name} implements and records any changes to documented procedures resulting from corrective action.

Corrective actions include

a)   the effective handling of reported nonconformities,

b)   proper investigation and recording of root cause,

c)   determining resolution for the cause,

d)   follow-up measures to insure effectiveness, and

e)   determination of preventive action(s).

> Customize this listing as necessary.

4.3   Preventive Action (8.5.3)

{Procedure Name and Number} defines the action *{Company Name}* takes to eliminate the cause(s) of potential nonconformities in order to prevent their occurrence.

Title:	Prepared By/Date:	Approved By/Date:	Effective Date:	Page:
				3 of 3
Improvement	Reviewed By/Date:	Approved By/Date:	Revision No.	Section No. S

{COMPANY NAME & Logo} — QUALITY SYSTEM MANUAL

{Add the following paragraph if it is a combined procedure:}

The Corrective and Preventive Action procedure is a combined Quality System Procedure, which makes a clear distinction between corrective action and preventive action and their inter-relationship.

Preventive actions are appropriate to the effects of the potential problems. Reference 2.4 defines requirements for

a)   determining potential nonconformities and their causes,

b)   evaluating the need for action to prevent occurrence of nonconformities,

c)   determining and implementing action needed,

d)   records of results of action taken, per Reference 2.2 (see paragraph 6.0 below), and

e)   reviewing preventive action taken.

{Company Name} implements and records any changes to documented procedures resulting from preventive action(s).

5.0   RESPONSIBILITIES

{State the responsibilities for the Corrective and Preventive Action System, for follow-up activities and effectiveness. See the following examples:}

Top management is responsible for ensuring action(s) are taken regarding continual improvement.

All employees are responsible to ensure quality, continual improvement, and customer satisfaction is addressed.

The *{Name of Department or Function}* issues all Corrective Action Requests and is responsible for following up to ensure that corrective and preventive action is in place and adjusting the internal audit frequency as may be required. See references 2.3 and 2.4.

Quality Assurance Department is responsible for the maintenance of corrective and preventive action records, and continual improvement records.

6.0   RECORDS

Quality Records for Corrective and Preventive Action are defined in Reference 2.3 and 2.4.

{COMPANY NAME & Logo}				QUALITY SYSTEM MANUAL	
Title: Glossary (Terms and Definitions)	Prepared By/Date:	Approved By/Date:	Effective Date:	Page: 1 of 7	
	Reviewed By/Date:	Approved By/Date:	Revision No.	Section No. T	
Applicability: This section is applicable to all *{Company Name}* operations.					

TERMS AND DEFINITIONS
(Note: Italicized terms are also defined in this Section.)

{Review terms and definitions in this section for applicability to your Quality System Manual, delete those that do not add value to its understanding and add those that are necessary to ensure understanding by an outside reader (italicized terms).}

AUDIT – Systematic, independent, and documented *process* for obtaining *audit evidence* and evaluating it objectively to determine the extent to which *audit criteria* are fulfilled [ISO 9000:2000 - 3.9.1].

AUDIT CRITERIA – Set of policies, *procedures,* or *requirements* used as a reference [ISO 9000:2000 - 3.9.3].

AUDIT CONCLUSION – Outcome of an *audit* provided by the *audit team* after consideration of the audit objectives and all *audit findings* [ISO 9000:2000 - 3.9.6].

AUDIT EVIDENCE - *Records*, statements of fact, or other *information* which are relevant to the *audit criteria* and verifiable [ISO 9000:2000 - 3.9.4]

AUDIT FINDING – Results of the evaluation of the collected *audit evidence* against *audit criteria.* (Note: Audit findings can indicate either conformity or nonconformity with audit criteria, or opportunities for improvement. [ISO 9000:2000 3.9.5]).

AUDIT PROGRAM – Set of one or more *audit*s planned for a specific time frame and directed towards a specific purpose. (Note: One auditor in the audit team is generally appointed as audit team leader) [ISO 9000:2000 - 3.9.2].

AUDIT TEAM – One or more *auditors* conducting an *audit* [ISO 9000:2000 - 3.9.10].

AUDITEE – *Organization* being audited [ISO 9000:2000 - 3.9.8].

AUDITOR – Person with the *competence* to conduct an *audit* [ISO 9000:2000 - 3.9.9].

CAPABILITY - Ability of an *organization*, *system*, or *process* to realize a *product* that will fulfill the *requirements* for that *product* [ISO 9000:2000 - 3.1.5]

CHARACTERISTIC – Distinguishing feature [ISO 9000:2000 - 3.5.1].

COMPETENCE – Demonstrated ability to apply knowledge and skills [ISO 9000:2000 – 3.9.12].

{COMPANY NAME & Logo}			QUALITY SYSTEM MANUAL		
Title:	Prepared By/Date:	Approved By/Date:	Effective Date:	Page: 2 of 7	
Glossary (Terms and Definitions)	Reviewed By/Date:	Approved By/Date:	Revision No.	Section No. T	

CONCESSION – Permission to use or release a *product* that does not conform to specified *requirements* [ISO 9000:2000 - 3.6.11].

CONFORMITY – Fulfillment of a *requirement* [ISO 9000:2000 - 3.6.1].

CONTINUAL IMPROVEMENT – A recurring activity to increase the ability to fulfill *requirements* [ISO 9000:2000 - 3.2.13]

CORRECTION – Action taken to eliminate a detected *nonconformity* [ISO 9000:2000 - 3.6.6].

CORRECTIVE ACTION - Action to eliminate the cause of a detected *nonconformity* or other undesirable situation (Note: There is a distinction between *correction* and *corrective action*)[ISO 9000:2000 - 3.6.5].

CUSTOMER – *Organization* or person that receives a *product* (or service) [ISO 9000:2000 - 3.3.5].

CUSTOMER SATISFACTION – Customer's perception of the degree to which the customer's *requirements* have been fulfilled [ISO 9000:2000 - 3.1.4].

DEFECT - Non-fulfillment of a *requirement* related to an intended or specified use (NOTE: The distinction between defect and nonconformity is important as it has legal connotations, particularly those associated with product liability issues; consequently, the term "defect" should be used with extreme caution)[ISO 9000:2000 - 3.6.3].

DESIGN AND DEVELOPMENT – Set of *processes* that transforms *requirements* into specified *characteristics* or into the *specification* of a *product, process,* or *system* [ISO 9000:2000 - 3.4.4].

DEVIATION PERMIT- Permission to depart from the originally specified *requirements* of a *product* prior to realization [ISO 9000:2000 - 3.6.12].

DOCUMENT – *Information* and its supporting medium [ISO 9000:2000 - 3.7.2].

EFFECTIVENESS - Extent to which planned activities are realized and planned results are achieved [ISO 9000:2000 - 3.2.14].

FOLLOW-UP AUDIT - A special audit performed to verify that corrective action has been implemented as scheduled and that the action was effective in preventing or minimizing recurrence.

{COMPANY NAME & Logo}			QUALITY SYSTEM MANUAL		
Title: Glossary (Terms and Definitions)	Prepared By/Date:	Approved By/Date:	Effective Date:	Page: 3 of 7	
	Reviewed By/Date:	Approved By/Date:	Revision No.	Section No. T	

INDEPENDENCE - Freedom from bias and external influence; provides for objectivity and impartiality.

INFORMATION - Meaningful data [ISO 9000:2000 - 3.7.1].

INFRASTRUCTURE - System of facilities, equipment, and services needed for the operation of an *organization* [ISO 9000:2000 - 3.3.3].

INSPECTION – Conformity evaluation by observation and judgement—accompanied, as appropriate, by measurement, testing, or gauging [ISO 9000:2000 - 3.8.2].

INSPECTION RECORD - Document stating results (data) concerning inspection activities.

LEAD AUDITOR - The individual who manages the *audit team* during an *audit*.

MANAGEMENT SYSTEM – A *system* to establish policy and objectives and to achieve those objectives [ISO 9000:2000 - 3.2.2].

MEASUREMENT CONTROL SYSTEM – Set of interrelated or interacting elements necessary to achieve *metrological confirmation* and continual control of measurement processes [ISO 9000:2000 - 3.10.1].

MEASUREMENT PROCESS – Set of operations to determine the value of a quantity [ISO 9000:2000 - 3.10.2].

METROLOGICAL CONFIRMATION – Set of operations required to ensure that *measuring equipment* conforms to the *requirements* for its intended use. (Note: Generally includes calibration or verification, any necessary adjustment or repair, and subsequent recalibration, comparison with the metrological requirements for the intended use of the equipment, as well as any required sealing and labeling) [ISO 9000:2000 - 3.10.3].

MEASURING EQUIPMENT – Measuring instrument, software, measurement standard, reference material, or auxiliary apparatus or combination thereof necessary to realize a *measurement process* [ISO 9000:2000 - 3.10.4].

METROLOGICAL CHARACTERISTIC – Distinguishing feature which can influence the results of measurement [ISO 9000:2000 - 3.10.5].

METROLOGICAL FUNCTION - Function with organizational responsibility for defining and implementing the *measurement control system* [ISO 9000:2000 - 3.10.6].

{COMPANY NAME & Logo}			QUALITY SYSTEM MANUAL		
Title:	Prepared By/Date:	Approved By/Date:	Effective Date:	Page: 4 of 7	
Glossary (Terms and Definitions)	Reviewed By/Date:	Approved By/Date:	Revision No.	Section No. T	

NONCONFORMITY – Non-fulfillment of a *requirement* [ISO 9000:2000 3.6.2].

OBJECTIVE EVIDENCE – Data supporting the existence or verity of something [ISO 9000:2000 - 3.8.1]

OBSERVATION – A concern or weakness detected in an element in the management system, but not a nonconformance; a condition that may become a nonconformance if not addressed; an opportunity for improvement.

OPENING MEETING – The introductory meeting between the auditor(s) and the auditee's representative, during which the overview of the planned audit is presented.

ORGANIZATION – Group of people and facilities with an arrangement of responsibilities, authorities, and relationships [ISO 9000:2000 - 3.3.1].

ORGANIZATIONAL STRUCTURE – Arrangement of responsibilities, authorities, and relationships between people [ISO 9000:2000 - 3.3.2].

PRE-AWARD SURVEY - An activity conducted prior to a contract award and used to evaluate the overall quality capability of a prospective supplier or contractor.

PREVENTIVE ACTION – Action to eliminate the cause of a potential *nonconformity* or other undesirable potential situation (Note: Preventive action is taken to prevent occurrence, whereas corrective action is taken to prevent recurrence) [ISO 9000:2000 - 3.6.4].

PROCEDURE - Specified way to carry out an activity or *process* [ISO 9000:2000 - 3.4.5].

PROCESS – Set of interrelated or interacting activities which transforms inputs into outputs. (Note 1: Inputs to a process are generally outputs from other processes. Note 2: Processes in an organization are generally planned and carried out under controlled conditions to add value. Note 3: A process where the conformity of the resulting product cannot be readily or economically verified is frequently referred to as a "special process") [ISO 9000:2000 - 3.4.1].

PRODUCT – Result of a *process*. (Note 1: There are four generic categories of product: 1) *Services*, 2) Software, 3) Hardware, 4) Processed materials [ISO 9000:2000 - 3.4.2].

Note: For the purposes of its ISO 9001 Certification, *{Company Name}*'s product consists of the

{COMPANY NAME & Logo}			QUALITY SYSTEM MANUAL		
Title: Glossary (Terms and Definitions)	Prepared By/Date:	Approved By/Date:	Effective Date:	Page: 5 of 7	
	Reviewed By/Date:	Approved By/Date:	Revision No.	Section No. T	

PROJECT – Unique *process*, consisting of a set of coordinated and controlled activities with start and finish dates, undertaken to achieve an objective conforming to specific *requirements*, including the constraints of time, cost, and resources [ISO 9000:2000 - 3.4.3].

QUALITY – Degree to which a set of inherent *characteristics* fulfills *requirements* [ISO 9000:2000 - 3.1.1].

QUALITY ASSURANCE – Part of *quality management* focused on providing confidence that quality *requirements* will be fulfilled [ISO 9000:2000 - 3.2.11].

QUALITY CONTROL – Part of *quality management* focused on fulfilling quality *requirements* [ISO 9000:2000 - 3.2.10].

QUALITY IMPROVEMENT – Part of *quality management* focused on increasing the ability to fulfill quality *requirements* [ISO 9000:2000 - 3.2.12].

QUALITY MANAGEMENT SYSTEM (QMS) – A *management system* to direct and control an *organization* with regard to *quality* [ISO 9000:2000 - 3.2.3].

QUALITY MANUAL (QM) - *Document* specifying the *quality management system* of an *organization* [ISO 9000:2000 - 3.7.4].

QUALITY OBJECTIVE - Something sought, or aimed for, related to quality (Note 1: Quality objectives are generally based on the organization's *quality policy*; Note 2: Quality objectives are generally specified for relevant functions and levels in the organization)[ISO 9000:2000 - 3.1.1].

QUALITY PLAN - *Document* specifying which *procedures* and associated *resources* shall be applied by whom and when to a specific *project, product, process,* or contract [ISO 9000:2000 - 3.7.5].

QUALITY PLANNING – Part of *quality management* focused on setting *quality objectives* and specifying necessary operational *processes* and related *resources* to fulfill the *quality objectives* [ISO 9000:2000 - 3.2.9].

QUALITY POLICY - The overall intentions and direction of an *organization* related to *quality* as formally expressed by *top management* [ISO 9000:2000 - 3.2.4].

RECORD - *Document* stating results achieved or providing evidence of activities performed [ISO 9000:2000 - 3.7.6].

{COMPANY NAME & Logo}			QUALITY SYSTEM MANUAL		
Title: Glossary (Terms and Definitions)	Prepared By/Date:	Approved By/Date:	Effective Date:	Page: 6 of 7	
	Reviewed By/Date:	Approved By/Date:	Revision No.	Section No. T	

RELEASE - Permission to proceed to the next stage of a process [ISO 9000:2000 - 3.6.13].

REQUIREMENT - Need or expectation that is stated, generally implied, or obligatory [ISO 9000:2000 - 3.1.2].

RESOURCES - People, time, money, buildings, equipment, and support activities, as necessary, that may be applied to a specific project, product, process, and/or contract in order to fulfill *requirements*.

REVIEW – Activity undertaken to determine the suitability, adequacy, and *effectiveness* of the subject matter to achieve established objectives [ISO 9000:2000 - 3.8.7].

ROOT CAUSE - The fundamental deficiency that results in a nonconformance that must be eliminated through corrective action to prevent recurrence of the same or similar nonconformance.

ROOT CAUSE ANALYSIS - Investigation to determine the fundamental deficiency that resulted in a nonconformity.

SERVICE – The result of at least one activity necessarily performed at the interface between the supplier and the customer and that is generally intangible. Provision of a service can involve: 1) Activity performed on a customer-supplied tangible product, 2) Activity performed on a customer-supplied intangible product, 3) Delivery of an intangible product, 4) Creation of ambience for the customer [ISO 9000:2000 - 3.4.2 Note 2].

SPECIFICATION – *Document* stating *requirements* [ISO 9000:2000 - 3.7.3].

SUPPLIER – *Organization* or person that provides a *product* [ISO 9000:2000 - 3.3.6].

SYSTEM - Set of interrelated or interacting elements [ISO 9000:2000 - 3.2.1]

TEST – Determination of one or more *characteristics* according to a *procedure* [ISO 9000:2000 - 3.8.3].

TOP MANAGEMENT – Person or group of people who directs and controls an *organization* at the highest level [ISO 9000:2000 - 3.2.7].

TRACEABILITY - Ability to trace the history, application, or location of that which is under consideration [ISO 9000:2000 - 3.5.4].

VALIDATION – Confirmation, through the provision of *objective evidence*, that the *requirements* for a specific intended use or application have been fulfilled [ISO 9000:2000 - 3.8.5].

{COMPANY NAME & Logo} QUALITY SYSTEM MANUAL

Title:	Prepared By/Date:	Approved By/Date:	Effective Date:	Page:
Glossary (Terms and Definitions)				7 of 7
	Reviewed By/Date:	Approved By/Date:	Revision No.	Section No. T

VERIFICATION – Confirmation, through the provision of *objective evidence*, that specified *requirements* have been fulfilled [ISO 9000:2000 - 3.8.4].

WORK ENVIRONMENT - Set of conditions under which work is performed (Note: Conditions include physical, social, psychological and environmental factors (temperature, recognition schemes, ergonomics and atmospheric composition)) [ISO 9000:2000 - 3.3.4].

{COMPANY NAME & Logo}				QUALITY SYSTEM MANUAL	
Title: Record of Revision	Prepared By/Date:	Approved By/Date:	Effective Date:	Page: 1 of 1	
	Reviewed By/Date:	Approved By/Date:	Revision No.	Section No. U	
Applicability: This section is applicable to all *{Company Name}* operations.					

Revision	Section	Detail	Effective Date
0	All	Initial Issue of the 9001:2000 transition revision to the QSM	

Appendix B

Quality Manual Configured to Option 2

{COMPANY NAME}

QUALITY MANAGEMENT

SYSTEM (QMS)

QUALITY MANUAL

Distribution Number: _____

Document Holder: _____

| Option 2 – ISO 9001:2000 |
| Standard Orientation |

{COMPANY NAME & Logo}				QUALITY SYSTEM MANUAL	
Title: Table of Contents	Prepared By/Date:	Approved By/Date:	Effective Date:	Page: 1 of 3	
	Reviewed By/Date:	Approved By/Date:	Revision No.	Section No. TOC	
Applicability: This section is applicable to all *{Company Name}* operations.					

This index lists the QMS requirements that comply with the ISO 9001:2000 requirements.

Clause Number	Title	Rev. No.	Rev. Date
1	Scope		
2	Normative Reference		
3	Terms and Definitions		

4	Quality Management System
	General Requirements (4.1)
	  ❑ Documentation Requirements (4.2)
	      ❑ General (4.2.1)
	      ❑ Quality Manual (4.2.2)
	      ❑ Control of Documents (4.2.3)
	  ❑ Control of Records (4.2.4)		

5	Management Responsibility
	  ❑ Management Commitment (5.1)
	  ❑ Customer Focus (5.2)
	  ❑ Quality Policy (5.3)
	  ❑ Planning (5.4)
	      ❑ Quality Objectives (5.4.1)
	      ❑ QMS Planning (5.4.2)
	  ❑ Responsibility, Authority and Communications (5.5)
	      ❑ Responsibility and Authority (5.5.1)
	      ❑ Management Representative (5.5.2)
	      ❑ Internal Communication (5.5.3)
	  ❑ Management Review (5.6)
	      ❑ General (5.6.1)
	      ❑ Input (5.6.2)
	      ❑ Output (5.6.3)		

{COMPANY NAME & Logo}			QUALITY SYSTEM MANUAL	
Title: Table of Contents	Prepared By/Date:	Approved By/Date:	Effective Date:	Page: 2 of 3
	Reviewed By/Date:	Approved By/Date:	Revision No.	Section No. TOC

This index lists the QMS requirements that comply with the ISO 9001:2000 requirements.

Title:	Prepared By/Date:	Approved By/Date:	Effective Date:	Page:
Table of Contents				3 of 3
	Reviewed By/Date:	Approved By/Date:	Revision No.	Section No. TOC

This index lists the QMS requirements that comply with the ISO 9001:2000 requirements.

Clause Number	Title	Rev. No.	Rev. Date

	❑ Production and Service Provision (7.5)
	    ❑ Control of Production and Service Provision (7.5.1)
	    ❑ Validation of Production and Service Provision (7.5.2)
	    ❑ Identification and Traceability (7.5.3)
	    ❑ Customer Property (7.5.4)
	    ❑ Preservation of Product (7.5.5)
	 ❑ Control of Monitoring and Measuring Devices (7.6)		

8	Measurement, Analysis and Improvement
	   ❑ General (8.1)
	   ❑ Monitoring and Measurement (8.2)
	    ❑ Customer Satisfaction (8.2.1)
	    ❑ Internal Audit (8.2.2)
	    ❑ Monitoring and Measurement of Processes (8.2.3)
	    ❑ Monitoring and Measurement of Product (8.2.4)
	   ❑ Control of Nonconforming Product (8.3)
	   ❑ Analysis of Data (8.4)
	   ❑ Improvement (8.5)
	    ❑ Continual Improvement (8.5.1)
	    ❑ Corrective Action (8.5.2)
	    ❑ Preventive Action (8.5.3)		

9	Record of Revision		

{COMPANY NAME & Logo}			QUALITY SYSTEM MANUAL		
Title: Scope	Prepared By/Date:	Approved By/Date:	Effective Date:	Page: 1 of 1	
	Reviewed By/Date:	Approved By/Date:	Revision No.	Section No. 1	
Applicability: This section is applicable to all *{Company Name}* operations.					

1.0 PURPOSE

This section establishes the basis of the *{Company Name}* Quality Management System (QMS).

2.0 REFERENCE DOCUMENTS

2.1 ISO 9001:2000 Clause 1

3.0 DEFINITIONS

3.1 See Section 3, Glossary, for definitions of italicized terms.

4.0 QMS REQUIREMENTS

4.1 Scope (1.0)

{Company Name} provides *{describe what the company does in one paragraph. See the following example:}*.

XYZ provides design and development engineering, material management, manufacturing and installation of modular structures for all industries.

This Quality System Manual specifies the requirements by which the QMS demonstrates *{Company Name}*'s ability to:

- consistently provide product that meets customer and applicable regulatory requirements, and

- enhance customer satisfaction through the effective application of the QMS, including processes for continual improvement of the system and the assurance of conformity to customer and applicable regulatory requirements.

5.0 RESPONSIBILITIES

Responsibilities and authorities are defined in paragraph 5 of each section of this Quality System Manual.

6.0 RECORDS

{COMPANY NAME & Logo}			QUALITY SYSTEM MANUAL	
Title: Normative Reference	Prepared By/Date:	Approved By/Date:	Effective Date:	Page: 1 of 1
	Reviewed By/Date:	Approved By/Date:	Revision No.	Section No. 2
Applicability: This section is applicable to all *{Company Name}* operations.				

1.0 PURPOSE

This section establishes *{Company Name}*'s Quality Management System (QMS) as the Normative Reference.

2.0 REFERENCE DOCUMENTS

2.1 Quality System Manual Section 4

3.0 DEFINITIONS

3.1 See Section 3, Glossary, for definitions of italicized terms.

4.0 QMS REQUIREMENTS

The *{Company Name}* Quality System Manual contains the requirements and supporting documentation, which demonstrates conformance to the ISO 9001:2000 QMS standard.

The Quality System Manual is a controlled document and acts as a normative document for the rest of the system.

{Company Name}'s QMS is established as defined in Reference 2.1.

5.0 RESPONSIBILITIES

Responsibilities and authorities are defined in paragraph 5 of each section of this Quality System Manual.

6.0 RECORDS

None.

{COMPANY NAME & Logo}			QUALITY SYSTEM MANUAL	
Title: Glossary Terms and Definitions	Prepared By/Date:	Approved By/Date:	Effective Date:	Page: 1 of 1
	Reviewed By/Date:	Approved By/Date:	Revision No.	Section No. 3
Applicability: This section is applicable to all *{Company Name}* operations.				

{This is the same as Section T of the Option 3 Configured Quality System Manual and therefore is not repeated here. For the Option 2 Configuration, instead of in Section T, it is placed here in Section 3, towards the front of the manual.}

{COMPANY NAME & Logo}				QUALITY SYSTEM MANUAL	
Title: Quality Management System	Prepared By/Date:	Approved By/Date:	Effective Date:		Page: 1 of 7
	Reviewed By/Date:	Approved By/Date:	Revision No.		Section No. 4
Applicability: This section is applicable to all {Company Name} operations.					

1.0   PURPOSE

This section establishes the requirements for {Company Name}'s Quality Management System (QMS).

2.0   REFERENCE DOCUMENTS

2.1   ISO 9001:2000 Clause 4

2.2   Quality System Manual Section 6,

2.3   QMS Procedure, Quality System Document Control

2.4   QMS Procedure, Quality Record Management

2.5   Quality System Manual Section 5, paragraph 4.3

2.6   Quality System Manual Section 5, paragraph 4.4

> Add the procedure number for each Quality System Procedure referenced.

{Add Subcontractor Control Procedure Reference if applicable, and monitoring, measuring, and analysis references (see 4.1e) below.}

3.0   DEFINITIONS

3.1   See Section 3, Glossary, for definitions of italicized terms.

4.0   QMS REQUIREMENTS

4.1   Quality Management System - General (4.1)

{Company Name} has established, documented, and implemented a Quality Management System and continually improves its effectiveness in accordance with the requirements of the ISO 9001:2000 Standard.

{Company Name} maintains its Quality Management System by

a)   identifying the processes needed for its QMS and their application throughout the organization,

b)   determining the sequence and interaction of these processes,

c)   determining the criteria and methods needed to ensure that both the operation and control of these processes are effective, as contained in *{add appropriate reference as may be applicable}*.

{COMPANY NAME & Logo}			QUALITY SYSTEM MANUAL		
Title: Quality Management System	Prepared By/Date:	Approved By/Date:	Effective Date:	Page: 2 of 7	
	Reviewed By/Date:	Approved By/Date:	Revision No.	Section No. 4	

  d) ensuring the availability of resources, per Reference 2.2, and information necessary to support the operation and monitoring of these processes,

  e) monitoring, measuring and analyzing these processes, per References {List the references here as may be applicable and include in Reference Section above}, and

  f) implementing actions necessary to achieve planned results and continual improvement of these processes.

{Company Name} manages the QMS processes in accordance with the requirements of the ISO 9001:2000 Standard.

<table><tr><td>If no outsourcing is done, use this paragraph or similar.</td></tr></table>

{Company Name} does not outsource any processes affecting product conformity with these requirements. Should any process be outsourced, *{Company Name}* will identify them and ensure control over such processes.

OR

<table><tr><td>If outsourcing is done, use this paragraph text or similar. List or reference the processes.</td></tr></table>

{Company Name} outsources certain processes that affect *product* conformity with requirements. *{Company Name}* ensures the control of these processes through the selection process … *{add a description of the means of control and the reference document that controls subcontractors.}*

{Company Name} outsources these processes:

  1)

<table><tr><td>Modify to fit organization.</td></tr></table>

  2)

{Company Name} ensures the control of these processes through subcontractor evaluation and selection processes, per Reference *{add reference here and above in References}*.

4.2 Documentation Requirements – General (4.2.1)

The *{Company Name}* QMS documentation includes:

  a) documented statements of a quality policy, per Reference 2.5, and quality objectives, per Reference 2.6,

  b) this Quality System Manual (see paragraph 4.3 below),

Title:	Prepared By/Date:	Approved By/Date:	Effective Date:	Page: 3 of 7
Quality Management System	Reviewed By/Date:	Approved By/Date:	Revision No.	Section No. 4

c)   documented procedures referenced within each Section of this Manual, where required by the ISO 9001:2000 Standard,

d)   documents needed by the *{Company Name}* organization to ensure the effective planning, operation and control of its processes, and

e)   records required by the ISO 9001:2000 Standard (see paragraph 4.5 below).

4.3   Quality Manual (4.2.2)

The Quality System Manual provides an overall description of the scope of the Quality Management System, the general quality policies, quality objectives and documented procedures (referenced by this manual), and a description of the interaction between the processes of the Quality Management System (QMS). The Quality System Manual is subject to internal and external controlled distribution.

{Company Name} has established and maintains this Quality Manual that includes:

a)   the scope of the QMS as defined in Section 2 as it applies to *{Company Name}*'s *{product(s)/service(s)}*.

The justification(s) for exclusion(s) claimed under Clause 1.2 of the ISO 9001:2000 Standard is/are detailed below:

> *{List the ISO 9001:2000 related exclusions here and the associated justification for each. Also state this in the appropriate section of the QSM. See the following two examples:}*
>
> 1)   *{Company Name}* does not hold any customer supplied property for exclusion of Clause 7.5.4, Customer Property.
>
> 2)   In the provision of design and development engineering, material management and program management XYZ does not use any monitoring and measuring devices; therefore, the requirements of Clause 7.6 are excluded.

b)   inclusion or reference to the documented procedures established for the QMS, and

c)   a description of the interactions between the processes of the QMS (see below and paragraph 4.6).

{COMPANY NAME & Logo}			QUALITY SYSTEM MANUAL		
Title:	Prepared By/Date:	Approved By/Date:	Effective Date:		Page: 4 of 7
Quality Management System	Reviewed By/Date:	Approved By/Date:	Revision No.		Section No. 4

{State here what the Company/Organization does relative to the scope of the ISO 9001:2000 Quality Management System. Include a simple flow diagram of the major process steps from input to delivery of the product and/or service.}

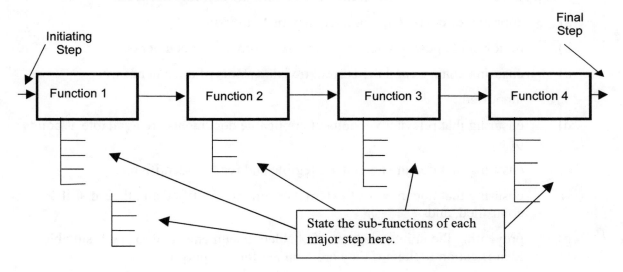

This diagram represents the overall high-level process of *{Company Name}* and the interconnections between the processes.

Title:	Prepared By/Date:	Approved By/Date:	Effective Date:	Page: 5 of 7
Quality Management System	Reviewed By/Date:	Approved By/Date:	Revision No.	Section No. 4

4.4   Control of Documents (4.2.3)

Documents required by the QMS are controlled as defined in Reference 2.3 above. Records are a special type of document and are controlled in accordance with Reference 2.4 above (see paragraph 4.5 below). Reference 2.3 defines the controls needed for

a)   approval of documents for adequacy prior to issue,

b)   review and update as necessary and re-approval of documents,

c)   ensuring changes and the current revision status of documents are

identified,

d)   ensuring that relevant versions of applicable documents are available at points of use,

e)   ensuring that documents remain legible and readily identifiable,

f)   ensuring that documents of external origin are identified and their distribution is controlled, and

g)   preventing the unintended use of obsolete documents, and to apply suitable identification to them if they are retained for any purpose.

A Master List has been established to identify the current revision of documents in order to control the issuance and revision status of the documents.

{If other than a Master List is used to track revisions, state the method here.}

4.5   Control of Records (4.2.4)

Records have been established and are maintained to provide evidence of conformity to requirements and of the effective operation of the QMS. Records are maintained legible, readily identifiable, and retrievable. Reference 2.4 defines the controls needed for the identification, storage, protection, retrieval, retention time, and disposition of records.

4.5.1   Documentation Structure (Optional)

The diagram below outlines the structure of *{Company Name}*'s QMS:

The Levels of documentation and instructions include:

{COMPANY NAME & Logo}			QUALITY SYSTEM MANUAL	
Title: Quality Management System	Prepared By/Date:	Approved By/Date:	Effective Date:	Page: 6 of 7
	Reviewed By/Date:	Approved By/Date:	Revision No.	Section No. 4

Level 1 – Quality System Manual – A description of *{Company Name}* method of establishing, implementing, and maintaining a Quality Management System that meets the requirements of the ISO 9001:2000 Standard.

Level 2 – Quality System Procedures – Procedures which describe the overall activities corresponding to the major sections of this Quality System Manual.

Level 3 – *{List and describe each level of the Quality Management System as it is applied to your organization. This structure shows the interrelationship between the parts of the QMS.}*

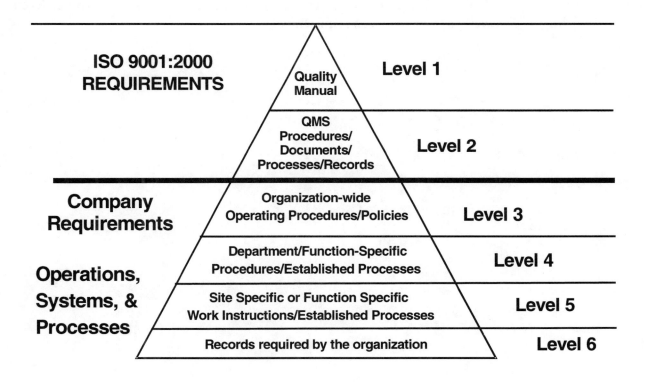

{Modify this diagram or use some other method to accurately display the interrelationship between all parts of the Quality Management System. }

Title:	Prepared By/Date:	Approved By/Date:	Effective Date:	Page: 7 of 7
Quality Management System	Reviewed By/Date:	Approved By/Date:	Revision No.	Section No. 4

5.0 RESPONSIBILITIES

The manager of each department is responsible for ensuring that issues of appropriate documents in their area are available for use, pertinent, and periodically reviewed for removal of all obsolete issues.

The establishment of the *{Company Name}* Quality Management System is the responsibility of Senior Management.

6.0 RECORDS

The control of quality records is stated in Reference 2.4.

Additional record requirements are contained in each respective procedure as well as their retention requirements.

> Modify these paragraphs as necessary to fully state Responsibilities and Records associated with the Quality Management System.

{COMPANY NAME & Logo}			QUALITY SYSTEM MANUAL	
Title: Management Responsibility	Prepared By/Date:	Approved By/Date:	Effective Date:	Page: 1 of 7
	Reviewed By/Date:	Approved By/Date:	Revision No.	Section No. 5
Applicability: This section is applicable to all *{Company Name}* operations.				

1.0 PURPOSE

This section establishes top management's responsibilities with regard to the continual improvement of *{Company Name}*'s Quality Management System and the enhancement of customer satisfaction.

2.0 REFERENCE DOCUMENTS

2.1 ISO 9001:2000 Clauses 5

2.2 Quality Manual Section 6

2.3 Quality Manual Section 7, paragraph 4.2

2.4 Quality Manual Section 8, paragraph 4.2

2.5 Quality Manual Section 7, paragraph 4.1(a)

2.6 Quality Manual Section 4, paragraph 4.1

2.7 Quality System Procedure, Control of Records

{List any other Quality System Procedure References that may apply.}

3.0 DEFINITIONS

3.1 See Section 3, Glossary, for definitions of italicized terms.

{Italicize those terms that appear in the Glossary.}

4.0 QMS REQUIREMENTS

4.1 Management Commitment (5.1)

Top management provides evidence of its commitment to the development and implementation of the QMS, and to continually improving the effectiveness of the QMS, by

a) communicating to all *{Company Name}* employees the importance of meeting customer as well as statutory and regulatory requirements,

b) establishing the quality policy (see paragraph 4.3 below) and ensuring that this policy is understood by all *{Company Name}* employees,

c) ensuring that the quality objectives are established (see paragraph 4.4 below)

{COMPANY NAME & Logo}			QUALITY SYSTEM MANUAL		
Title: Management Responsibility	Prepared By/Date:	Approved By/Date:	Effective Date:	Page: 2 of 7	
	Reviewed By/Date:	Approved By/Date:	Revision No.	Section No. 5	

d)   conducting management reviews, (see paragraph 4.9 below), and

e)   ensuring the availability of resources, per Reference 2.2.

{Add any additional evidence of management commitment that the organization may perform.}

4.2   Customer Focus (5.2)

Top management ensures that customer requirements are determined, per Reference 2.3. These requirements are met with the aim of enhancing the satisfaction of our customer per Reference 2.4 above.

4.3   Quality Policy (5.3)

This Quality System Manual is issued to describe the quality system employed by *{Company Name}*. Top Management of *{Company Name}* ensures that the Quality Policy

Make sure that the Quality Policy addresses items a), b), and c) in its text.

a)   is appropriate to the purpose of the organization,

b)   includes a commitment to comply with requirements and continually improve the effectiveness of the QMS,

c)   provides a framework for establishing and reviewing quality objectives,

Make sure that d) and e) are done and documented.

d)   is communicated and understood within the organization, and

e)   is reviewed for continuing suitability.

4.3.1   The following is the Quality Policy adopted by *{Company Name}*:

{State the organization's Quality Policy here exactly as it is. It is important that all distributed copies match the one contained here at all times.}

{COMPANY NAME & Logo}				QUALITY SYSTEM MANUAL	
Title: Management Responsibility	Prepared By/Date:	Approved By/Date:	Effective Date:		Page: 3 of 7
	Reviewed By/Date:	Approved By/Date:	Revision No.		Section No. 5

4.3.2 Quality Policy Implementation

The ways in which *{Company Name}*'s quality policy is implemented include:

{list the ways in which the quality policy is implemented. Customize the following examples as necessary:}

a) our commitment to continual improvement,

b) making the quality policy available,

c) providing a framework for establishing and reviewing objectives,

d) review of the Quality Management System by top management,

e) audits of the Quality Management System,

f) the organization, responsibility, and interfaces of various functions being defined and documented,

g) our equipment and facilities being suited for their intended purpose,

h) our employees possessing sound skills in their own areas of responsibility and being offered the opportunity for the necessary training to ensure that they are capable to achieve quality in the work they perform.

4.4 Quality Objectives (5.4.1)

It is the responsibility of *{Company Name}*'s top management to ensure that quality objectives, including those needed to meet work related requirements and in support of the organizational objectives, are established at relevant functions and levels within the organization. These objectives are measurable and consistent with the quality policy stated above.

The overall quality objectives are as follows:

{List the organization's quality objectives here. They must be obtainable and measurable. Sample objectives are shown below. Customize as needed.}

a) the provision of superior products and services to our customers,

b) continual improvement of our Quality Management System,

c) customer satisfaction as a paramount goal,

d) maintain the ISO 9001:2000 Certification,

e) create and maintain a work environment for our employees that encourages innovative thinking, leadership, decision making, and a commitment to continual improvement,

{COMPANY NAME & Logo}				QUALITY SYSTEM MANUAL	
Title: Management Responsibility	Prepared By/Date:	Approved By/Date:	Effective Date:	Page: 4 of 7	
	Reviewed By/Date:	Approved By/Date:	Revision No.	Section No. 5	

f)   work with suppliers to ensure continuous adherence to *{Company Name}*'s requirements.

In addition, quality objectives, including those needed to meet requirements for *product* per Reference 2.5, have been established within the below-listed functions and levels of *{Company Name}*:

{List the functions here, if practical, or reference where they are listed or stated.}

4.5   Quality Management System Planning (5.4.2)

{Company Name}'s top management ensures that:

a)   the planning of the QMS is carried out in order to meet the requirements given per Reference 2.6, as well as the quality objectives listed above, and

b)   the integrity of the QMS is maintained when changes to the QMS are planned and implemented.

4.5.1   Plan Development

{Add additional specific company information relative to Planning such as 4.5.1 Plan Development.}

4.6   Responsibility and Authority (5.5.1)

Modify this paragraph to fit the organization, but address all issues contained therein.

Top management within *{Company Name}* defines and communicates the responsibilities and authorities of all employees within the organization. Organizational relationships within the company are described in the organizational charts. Specific responsibilities and authorities for such activity affecting quality are defined in the respective job description and in paragraph 5 of each Quality System Manual Section and in each Quality System Procedure.

4.7   Management Representative (5.5.2)

The overall responsibility for quality at *{Company Name}* rests with the *{Title of top management person}* of *{Company Name}* who has appointed the *{Functional Title of person}* who, irrespective of other responsibilities, has responsibility and authority that includes

a)   ensuring that processes needed for the QMS are established, implemented, and maintained,

{COMPANY NAME & Logo}				QUALITY SYSTEM MANUAL	
Title: Management Responsibility	Prepared By/Date:	Approved By/Date:	Effective Date:	Page: 5 of 7	
	Reviewed By/Date:	Approved By/Date:	Revision No.	Section No. 5	

b) reporting on the performance of the QMS to the President, including any need for improvement, and

c) ensuring the promotion and awareness of customer requirements throughout the *{Company Name}* organization.

{Provide descriptions of other QMS related job functions such as Quality Assurance Manager. Create a paragraph for each—4.7.1, 4.7.2, etc.}

Example

4.7.1 Quality Assurance Manager

The Quality Assurance Manager of each facility within the *{Name of organization}* will be the management representative for the ISO 9000 Quality Management System. The Management Representative is responsible for ensuring that the quality management system is established and maintained according to the ISO 9000 Standard, and has the following responsibilities:

a) coordinate Quality Assurance requirements with other departments;

b) ensure adequate training is given to Quality Department personnel;

c) establish quality policies and procedures to meet contractual requirements;

d) provide functional counseling and guidance on preparation of inspection and test plans;

e) ensures the appropriate quality representative participates in design review;

f) interpret quality requirements of contracts and notify affected areas of any changes;

g) report on the performance of the quality system to management for review.

The Quality Assurance Manager is responsible for chairing the Quality Management System Review Meeting.

4.8 Internal Communication (5.5.3)

Top management ensures that appropriate communication processes are established within the organization. These processes ensure that communication takes place regarding the effectiveness of the QMS.

Title: Management Responsibility	Prepared By/Date:	Approved By/Date:	Effective Date:	Page: 6 of 7
	Reviewed By/Date:	Approved By/Date:	Revision No.	Section No. 5

4.9 Management Review – General (5.6.1)

Top management reviews *{Company Name}*'s QMS on an annual basis to ensure its continuing suitability, adequacy, and effectiveness. This review includes assessing opportunities for improvement and the need for changes to the quality management system, including the quality policy and quality objectives. Records from these reviews are maintained per Reference 2.7 (see paragraph 6.0 below).

4.10 Review Input (5.6.2)

Inputs to the management review include information on

a)   Results of audits,

b)   Customer feedback,

c)   Process performance and product conformity to requirements,

d)   Status of corrective and preventive actions,

e)   Follow-up actions from previous management reviews,

f)   Changes that could affect the QMS, and

g)   Recommendations for improvement.

4.11 Review Output (5.6.3)

The outputs from the review include all decisions and actions related to

a)   Improvement of the effectiveness of the QMS and its processes,

b)   Improvement of *product* related to customer requirements, and

c)   Resource needs.

Title:	Prepared By/Date:	Approved By/Date:	Effective Date:	Page: 7 of 7
Management Responsibility	Reviewed By/Date:	Approved By/Date:	Revision No.	Section No. 5

5.0　RESPONSIBILITIES

{State here the responsibilities for Management Commitment, Customer Focus, Quality Policy, Quality Objectives, QMS Planning, Responsibilities and Authorities, Management Representative, Internal Communication, and Management Review. Refer to those documents that contain the listed responsibilities as may be applicable. Include the references in Section 2 above. See some examples and suggestions below.}

{State the responsibilities here if not clearly stated in the text of paragraph 4.0.}

It is the responsibility of top management to ensure customer focus and internal communication throughout the organization.

The *{Name of Function, such as Quality Assurance Manager}* is responsible for chairing the Quality System Management Review Meeting. Top management is responsible for reviewing the quality management system and to ensure its continuing suitability, adequacy, and effectiveness.

{Name the function responsible for chairing the Management Review Meeting as well as for maintaining the records and actions items resulting from the review. Modify these paragraphs as necessary to adequately fit your organization.}

QMS Planning is the responsibility of *{list the responsibility for QMS Planning}*.

6.0　RECORDS

Records of management reviews are maintained by *{Function, such as Quality Assurance Manager}* in accordance with Reference 2.7 and include Minutes of Management Review meetings, which include actions, follow-up, and effectiveness of the results of the management reviews.

Records associated with QMS Planning are maintained by *{state where Records associated with QMS Planning are maintained or equivalent}*.

{COMPANY NAME & Logo}			QUALITY SYSTEM MANUAL	
Title: Resource Management	Prepared By/Date:	Approved By/Date:	Effective Date:	Page: 1 of 3
	Reviewed By/Date:	Approved By/Date:	Revision No.	Section No. 6
Applicability: This section is applicable to all {Company Name} operations.				

1.0   PURPOSE

This section establishes the requirements for management of the *resources* that are essential to the implementation and continual improvement of the QMS.

2.0   REFERENCE DOCUMENTS

2.1   ISO 9001:2000 Clause 6

2.2   Quality Manual Section 4, Paragraph 4.5

2.3   Quality Manual Section 7, Paragraph 4.1

{Reference any organization-specific supporting procedures here.}

3.0   DEFINITIONS

3.1   See Section 3, Glossary, for definitions of italicized terms.

4.0   QMS REQUIREMENTS

4.1   Provision of Resources – General (6.1)

{Company Name} identifies resource requirements and provides resources needed to implement and maintain the QMS, to continually improve its effectiveness, and to enhance customer satisfaction by meeting their requirements. When resource requirements change, management ensures that adequate resources are allocated.

4.2   Human Resources – General (6.2.1)

Personnel performing work affecting product quality have been determined to be competent on the basis of appropriate education, training, skills, and experience.

4.3   Competence, Awareness and Training (6.2.2)

All employees performing work affecting product or service quality are verified to be competent in their specific job assignments on the basis of appropriate *education, training, skills,* and *experience.* All employees receive instruction in the QMS applicable to their specific work assignments. Personnel performing certain specialized activities identified and addressed in the QMS are formally qualified to perform those designated activities.

{The above or below paragraph may suffice as applicable. Modify or expand as necessary to show how the organization addresses this subject.}

{COMPANY NAME & Logo}   QUALITY SYSTEM MANUAL

Title: Resource Management	Prepared By/Date:	Approved By/Date:	Effective Date:	Page: 2 of 3
	Reviewed By/Date:	Approved By/Date:	Revision No.	Section No. 6

{Company Name}:

a)   determines the necessary competence for personnel performing work affecting product quality,

b)   provides training or taken other actions to satisfy these needs,

c)   evaluates the effectiveness of the actions taken,

d)   ensures that its personnel are aware of the relevance and importance of their activities and how they contribute to the achievement of the quality objectives, and

e)   maintains appropriate records of education, training, skills, and experience (see paragraph 6.0 below).

> Modify as necessary to reflect how the organization accomplishes this function.

The *{Name of Department}* screens all applicants to ensure that all personnel are adequately qualified on the basis of appropriate skills assessment, education, training, and/or experience required.

As part of the orientation process, all new employees receive the following instruction as a minimum:

{List as may be appropriate}

4.4   Infrastructure (6.3)

> Customize these paragraphs but maintain the main content items.

{Company Name} determines, provides and maintains the infrastructure needed to achieve conformity to *product* requirements. The infrastructure includes

a)   buildings, workspace, and associated utilities,

b)   *process equipment* (hardware and software), and

c)   *supporting services* (such as *transport* or communication)

4.5   Work Environment (6.4)

{Company Name} determines and manages the work environment needed to achieve conformity to *product* requirements.

{COMPANY NAME & Logo}				QUALITY SYSTEM MANUAL	
Title: Resource Management	Prepared By/Date:	Approved By/Date:	Effective Date:	Page: 3 of 3	
	Reviewed By/Date:	Approved By/Date:	Revision No.	Section No. 6	

5.0   RESPONSIBILITIES

{Identify responsibilities for training requirements, identification, and implementation. Modify the following examples as necessary.}

{Company Name} management is responsible for ensuring employee competence, awareness and training, and to establish the infrastructure and work environment needed to achieve conformity to product requirements.

The _{Name of Department or Function}_ is responsible for documenting the training of employees as requirements are identified. Job descriptions may be used as guidelines for training requirements.

6.0   RECORDS

{State which training records are maintained and where they are located. Modify the following example as necessary.}

Data on education, training, skills, and experience is recorded and maintained by the _{Name of Department or Function}_ in accordance with Reference 2.2.

{COMPANY NAME & Logo}		QUALITY SYSTEM MANUAL			
Title: Product Realization	Prepared By/Date:	Approved By/Date:	Effective Date:	Page: 1 of 13	
	Reviewed By/Date:	Approved By/Date:	Revision No.	Section No. 7	
Applicability: This section is applicable to all *{Company Name}* operations.					

1.0 PURPOSE

This section establishes the requirements for planning and developing the processes needed for *product realization*. Planning of product realization is consistent with the requirements of all other sections of the Quality System Manual.

2.0 REFERENCE DOCUMENTS

2.1 ISO 9001:2000 Clause 7

2.2 Quality Manual Section 4, paragraph 4.1

2.3 Quality Manual Section 4, paragraph 4.3

2.4 Quality Manual Section 4, paragraph 4.5

{Reference any organization-specific supporting procedures here.}

{Add Operating Procedure References here that apply to this section.}

3.0 DEFINITIONS

3.1 See Section 3, Glossary, for definitions of italicized terms.

4.0 QMS REQUIREMENTS

4.1 Planning of Product Realization (7.1)

{State what your company does in words. This should match the scope of the ISO Certificate. Customize as appropriate.}

{Company Name} plans and develops the processes needed for product realization. Planning of product realization is consistent with the requirements of the other processes of the QMS defined in Reference 2.2.

In planning product realization, *{Company Name}* determines the following:

a) quality objectives and requirements for the product;

b) the need to establish processes, documents, and provide resources specific to the product;

c) required verification, validation, monitoring, inspection, and test activities specific to the product and the criteria for product acceptance;

d) records needed to provide evidence that the realization processes and resulting product meet the requirements, per Reference 2.5.

The output of this planning is in a form suitable for *{Company Name}*'s method of operations.

{Include a simple flow chart that shows the overall process if desired to help clarify the Product Realization Process.}

> If any items are not appropriate, modify or delete them.

{COMPANY NAME & Logo}			QUALITY SYSTEM MANUAL		
Title: Product Realization	Prepared By/Date:	Approved By/Date:	Effective Date:		Page: 2 of 13
	Reviewed By/Date:	Approved By/Date:	Revision No.		Section No. 7

4.2 Determination of Requirements Related to the *Product* (7.2.1)

> Modify this paragraph to fit the organization.

{Company Name} has established procedures detailing the methods for reviewing proposals and contracts to ensure that *{Company Name}* has the capability to meet all customers' specified requirements.

{Customize the following paragraph based on the product or service output of the organization:}

{Company Name} determines the requirements specified by the customer, including the requirements for delivery and post-delivery activities. Requirements not stated by the customer but necessary for specified use or intended use are reviewed and resolved prior to the delivery of the *{product or service}*. Any statutory or regulatory requirements are determined and acted upon by *{Company Name}* as well as any company-specific requirements.

{Add any additional product related requirements here. Modify the following example to fit the organization.}

Before acceptance, the Sales Department reviews contracts, at a minimum, for pricing, quantities, and ship-dates. Appropriate departments are consulted as necessary during the Contract Review.

4.3 Review of requirements related to the *product* (7.2.2)

{Company Name} reviews the requirements related to its product. This review is conducted prior to *{Company Name}*'s commitment to supply the product to the customer (e.g. submission of tenders, acceptance of contracts or orders, acceptance of changes to contracts or orders) and ensures that

a)   product requirements are defined,

b)   contract or order requirements differing from those previously expressed are resolved, and

c)   the organization has the ability to meet the defined requirements.

Records of the results of the review and actions arising from the review are maintained (see paragraph 6.0 below).

{COMPANY NAME & Logo}			QUALITY SYSTEM MANUAL		
Title: Product Realization	Prepared By/Date:	Approved By/Date:	Effective Date:		Page: 3 of 13
	Reviewed By/Date:	Approved By/Date:	Revision No.		Section No. 7

Where the customer provides no documented statement of requirement, the customer requirements are confirmed by *{Company Name}* before acceptance.

Where product requirements are changed, *{Company Name}* ensures that relevant documents are amended and that relevant personnel are made aware of the changed requirements.

4.4   Customer Communication (7.2.3)

{Company Name} determines and implements effective arrangements for communicating with customers in relation to

a)   product information,

b)   inquiries, contracts or order handling, including amendments, and

c)   customer feedback, including customer complaints.

{Company Name} accomplishes customer product communications through *{complete the sentence to fit the organization}*.

4.5   Design and Development Planning (7.3.1)

Design and Development Planning establishes the requirements for the design and development of *product* related to *{state that for which the Design and Development effort is applicable, such as the product or business}*.

{Company Name} plans and controls the design and development of product. During the design and development planning, *{Company Name}* determines

a)   the design and development stages,

b)   the review, verification, and validation that are appropriate to each design and development stage, and

c)   the responsibilities and authorities for design and development.

{Company Name} manages the interfaces between different groups involved in design and development to ensure effective communication and clear assignment of responsibility.

Planning output is updated, as appropriate, as the design and development progresses.

Title:	Prepared By/Date:	Approved By/Date:	Effective Date:	Page:
Product Realization				4 of 13
	Reviewed By/Date:	Approved By/Date:	Revision No.	Section No. 7

4.6   Design and Development Inputs (7.3.2)

Inputs relating to product requirements are determined and records maintained (see paragraph 6.0 below). Inputs include

a)   functional and performance requirements,

b)   applicable statutory and regulatory requirements,

c)   information derived from previous similar designs (where applicable), and

d)   other requirements essential for design and development.

These inputs are reviewed for adequacy by *{Name of function}* to ensure that requirements are complete, unambiguous, and not in conflict with each other.

4.7   Design and Development Outputs (7.3.3)

The outputs of design and development are provided in a form that enables verification against the design and development inputs and are approved prior to release. Design and development outputs

a)   meet the input requirements for design and development,

b)   provide appropriate information for purchasing, production, and for service provision,

c)   contain or reference product acceptance criteria, and

d)   specify the characteristics of the product that are essential for its safe and proper use.

4.8   Design and Development Review (7.3.4)

At suitable stages, systematic reviews of design and development are performed in accordance with planned arrangements, per paragraph 4.1 above,

a)   to evaluate the ability of the results of design and development to fulfil requirements, and

b)   to identify any problems and propose necessary actions.

Participants in such reviews include representatives of functions concerned with the design and development stage(s) being reviewed.

{COMPANY NAME & Logo}		QUALITY SYSTEM MANUAL		
Title: Product Realization	Prepared By/Date:	Approved By/Date:	Effective Date:	Page: 5 of 13
	Reviewed By/Date:	Approved By/Date:	Revision No.	Section No. 7

Records of the results of the reviews and any necessary actions are maintained (see paragraph 6.0 below).

4.9   Design and Development Verification (7.3.5)

Verification is performed in accordance with planned arrangements, per paragraph 4.1 above, to ensure that the design and development outputs have satisfied the design and development input requirements. Records of the results of the verification and any necessary actions are maintained (see paragraph 6.0 below).

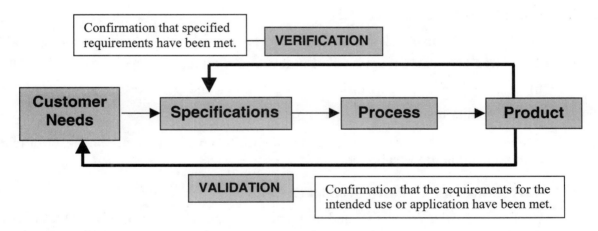

4.10   Design and Development Validation (7.3.6)

Design and development validation is performed in accordance with planned arrangements, per paragraph 4.1 above, to ensure that the resulting product is capable of meeting the requirements for the specified application or intended use, where known. Wherever practicable, validation is completed prior to the delivery or implementation of the product. Records of the results of validation and any necessary actions are maintained (see paragraph 6.0 below).

4.11   Control of Design and Development Changes (7.3.7)

Design and development changes are identified and records maintained. The changes are reviewed, verified, and validated, as appropriate, and approved before implementation. The review of design and development changes includes evaluation of the effect of the changes on constituent parts and product already delivered. Records of the results of the review of changes and any necessary actions are maintained (see paragraph 6.0 below).

{COMPANY NAME & Logo}			QUALITY SYSTEM MANUAL		
Title: Product Realization	Prepared By/Date:	Approved By/Date:	Effective Date:	Page: 6 of 13	
	Reviewed By/Date:	Approved By/Date:	Revision No.	Section No. 7	

4.12 Purchasing Process (7.4.1)

> Describe the type and extent of control.

It is the policy of {Company Name} to ensure that all purchased products conform to specified purchase requirements. The type and extent of control applied to the supplier and the purchased product is dependent upon the effect of the purchased product on subsequent product realization or the final product. {Company Name} evaluates and selects suppliers based on their ability to supply product in accordance with {Company Name}'s requirements. Criteria for selection, evaluation, and re-evaluation are established. Records of the results of evaluations and any necessary actions arising from the evaluation are maintained (see paragraph 6.0 below).

4.13 Purchasing Information (7.4.2)

Purchasing information describes the product to be purchased including, where appropriate,

a)   requirements for approval of product, procedures, processes, and equipment,

b)   requirements for qualification of personnel, and

c)   quality management system requirements.

{Company Name} ensures the adequacy of specified purchase requirements prior to their communication to the supplier.

4.14 Verification of Purchased Product (7.4.3)

{Company Name} establishes and implements the inspection or other activities necessary for ensuring that purchased product meets specified purchase requirements. Where the organization or its customer intends to perform verification at the supplier's premises, {Company Name} states the intended verification arrangements and method of product release in the purchasing information.

{COMPANY NAME & Logo}			QUALITY SYSTEM MANUAL		
Title: Product Realization	Prepared By/Date:	Approved By/Date:	Effective Date:		Page: 7 of 13
	Reviewed By/Date:	Approved By/Date:	Revision No.		Section No. 7

4.15   Control of Production and Service Provision (7.5.1)

This section establishes the requirements for *production and service provision* related to the *{state the scope of ISO Certification here (describe the Company business specifically detailing the scope of the ISO Certification)}*.

{Company Name} plans and carries out production and service provision under controlled conditions. Controlled conditions include, as applicable

a)   the availability of information that describes the characteristics of the product,

b)   the availability of work instructions, as necessary,

c)   the use of suitable equipment,

d)   the availability and use of monitoring and measuring devices,

e)   the implementation of monitoring and measurement, and

f)   the implementation of release, delivery, and post-delivery activities.

{Add descriptive paragraph here that describes how the procedures/work instructions are communicated to the required operations. If there are additional documents that control production, list them here as well.}

| Example |

Quality Assurance, Manufacturing Engineering, and/or Production communicate work instructions to required operations functions. In addition to work instructions, illustrations and samples may also be provided to show workmanship criteria.

4.16   Validation of Processes for Production and Service Provision (7.5.2)

{Company Name} validates any processes for production and service provision where the resulting output cannot be verified by subsequent monitoring or measurement. This includes any processes where deficiencies become apparent only after the product is in use or the service has been delivered.

{COMPANY NAME & Logo}			QUALITY SYSTEM MANUAL		
Title: Product Realization	Prepared By/Date:	Approved By/Date:	Effective Date:	Page: 8 of 13	
	Reviewed By/Date:	Approved By/Date:	Revision No.	Section No. 7	

Validation demonstrates the ability of these processes to achieve planned results. {Company Name} establishes arrangements for these processes including, as applicable

a)   defined criteria for review and approval of the processes,

b)   approval of equipment and qualification of personnel,

c)   use of specific methods and procedures,

d)   requirements for records (see paragraph 6.0 below), and

e)   revalidation.

{Describe further how Validation occurs relative to the Production and Service Provision. See examples provided below.}

Processes are periodically reviewed by the Manufacturing Engineering Department through Maintenance Records, Statistical Charting, and First Part Inspections.

In-process functional tests are uniquely identified by the individual performing the tests. Test results are documented in accordance with control plans or inspection instructions.

Examples

Final inspection includes verification that appropriate in-process inspections and tests are performed. No product is to be sent to stock without an acceptance stamp affixed.

Final inspection is performed as described in control plans and/or inspection instructions to ensure that all customer-specified requirements are satisfied.

Inspection and test results are documented in the form of inspection and test reports. Final inspection and test results are also recorded.

Any product found to be nonconforming is handled as described in Section 16 of this manual.

{COMPANY NAME & Logo}			QUALITY SYSTEM MANUAL	
Title: Product Realization	Prepared By/Date:	Approved By/Date:	Effective Date:	Page: 9 of 13
	Reviewed By/Date:	Approved By/Date:	Revision No.	Section No. 7

4.17 Identification and Traceability (7.5.3)

Where appropriate, *{Company Name}* identifies the product by suitable means throughout product realization. This includes identification of product status with respect to monitoring and measurement requirements. Where traceability is a requirement, *{Company Name}* controls and records the unique identification of the product (see paragraph 6.0 below).

{Add additional descriptive paragraphs that describe the identification and traceability provided by the company of product as may be applicable. If this section is not applicable, such as in the case of a service company, so state.}

4.18 Customer Property (7.5.4)

{Company Name} exercises care with customer property while it is under the organization's control or being used by the organization. Processes are in place to identify, verify, protect, and safeguard customer property provided for use or incorporation into the product. If any customer property is lost, damaged, or otherwise found to be unsuitable for use, this situation is reported to the customer and records maintained (see paragraph 6.0 below).

{Modify the above paragraph to adequately describe what is done relative to customer property. If it does not apply, state that it does not apply and justify the statement.}

4.19 Preservation of Product (7.5.5)

{Company Name} preserves the conformity of product during internal processing and delivery to the intended destination. This preservation includes identification, handling, packaging, storage, and protection of all tangible aspects of our product. Preservation also applies to the constituent parts of the product.

{Add additional paragraphs here to describe or reference an associated procedure for the handling, storage, packaging, preservation, and delivery requirements of the company as may be appropriate.}

4.20   Control of Monitoring and Measuring Devices (7.6)

{Company Name} determines the monitoring and measurement to be undertaken and the monitoring and measuring devices needed to provide evidence of conformity of product to determined requirements, per paragraph 4.2 above. _{Company Name}_ establishes processes to ensure that monitoring and measurement can be carried out and are carried out in a manner that is consistent with the monitoring and measurement requirements.

Where necessary to ensure valid results, measuring equipment is

a)   calibrated or verified at specified intervals, or prior to use, against measurement standards traceable to international or national measurement standards. Where no such standards exist, the basis used for calibration or verification is recorded;

b)   adjusted or re-adjusted as necessary;

c)   identified to enable the calibration status to be determined;

d)   safeguarded from adjustments that would invalidate the measurement result;

e)   protected from damage and deterioration during handling, maintenance, and storage.

In addition, _{Company Name}_ assesses and records the validity of the previous measuring results when the equipment is found not to conform to requirements and takes appropriate action on the equipment and any product affected. Records of the results of calibration and verification are maintained (see paragraph 6.0 below).

When used in the monitoring and measurement of specified requirements, the ability of computer software to satisfy the intended application is confirmed prior to initial use and reconfirmed as necessary.

{COMPANY NAME & Logo}			QUALITY SYSTEM MANUAL		
Title: Product Realization	Prepared By/Date:	Approved By/Date:	Effective Date:		Page: 11 of 13
	Reviewed By/Date:	Approved By/Date:	Revision No.		Section No. 7

5.0 RESPONSIBILITIES

R&D has the responsibility for effective planning, design inputs, design outputs and review, verification and validation, and changes associated with the design and development for *{Company Name}* products.

{State here the responsibility for the various Design and Development functions. An example statement is given for reference. Include Design and Development Planning, Design and Development Inputs, Design and Development Outputs, Design and Development Review, Design and Development Verification, Design and Development Validation, and Control of Design and Development Changes.}

{Department Name} has the responsibility for the Purchasing Process.

{State the responsibilities for the Purchasing Process, Purchasing Information, and the Verification of Purchased Product here.}

Planning of Product Realization is the responsibility of *{Name of Departments/Functions}*.

{Name the Departments/Functions responsible for the Purchasing Process, including determination of requirements and review of requirements related to the product as may be applicable. Reference associated procedures and include in the references above.}

{COMPANY NAME & Logo}			QUALITY SYSTEM MANUAL		
Title: Product Realization	Prepared By/Date:	Approved By/Date:	Effective Date:	Page: 12 of 13	
	Reviewed By/Date:	Approved By/Date:	Revision No.	Section No. 7	

The responsibility for Customer Communication is that of the *{Name of Department(s) or Function(s)}*.

| Example |

The Sales Department and the National Order Center share the responsibility for determination and review of the requirements related to the product as well as customer communications.

Identification and Traceability is the responsibility of *{Name of Department(s) or Function(s)}*.

Customer Property and Preservation of product is the responsibility of *{Name of Department(s) or Function(s)}*.

Control of Monitoring and Measuring Devices is the responsibility of *{Name of Department(s) or Function(s)}*.

{Add the appropriate responsible parties or reference to specific procedures that have the responsibilities stated.}

6.0   RECORDS

Records associated with Product design are maintained in accordance with Section 7 of this manual and are the responsibility of the *{Name of Function}* Department.

{State here what records are maintained and who is responsible for such.}

The *{responsible Department or Function}* is responsible for the records needed to provide evidence that the product realization process and resulting product meet requirements.

{Modify the above paragraph as necessary to reflect who maintains the associated records.}

The Quality Assurance Department is responsible for maintaining equipment calibration, per *{Procedure Reference Number}*.

{COMPANY NAME & Logo}			QUALITY SYSTEM MANUAL		
Title: Product Realization	Prepared By/Date:	Approved By/Date:	Effective Date:	Page: 13 of 13	
	Reviewed By/Date:	Approved By/Date:	Revision No.	Section No. 7	

<table>
<tr><td>Examples</td><td>It is the responsibility of everyone using the measuring and test equipment to verify that the calibration status is current.</td></tr>
</table>

It is the responsibility of everyone using the measuring and test equipment to verify that the calibration status is current.

{State the responsible function for the Control of Monitoring and Measuring Devices here. See the example provided above.}

The results of calibration and verification are recorded on documents maintained in accordance with the requirements of *{Procedure Reference Number}*.

{State the related records associated with the Control of Monitoring and Measuring Devices here or reference where the records are so stated. See the example provided above.}

{COMPANY NAME & Logo}			QUALITY SYSTEM MANUAL		
Title: Measurement, Analysis, and Improvement	Prepared By/Date:	Approved By/Date:	Effective Date:		Page: 1 of 7
	Reviewed By/Date:	Approved By/Date:	Revision No.		Section No. 8
Applicability: This section is applicable to all *{Company Name}* operations.					

1.0 PURPOSE

This section establishes the *requirements* for the measurement, analysis, and improvement of the QMS processes.

2.0 REFERENCE DOCUMENTS

2.1 ISO 9001:2000 Clause 8.1

2.2 Quality Manual Section 7, paragraph 7.1

2.3 Quality Manual Section 4, paragraph 4.5

{For the following procedures, add the correct reference procedure names and numbers for your organization, as applicable:}

2.4 QMS Procedure *{"Internal Audits"}*

2.5 QMS Procedure *{"Control of Nonconforming Product"}*

2.6 QMS Procedure *{"Corrective Action"}*

2.7 QMS Procedure *{"Preventive Action"}*

3.0 DEFINITIONS

3.1 See Section 3, Glossary, for definitions of italicized terms.

4.0 QMS REQUIREMENTS

4.1 Measurement, Analysis and Improvement – General (8.1)

{Company Name} plans and implements the monitoring, measurement, analysis, and improvement processes needed to demonstrate conformity of the product and to ensure conformity of the Quality Management System.

{Company Name} uses the following to demonstrate and ensure conformity of the product:

{List here the methods that the Company uses to demonstrate and ensure conformity of the product. Examples are provided below.}

a) Production Concern Process
b) Inspection
c) Warranty analysis
d) Customer feedback
e) Nonconformity analysis
f) Product audits

{COMPANY NAME & Logo}			QUALITY SYSTEM MANUAL		
Title: Measurement, Analysis, and Improvement	Prepared By/Date:	Approved By/Date:	Effective Date:	Page: 2 of 7	
	Reviewed By/Date:	Approved By/Date:	Revision No.	Section No. 8	

{Company Name} ensures conformity of the Quality Management System through:

- a) Internal audits
- b) External audits
- c) Safety audits
- d) Management reviews
- e) Analysis of nonconformances
- f) Corrective action data
- g) Customer feedback

{Add any others that may be applicable.}

> **Adjust listing as is applicable.**

{Company Name} uses the Management reviews, results of internal and external audits, results of nonconformance, corrective action, preventive action analysis, and customer feedback to continually improve the effectiveness of the Quality Management System.

This includes the determination of applicable methods, including statistical techniques, and the extent of their use.

4.2 Customer Satisfaction (8.2.1)

> **Add to and adjust as is applicable to the organization.**

As one of the measurements of the performance of the QMS, {Company Name} monitors information relating to customer perception as to whether the organization has met customer requirements. The methods for obtaining and using this information have been determined and include:

- a) Controlled customer perception survey
- b) Customer complaints
- c) Direct customer communication/feedback
- d) Customer visits

{COMPANY NAME & Logo}			QUALITY SYSTEM MANUAL	
Title:	Prepared By/Date:	Approved By/Date:	Effective Date:	Page: 3 of 7
Measurement, Analysis, and Improvement	Reviewed By/Date:	Approved By/Date:	Revision No.	Section No. 8

4.3   Internal Audit (8.2.2)

{Company Name} conducts internal audits at planned intervals to determine whether the QMS

a)   conforms to the planned arrangements, per Reference 2.2, to the requirements of the ISO 9001:2000 Standard, and to the QMS requirements established within this Manual, and

b)   is effectively implemented and maintained.

An audit program is planned, taking into consideration the status and importance of the processes and areas to be audited as well as the results of previous audits. The audit criteria, scope, frequency, and methods are defined per Reference 2.4. Selection of auditors and the conduct of audits ensure objectivity and impartiality of the audit process. Auditors do not audit their own work.

The responsibilities and requirements for planning and conducting audits, and for reporting results and maintaining records (see paragraph 6.0 below), are defined in Reference 2.4.

The management responsible for the area being audited ensures that actions are taken without undue delay to eliminate detected nonconformities and their causes. Follow-up activities include the verification of the actions taken and the reporting of verification results, per paragraph 4.9 below.

4.4   Monitoring and Measurement of Processes (8.2.3)

Modify and add to listing as is applicable.

{Company Name} applies suitable methods for monitoring and, where applicable, measurement of the QMS processes. These methods include internal audit results, Management Reviews, supplier performance, and customer feedback. These methods demonstrate the ability of the processes to achieve planned results. When planned results are not achieved, correction and corrective action is taken, as appropriate, to ensure conformity of the product.

{COMPANY NAME & Logo}			QUALITY SYSTEM MANUAL		
Title: Measurement, Analysis, and Improvement	Prepared By/Date:	Approved By/Date:	Effective Date:		Page: 4 of 7
	Reviewed By/Date:	Approved By/Date:	Revision No.		Section No. 8

4.5   Monitoring and Measurement of Product (8.2.4)

{Company Name} monitors and measures the characteristics of the product to verify that product requirements have been met. This is carried out at appropriate stages of the product realization process in accordance with the planned arrangements, per Reference 2.2.

Evidence of conformity with the acceptance criteria is maintained (See paragraph 6.0 below). These records indicate the person(s) authorizing release of product.

Product release and service delivery do not proceed until all the planned arrangements have been satisfactorily completed, per Reference 2.2, unless otherwise approved by a relevant authority, and where applicable by the customer.

4.6   Control of Nonconforming Product (8.3)

{Company Name} ensures that product which does not conform to product requirements is identified and controlled to prevent its unintended use or delivery. The controls and related responsibilities and authorities for dealing with nonconforming product are defined in Reference 2.5.

{Company Name} deals with nonconforming product by one or more of the following ways:

a)   by taking action to eliminate the detected nonconformity;

b)   by authorizing its use, release, or acceptance under concession by a relevant authority and, where applicable, by the customer;

c)   by taking action to preclude its original intended use or application.

Records of the nature of nonconformities and any subsequent actions taken, including concessions obtained, are maintained (see paragraph 6.0 below). When nonconforming product is corrected, it is subject to re-verification to demonstrate conformity to the requirements. When nonconforming product is detected after delivery or use has started, *{Company Name}* takes action appropriate to the effects, or potential effects, of the nonconformity.

{COMPANY NAME & Logo}			QUALITY SYSTEM MANUAL		
Title: Measurement, Analysis, and Improvement	Prepared By/Date:	Approved By/Date:	Effective Date:	Page: 5 of 7	
	Reviewed By/Date:	Approved By/Date:	Revision No.	Section No. 8	

4.7 Analysis of Data (8.4)

{Company Name} determines, collects, and analyzes appropriate data to demonstrate the suitability and effectiveness of the QMS and to evaluate where continual improvement of the effectiveness of the QMS can be made. This includes data generated as a result of monitoring and measurement and from other relevant sources.

The analysis of data provides information relating to

a)   customer satisfaction, per paragraph 4.2 above,

b)   conformance to product requirements, per Reference 2.2,

c)   characteristics and trends of processes and products including opportunities for preventive action, and

d)   suppliers.

4.8 Continual Improvement (8.5.1)

{Company Name} continually improves the effectiveness of its QMS through the use of the quality policy, quality objectives, audit results, analysis of data, corrective and preventive actions, and management review.

4.9 Corrective Action (8.5.2)

{Company Name} takes action to eliminate the cause of nonconformities in order to prevent recurrence. Corrective actions are appropriate to the effects of the nonconformities encountered. Reference 2.6 defines requirements for:

a)   reviewing nonconformities (including customer complaints),

b)   determining the causes of non-conformities,

c)   evaluating the need for action to ensure that nonconformities do not recur,

d)   determining and implementing action needed,

e)   records of the results of action taken (see paragraph 6.0 below), and

f)   reviewing corrective action taken.

> Sample
> Statements

{COMPANY NAME & Logo}			QUALITY SYSTEM MANUAL	
Title: Measurement, Analysis, and Improvement	Prepared By/Date:	Approved By/Date:	Effective Date:	Page: 6 of 7
	Reviewed By/Date:	Approved By/Date:	Revision No.	Section No. 8

4.10 Preventive Action (8.5.3)

{Company Name} determines action to eliminate the causes of potential nonconformities in order to prevent their occurrence. Preventive actions are appropriate to the effects of the potential problems. Reference 2.7 defines requirements for:

a) determining potential nonconformities and their causes,

b) evaluating the need for action to prevent occurrence of nonconformities,

c) determining and implementing action needed,

d) records of results of action taken (see paragraph 6.0 below), and

e) reviewing preventive action taken.

5.0 RESPONSIBILITIES

> Customize Paragraph 5.0 as necessary.

Top management is responsible for ensuring action(s) are taken regarding continual improvement.

{State the responsibilities for the Corrective and Preventive Action System, for follow-up activities and effectiveness.}

All employees are responsible to ensure quality, continual improvement, and customer satisfaction is addressed.

The *{Name of Department or Function}* issues all Corrective Action Requests and is responsible for follow-up to ensure that corrective and preventive action is in place, and for adjusting internal audit frequency as may be required. See references 2.3 and 2.4.

Quality Assurance Department is responsible for the maintenance of corrective action records, preventive action records, and continual improvement records.

> Examples

The *{Name of Department or Function}* is responsible for monitoring, measuring, and analyzing the data to ensure product conformity and continual improvement of the QMS.

The *{Name of Department or Function}* recommends action(s) based on the results of the monitoring, measuring, and analysis results dependent upon the criticality of the finding. The determination of applicable methods, including statistical techniques, and the extent of their use is the responsibility of the *{Name of Department or Function}*.

Management is responsible for follow through of recommended action(s).

{COMPANY NAME & Logo}			QUALITY SYSTEM MANUAL	
Title: Measurement, Analysis, and Improvement	Prepared By/Date:	Approved By/Date:	Effective Date:	Page: 7 of 7
	Reviewed By/Date:	Approved By/Date:	Revision No.	Section No. 8

The *{Name of Department or Function}* is responsible for all aspects of internal audits (see reference 2.5).

Customize Paragraph 5.0 as necessary.

The *{Name of Department or Function}*, in conjunction with *{manufacturing}*, is responsible for monitoring and measurement processes, and follow-up action(s).

Management is responsible for action(s) as a result of the internal audits.

The *{Name of Department or Function}* is responsible for all aspects of customer satisfaction.

6.0   RECORDS

The following records are maintained in accordance with Reference 2.3

Customize Paragraph 6.0 as necessary.

The *{Name of Department or Function}* maintains all monitoring and measurement records.

The *{Name of Department or Function}* maintains all customer satisfaction records in accordance with Section 7 of this Manual:

Quality Records for Corrective and Preventive Action are defined in Reference 2.3 and 2.4.

The results of internal audits are maintained by the *{Name of Department or Function}*.

Evidence of conformity with the acceptance criteria and the function authorizing release of product is *{Complete this statement}*.

The nature of nonconformities and any subsequent actions taken, including concessions obtained, are the responsibility of *{Name of Department or Function}*.

{COMPANY NAME & Logo}					QUALITY SYSTEM MANUAL

Title:	Prepared By/Date:	Approved By/Date:	Effective Date:	Page:
Record of Revisions				1 of 1
	Reviewed By/Date:	Approved By/Date:	Revision No.	Section No. 9

Applicability:	This section is applicable to all *{Company Name}* operations.

Revision	Section	Detail	Effective Date
0	All	Initial Issue of the 9001:2000 transition revision to the QSM	

References

Camp, Robert C. *Benchmarking: The Search for Industry Best Practices That Lead to Superior Performance*. Milwaukee, WI: Quality Press, 1989.

Crosby, Philip B. *Quality Is Free*. New York: McGraw Hill, 1979.

Eicher, L. D. *Quality Management in the 90s: The ISO Phenomena*. Quality Forum, Vol. 10, No. 2, 1992.

Gale, Bradley T., and Robert Chapman Wood, *Managing Customer Value: Creating Quality and Service That Customers Can See*. Free Press, 1994.

Malcolm Baldrige National Quality Award. 2001 Criteria for Performance Excellence.

Rudy, Keith L. *Management Innovations, An Interpretation of ISO 9000*. A Presentation on ISO 9000 at the Fourth Annual Spring Accounting Expo, Houston, TX, 1993.

Total Quality, An Executive's Guide for the 1990s. The Ernst and Young Quality Improvement Consulting Group, Dow Jones-Irwin/Apics Series in Production Management, 1990.

Why, 28 May 2001. Taken from notes of 55th ASQ Quality Congress, May 7-8, 2001, Charlotte, NC.

Index

Government Institutes Mini-Catalog

PC #	ENVIRONMENTAL TITLES	Pub Date	Price*
629	ABCs of Environmental Regulation	1998	$65
672	Book of Lists for Regulated Hazardous Substances, 9th Edition	1999	$95
4100	⊙ CFR Chemical Lists on CD ROM, 1999-2000 Edition	1999	$125
512	Clean Water Handbook, Second Edition	1996	$115
581	EH&S Auditing Made Easy	1997	$95
673	E H & S CFR Training Requirements, Fourth Edition	2000	$99
825	Environmental, Health and Safety Audits, 8th Edition	2001	$115
548	Environmental Engineering and Science	1997	$95
643	Environmental Guide to the Internet, Fourth Edition	1998	$75
820	Environmental Law Handbook, Sixteenth Edition	2001	$99
688	EH&S Dictionary: Official Regulatory Terms, Seventh Edition	2000	$95
821	Environmental Statutes, 2001 Edition	2001	$115
4099	⊙ Environmental Statutes on CD ROM for Windows-Single User, 1999 Ed.	1999	$169
707	Federal Facility Environmental Compliance and Enforcement Guide	2000	$115
708	Federal Facility Environmental Management Systems	2000	$99
689	Fundamentals of Site Remediation	2000	$85
515	Industrial Environmental Management: A Practical Approach	1996	$95
510	ISO 14000: Understanding Environmental Standards	1996	$85
551	ISO 14001: An Executive Report	1996	$75
588	International Environmental Auditing	1998	$179
518	Lead Regulation Handbook	1996	$95
608	NEPA Effectiveness: Mastering the Process	1998	$95
582	Recycling & Waste Mgmt Guide to the Internet	1997	$65
615	Risk Management Planning Handbook	1998	$105
603	Superfund Manual, 6th Edition	1997	$129
685	State Environmental Agencies on the Internet	1999	$75
566	TSCA Handbook, Third Edition	1997	$115
534	Wetland Mitigation: Mitigation Banking and Other Strategies	1997	$95

PC #	SAFETY and HEALTH TITLES	Pub Date	Price*
697	Applied Statistics in Occupational Safety and Health	2000	$105
547	Construction Safety Handbook	1996	$95
553	Cumulative Trauma Disorders	1997	$75
663	Forklift Safety, Second Edition	1999	$85
709	Fundamentals of Occupational Safety & Health, Second Edition	2001	$69
612	HAZWOPER Incident Command	1998	$75
662	Machine Guarding Handbook	1999	$75
535	Making Sense of OSHA Compliance	1997	$75
718	OSHA's New Ergonomic Standard	2001	$95
558	PPE Made Easy	1998	$95
683	Product Safety Handbook	2001	$95
598	Project Mgmt for E H & S Professionals	1997	$85
658	Root Cause Analysis	1999	$105
552	Safety & Health in Agriculture, Forestry and Fisheries	1997	$155
669	Safety & Health on the Internet, Third Edition	1999	$75
668	Safety Made Easy, Second Edition	1999	$75
590	Your Company Safety and Health Manual	1997	$95

Government Institutes

4 Research Place, Suite 200 • Rockville, MD 20850-3226
Tel. (301) 921-2323 • FAX (301) 921-0264
Email: giinfo@govinst.com • Internet: http://www.govinst.com

Please call our customer service department at (301) 921-2323 for a free publications catalog.

CFRs now available online. Call (301) 921-2355 for info.

*All prices are subject to change. Please call for current prices and availablity.

Government Institutes Order Form

4 Research Place, Suite 200 • Rockville, MD 20850-3226
Tel (301) 921-2323 • Fax (301) 921-0264
Internet: http://www.govinst.com • E-mail: giinfo@govinst.com

4 EASY WAYS TO ORDER

1. Tel: **(301) 921-2323**
Have your credit card ready when you call.

2. Fax: **(301) 921-0264**
Fax this completed order form with your company purchase order or credit card information.

3. Mail: **Government Institutes Division**
ABS Group Inc.
P.O. Box 846304
Dallas, TX 75284-6304   USA

Mail this completed order form with a check, company purchase order, or credit card information.

4. Online: Visit http://www.govinst.com

PAYMENT OPTIONS

❏ **Check** *(payable in US dollars to **ABS Group Inc. Government Institutes Division**)*

❏ **Purchase Order** *(This order form must be attached to your company P.O. Note:All International orders must be prepaid.)*

❏ **Credit Card** ☐ VISA ☐ MasterCard ☐ AMERICAN EXPRESS

Exp. ___ /____

Credit Card No. _____

Signature _____

(Government Institutes' Federal I.D.# is 13-2695912)

CUSTOMER INFORMATION

Ship To: (Please attach your purchase order)

Name _____

GI Account # (*7 digits on mailing label*) _____

Company/Institution _____

Address _____
(Please supply street address for UPS shipping)

City _____ State/Province _____

Zip/Postal Code _____ Country _____

Tel ( )_____

Fax ( )_____

E-mail Address _____

Bill To: (if different from ship-to address)

Name _____

Title/Position _____

Company/Institution _____

Address _____
(Please supply street address for UPS shipping)

City _____ State/Province _____

Zip/Postal Code _____ Country _____

Tel ( )_____

Fax ( )_____

E-mail Address _____

Qty.	Product Code	Title	Price

30 DAY MONEY-BACK GUARANTEE

If you're not completely satisfied with any product, return it undamaged within 30 days for a full and immediate refund on the price of the product.

Subtotal _____

MD Residents add 5% Sales Tax _____

Shipping and Handling (see box below) _____

Total Payment Enclosed _____

SOURCE CODE: BP03

Shipping and Handling	**Sales Tax**
Within U.S:	Maryland 5%
1-4 products: $6/product	Texas 8.25%
5 or more: $4/product	Virginia 4.5%
Outside U.S:	
Add $15 for each item (Global)	